3,000 "Coffee Breaks"

A Ventriloquist's Journey on the Gerson Alternative Cancer Therapy

by

James Wedgwood

3,000 "Coffee Breaks"

by

James Wedgwood

Published by Knock Wood LLC, St. Paul, MN

ISBN 978-0-578-09758-9

Proudly printed in the United States of America

Edited by
Patricia Walker and **Delores Nordstrom**

Cover Art and Photographs by
James Wedgwood

Coffee Cup Graphic by
Nancy LaRoche

For more information on The Gerson Therapy
please visit **www.gerson.org** or contact:

The Gerson Institute
P.O. Box 161358
San Diego, CA 92176

Dedicated with great appreciation and love to

Gail

Contents

Contents cont'd

Preface

As I write this, it is almost nine years since my journey with The Gerson Therapy began. I would have liked to have finished this book much sooner but a move, my career, my parents care and the day to day exercise of life somehow kept completion at arms length, never quite close enough to fully embrace.

Of course, truth be told, part of the delay was my own fear of publishing a book, knowing it will resonate deeply with some, but not at all with others, and will lead me on a path hopefully for better but paved with the insecurity of the unknown.

So be it. Fear is never a good reason for not trying.

My hope is at the least the book will be helpful to anyone trudging through the abyss that defines serious illness, to let them know they are not alone on the tsunami of emotions and trials that they could not have even imagined pre-diagnoses. And that amidst the turmoil, there can be hope, growth and laughter.

At the most, I hope it will present an alternative to those seeking other possibilities besides traditional western medicine. Not to condemn western medicine, not at all. I have close friends and family who have benefited greatly from traditional healing methods.

But there are options to pills, chemo, and radiation and they need to be presented, explored and embraced as a valid alternatives.

I must emphasize, what follows is the story of my journey on the Gerson Therapy. It is not nor intended to be in any way a handbook for the Therapy's application.

If you have been diagnosed with a serious or any illness, you must consult your physician. This book is not designed to convey medical advice. It is only the story of the choices I made and where those choices led me.

Also, I have changed the names of all patients and physicians to protect their privacy.

Okay, the official sounding disclaimery statements to cover my derriere are finished.

I need to change gears and send you off on my journey with a positive note. If any part of *3,000 "Coffee Breaks"* helps you in a healing process, be it emotional or physical, as a patient or loved one, if it brings a smile to your face in a time of turmoil, or alternately a cathartic tear, if it helps you feel not quite so isolated in the face of chaos, I will have achieved my goal.

Writing it did just that for me.

James Wedgwood

Chapter One

Randy

The best friend in all my life was Randy Milner. In 1968 when my family moved back to Indiana, I went out for wrestling and he was on the team. He weighed a whopping 87 pounds and I a massive 98!

We definitely were not the bruisers of the 8th grade.

He wrestled varsity, mainly because there were no other 87-pounders at our school, and won a lot of matches just because the other team didn't have anyone in his weight class.

Lacking even the remotest inkling of a killer instinct, I was fated to be a second stringer. Oh, I was fit and athletic enough and I was very quick. It was just that for some weird reason I felt guilty about kicking the other guy's ass. In my 8th grade world view, I just kind of wanted everyone to get along, which pretty much doomed me to sports mediocrity throughout my junior high and high school years. But it was still fun, and dealing with an overzealous coach, nausea inducing practices, and general harassment in the locker room was seen as a character building rite of male passage at the time. Even if you stunk, you still had a sense of confidence and pride just from surviving the ordeal.

In addition to wrestling and our diminutive size, Randy and I both played drums and shared a love for photography. With that much in common, it would have been odd not to become best friends, and although we didn't know it at the time, we would carry each other through three decades of schooling, jobs, marriages and divorces.

For all the firsts of adolescence he was there to commiserate: girls, grades, zits and embarrassingly late arriving puberty. Perhaps overcompensating for our munchkinesque stature, we became the clowns of the marching band, mercilessly tormenting the drum major and playing dumb attention getting tricks on the girls drill team, since at that age we had no clue how to actually talk with women.

At night we tooled around in Randy's father's 1960 Renault, which was a French Beetle looking thing only smaller and colder! We even put a big key on the back and pretended to wind it up behind our school, seeing if any gullible girls would buy our story of a large watch spring hidden under the hood. I think we told one 15 year old that the thing was actually an oversized music box that given enough turns of the key, would crank out "In A-Gadda-Da-Vida" in delicate bell tones.

When we had dates, my father's metallic green '68 Nova was the ride of choice and our favorite "make-out-steam-up-the-windows" vehicle with its reasonably spacious vinyl bench seats in the back and front. To attempt that type of activity in the Renault, especially in the front seat with it's gear shift and parking brake lever protruding prominently between the buckets, was to invite almost certain debilitating injuries in the bodily areas most prized by an adolescent young man.

His father, being a printer, helped us put together a business card with a photo of me on the left sitting in a trash can and Randy in a faux fur coat and derby on the right, with our "Services" listed in the middle. I think pilots and photographers were on that dubious roster. When I asked how we could be pilots, Randy simply replied, "We pile it here, and we pile it there," quoting what I believe is an ancient vaudeville routine. Not so funny now, but at that age we thought it was hilarious.

In the middle of the card with the big wind-up key protruding prominently from the back was the Renault, billed as "Our Limousine Service."

He was the first guy I would call about some new girl I liked, although at that time it was more like, "Well, like . . . she's kinda fun." Years later that same conversation would be, "Well, I think, of course, the only reason I'm attracted to her is some latent Jungian maternal association."

We even had codes to refer various parts of the female anatomy so no one would know what we were discussing.

All of this was typical teenage stuff. It was also the "stuff" that was cementing what would become a lifelong bond built on history, personal trials, and trust.

Randy went to my university, Indiana at Bloomington, for a year. Among several misadventures was him hiding in the sunken corner of a guy's waterbed while the guy was in the shower. The unsuspecting victim came back from the bathroom, which was down the hall, got into bed, (I was discretely watching from a closet) turned off the light and after about ten minutes Randy reached out and grabbed him!

The effect was far better than even the decapitated

thoroughbred's head scene in "The Godfather." Our foil's screams woke up the entire floor, and the playful wrestling match that ensued broke a full length mirror that to this day only God knows who paid for.

Randy finished college at another school to better pursue his major and work.

We each got married a couple of years after graduation and neither one of us could fathom what that was all about. Both of our wives dumped us within a year of each other, mine leaving me in Minneapolis where we had moved to pursue glamorous, exhilarating careers in the performing arts (I ended up waiting tables at something like "Burrito Bob's"). Randy came home from work one day to find an empty trailer home – his wife having bailed on him with his only daughter, all their furniture and the cat.

After that we each got involved in our own versions of life reconstruction. Through odd circumstances I became a professional ventriloquist, rekindling a childhood hobby into a surprisingly lucrative and fun avenue of self-employment, while Randy pursued a nursing degree and continued his work as a parole officer. While good things began happening to us, our careers, relationship recovery, a lot of growing up to do, and 600 miles of Midwest farmland in between Indy and the Twin Cities caused us to lose touch.

But one day when I was back in town visiting my folks, I called him for lunch. We chatted about all the incredibly fun and stupid stuff we'd done in high school and college, gave each other grief about our hairlines or lack thereof, and tried to figure out what the hell was up with us and women.

The embers of our old friendship began to glow again . . . rekindled by memories of laughter, lasciviousness and loss, but tempered by the realities of adult responsibility.

He and his new wife came up to Minnesota for a visit, I and my new wife went down to Indiana.

It culminated in he and I taking two great trips together to Vegas and LA that I cherish all the more . . . knowing what I do now.

We did mostly typical vacation stuff and a little of "What happens in Vegas stays in Vegas." Needless to say, we had a great time. I felt so fortunate to have him back in my life, the one person in the world I had so much history with and who consequently knew and understood my life process so well. Communication and reactions to whatever situation we found ourselves in became almost telepathic, and complete trust was implicit.

He was the one person I could tell anything to: marital issues, work insecurities, hopes, dream, fears and nightmares. He could give me a context to explore them and then give me joking crap about it. There was no one else like him . . . not in my life anyway.

Gail, my current and wonderful wife and I met him and his wife Misty for New Year's '93/'94 at the Palmer House in Chicago. He and I both wore newly acquired tuxes, Randy accenting his with Army boots. He referred to Gail's cleavage as her "pendulousity" and Misty's feathery ensemble as her "Chicken Dress." It was vintage Randy.

I looked forward to more good times with him in the New

Year, and as the decades of our lives rolled on.

But in June of '94 during a normal touch-in phone call he mentioned almost in passing that during a routine physical they had found blood in his urine. "OK" I thought, "No big deal. Urinary problems? Bladder infection? Bruise? Ah, no biggy." Anything serious never entered my mind.

A few days later though, I got not "a" call, but "The Call," the one you never, no matter how much you want to, can completely obliterate from your scarred psyche. It's the one you instantly know will change you and your existence forever, and yet you remain in a state of denial as long as your rational mind will allow because if you let your new reality seep in through the cracks, it will dissolve your being like a sugar cube in scalding coffee, never to be completely whole again.

My lifelong friend, my Dramamine through the roller coaster of existence, the closest thing to a "brother" I had, at 39 years old had a tennis ball sized malignant tumor engulfing his right kidney.

Shit. Damn. No frickin' way!

During that phone conversation with him there were the ever awkward, "Uh . . . OK . . . uh, wow . . . OK . . . OK . . . uh, yeah," stammerings that those who have been through this know all too well. Somehow through the tongue numbing shock I mustered, "So what happens next?"

He was immediately scheduled for surgery. I flew down to see him the day after in the hospital. He was in great spirits, his usual laughing, joking self, giving everyone within range all the grief he could, playing patient and consoler at the same time.

I pulled his mother aside to get the prognosis. Ruth and Bob, Randy's parents, had been my second mom and dad growing up. I love them like my own folks. We tacitly knew, without words, the seriousness of the situation, despite Randy's attempts to keep the mood in the room jovial.

She said they had done a complete nephrectomy (removed the kidney), and the surgery itself had gone well. And then she uttered the words that everyone who has gone through this prays they won't hear, "The cancer has spread to his lymph nodes."

Shit. Damn. I knew all too clearly what this meant. Those little bastard cancer cells were just floating throughout his body looking for a warm cozy place to set up shop.

Even though they had "gotten all of it," referring to the main tumor (I dread hearing that stupid phrase too!), there were quite possibly hundreds of little time bombs still in him, God only knows where, just waiting to go ape shit at the first opportunity.

I walked back into Randy's room from the hall where Ruth and I had been talking, and as I saw him laughing and joking, I put on my best game face and joined the BS-ing.

Most of his family was there as was Randy's and my high school buddy, Rob.

The whole scene was so macabre, like a great fun reunion

that was making me sick to my stomach.

Honestly, on the outside I was smiling while inside my guts were roiling and my spirit was staggering into a depression that would end up lasting two years.

Of course I hoped for "The Miracle," but I braced for Armageddon.

When it was time for me to go I hugged his mom and dad and Misty, but with a bit more intensity, a bit more holding on than normal goodbye hugs. These were hugs full of history, love, fear and insecurity, but at the same time trying very hard not to betray any hint of desperation.

I left after hugging Randy, but with him I tried not to belabor the embrace. Everything had to seem OK. To emphasize that, I made a point to give him grief about being shaved, everywhere, for surgery. He said something like, "You only wish you could see that!"

If he was scared he didn't let on. Or perhaps he was just a better actor than the rest of us.

Or maybe, just maybe, things would be OK, and somehow he intrinsically knew. Maybe he would be "The Miracle" . . . maybe.

After a few weeks off Randy went back to his job at a nursing home. Shortly before his diagnosis he had completed his R.N. degree and was very proud of that fact. He had no other treatment after surgery because for kidney cancers chemo doesn't work. It's hack it out, cross your fingers and pray like hell!

I called him frequently during his convalescence, and made a point to visit Indy as much as I could to lend moral support, and just in case at some point there would be no Randy there to visit.

He seemed to be doing OK, although we were all still nervous.

As anyone who has gone through this knows, when a loved one is diagnosed with any life-threatening illness, you immediately want to help, to have a magic wand and make them better; click your heels three times and you're back in Kansas with a healthy body, finding out it really was just a bad dream.

I desperately wanted that to be the case with Randy. I wanted this all to mysteriously disappear and for him to live - admittedly as much for my sake as for his. The comfort and rapport I knew with him could never be duplicated.

And deep down I knew half of me would die with him if he checked out.

Randy, the catalyst for 26 years of memories, joys and future adventures would be gone. I couldn't let that happen! I had to at least tell him about what might be his medical "Ace in the Hole."

In the early eighties I had chanced upon the book *Cancer Winner*, by Jaquie Davison.[1] Its cover jumped out at me, almost mystically, from a shelf in the health food section of a local grocery store. As I thumbed through the large paperback, it described a bizarre but captivating cancer treatment called The Gerson Therapy.[2] With lettuce, carrot, and raw liver juices combined with coffee enemas to pull out the toxins, the author had recovered from a cancer so vicious it almost certainly guarantees a death certificate to anyone who gets it.

The entire premise is to put one's body into healing over-drive, super boosting the immune system, altering the very chemistry of the cells so the body can push out the poisons attacking it, and then put them into the bloodstream for elimination.

That's where the coffee enemas come in. They stimulate the bile ducts and ducts in the liver and gall bladder to pump all the poisons and toxic material out into the colon where they are then excreted.

The therapy was developed by Dr. Max Gerson. As a young physician in 1920's Germany he had been plagued by severe migraine headaches and began pursuing a cure.

He discovered that by radically changing his diet he could eliminate them. Over the ensuing decades he expanded on this premise and developed a therapy that has proved successful on a variety of illnesses including not only cancer, but TB and MS as well. Indeed, his own daughter Charlotte, who currently oversees the Gerson Institute, was cured of bone tuberculosis using his methods.

For some reason his work resonated with me on several levels. The logic of boosting the body's defenses rather than poisoning them with chemo and radiation just made sense, and was dramatically reinforced by Jaquie's astounding recovery.

I purchased Dr. Gerson's summary of his work, *A Cancer Therapy: Results of Fifty Cases*, which he presented to the U.S. Senate in public hearings during July of 1946. While many of the technical aspects were over my head at that time, I never forgot about it.

When two favorite aunts came down with cancer, one with colon, the other with pancreatic, I sent them copies of Jaquie's and Dr. Gerson's book - at the very least to present another option, at the most to save their lives. They both passed away without pursuing the therapy. Would it have helped them? I don't know, but I would have loved to have found out.

I mentioned the therapy to anyone I knew who was diagnosed with cancer over the next several years, familiarizing myself with it more and more with each case that crossed my path, and gave books to anyone who wanted additional in-depth information. But still, no one actually did it.

Did folks just not want to think outside the traditional box of American medicine?

Was the arduous nature of the process just too much to even contemplate?

Before Randy had surgery I mentioned the Gerson Therapy to him. I didn't push it because he was under a lot of stress and his long-term prognosis was unknown at that time.

Plus, as I mentioned earlier, he had just gotten his nursing degree a few months before and was understandably engulfed in traditional approaches to healing. I'm sure carrot juice and rectal coffee sounded like voodoo to him. Still, graciously, he let me send him the books anyway.

After he went back to work we all thought maybe, just maybe, things were OK. There weren't immediate signs of cancer elsewhere in his body and hopefully we would all be moving on beyond this immense, frightening, bump in the road, and by the end of the year be laughing over beers about Randy being shaved "everywhere" for surgery.

But in the early fall, that bump in the road became a dead end. Randy and his wife lived in the country. He told her he was going for a walk and almost as if he had a premonition said, "If I don't come back, come looking for me." Out in one of his fields he began to feel woozy. He passed out.

He awoke with gnats buzzing about his face and a terrified Misty yelling for him, having taken his prophetic words to heart.

He had suffered a stroke caused by one of three tumors in his brain. His speech became slightly slurred and he had a pronounced limp in his right leg.

They tried radiation on what Randy called his "trifecta," with limited success. In a preemptive strike against radiation induced hair loss, he shaved his head, making him look like some kind of Hoosier Lex Luther.

He told me later he was terrified the "trifecta" would make him a vegetable.

When I got the news I couldn't eat for two days and the

world in my eyes seemed like a viciously cruel place. Thirty-nine was too young for this to happen to anyone, especially someone as vibrantly engaged with his life and the lives of his family, friends and coworkers as Randy.

And selfishly, I felt it was too young to happen to me. People aren't supposed to lose their best buddies until well after they've pinched a few aides in the nursing home together, or at the very least spent several Tuesday mornings BS-ing at the local pancake house with other octogenarians about what was, is, and could have been.

I went down to visit him as soon as I could. Fortunately by then he was ambulatory with a cane and we went to see a llama he and Misty were thinking about buying, Woolly Bully. As we walked into the farm where Woolly was kept, I watched Randy gimping along, bald and slowly losing the beautiful vitality that had buoyed me up on so many occasions. It was ripping me in half, but I couldn't lose it, not now, not here. I needed to be his life preserver and at least attempt to keep his spirits afloat, not the other way around.

We reminisced, trying to analyze why we were the way we were, musing over past girlfriends, comparing and contrasting our parents, and eventually addressing the reality of his current situation.

The only thing I could do to give me any sense of control over the encroaching chaos of his illness was to bring the Gerson Therapy again to the table. I had nothing to lose. I always did it lightly and he would joke back his refusal. This time I offered to go with him to the Gerson clinic in Mexico, but I think the image of the proverbial "Mexican Cancer

Clinic" just reinforced his image of the therapy as quackery.

He continued to lose stamina and mobility. In October, Gail and I went down to help build a fence for the now purchased Wooly Bully. Most of Randy's family and our friend Rob were there and Randy got around on an electric cart. He wore a sultanesque wrap on his head and dark glasses, because his skin and eyes were becoming increasingly sensitive to sunlight, although he did manage to operate the rented posthole digger hooked to his tractor pretty well.

We again joked about Gerson. I got creative and told him, "Look, if you go on it and live, I'll pay for it. If you go on it and die on me, then it's your nickel," trying humorously to convey my confidence in Dr. Gerson's and Jaquie's books which I had by then re-read and studied. But realistically, I knew he'd never go to Mexico. It wasn't his choice and it wasn't my call.

The helplessness of not being able to do anything to save him was the most frustrating conundrum in my life to that point. The universe was forcing me to just stand by and watch him go down.

He was sentenced to die, convicted of nothing.

During those days, God was not on my "Friends and Family" list.

A week or so later, masses showed up in his lungs and liver. The last time I saw him alive was at Thanksgiving, roughly six months after his initial diagnosis. Misty was understandably restricting his calls and visits. He only had energy for about 10 minutes. With his gray/black deeply sunken eyes, and waxy, pallid skin tone, he looked like a B movie zombie.

The worst moments in my life have been when I know I am seeing someone for the last time. Maybe if you just hug them hard enough you can keep them from going. Gail had to drive me from his place because I was weeping so hard. The tears were the deep kind, like a wild coyote dying in a leg trap.

I felt so utterly helpless, angry and cheated. And I knew I would feel like this for a long time.

On December 11th, I got the call that Randy was dead. He passed on with his family and Rob at his side. There were two days of reviewal. Of course Misty was there - as were Randy's ex-wife and enough of his old girlfriends that had he been alive, the stress might have killed him anyway.

The line of cars to the cemetery was huge, a testament to his magnetic personality that refused to be diminished by the frigid, drizzly, December day. I was so punchy by the end of it all that with just a few family and friends around who I knew would get the joke, I threw my voice into the casket at the graveside saying, "Hey, let me outta here! I'm not dead yet! I gotta take a dump!"

They loved it and we all needed the release, no matter how macabre the joke. Randy would have enjoyed it too, had he been able to hear it, as he lay there along with half my soul in that dark blue, cold, metal casket.

If Randy had done Gerson right away would he have

lived? Truly God (who I have by this time forgiven) only knows. I wished I had forced the issue, but people choose what's right for them and we have to respect that. The world obviously doesn't revolve around just what I want, even though in Randy's case, I sure wished it did.

But maybe, just maybe, if I couldn't save Randy, I could save someone else.

---

1. Jaquie Davison, *Cancer Winner: How I Purged Myself of Melanoma* (Pierce City, MO: Pacific Press, 1977).

2. Max Gerson M.D., *A Cancer Therapy: Results of Fifty Cases and the Cure of Advanced Cancer by Diet Therapy,* 6th ed. (San Diego: Gerson Institute, 2002).

Chapter Two

Cathy

After Randy died, I always had the fear that I'd have to go through it all again. Would it be a parent? My sister? Another close friend?

But outwardly, I let myself believe the illusion that one close loss younger than 50 would be it. Randy's early excruciatingly painful exit had to be just an aberration.

21st Century medicine was good enough that I would be spared that agony again. With luck, my immediate circle of friends and family would live at least well into our seventh decades, with plenty of senior moments and Depends jokes along the way to cushion the inevitable journey down Wrinkles Road and Hoveround Highway.

In other words, we'd be ready: "OK, it was a good life and this IS when things start breaking down," and "We may not like it, but it is the natural course of things," would be thoughts we'd begrudgingly resign ourselves to.

In the late 90's, Gail and I had a good network of folks around us between the ages of 45 and 55: Baby Boomers who grew up on "Leave It to Beaver" and "Gilligan's Island," the Kennedy assassination and the Cuban Missile Crisis. We rebelled against the system with the Beatles, and bought back in with our 401Ks.

One of the most effervescent of this peer group was Gail's sister Cathy. They grew up together in Richfield, Minnesota, a classic post-war working class suburb of Minneapolis.

Cathy was cute, full of personality, and definitely a favorite of the boys.

And of Gail's three siblings, Cathy was the one that eventually most resembled her. As adults they were often mistaken for one another, even though growing up, Gail was far shyer than her outgoing sister.

Cathy was generally easy going and light hearted . . . unless you added foreign ingredients or otherwise modified her Famous Chili Recipe! Then you were on your own! Other people would fade into the woodwork in terror as you tried to reconcile your trespass with a beet faced, fuming Cathy!

Cathy enjoyed her career as a dental hygienist and with her husband Bob, was raising two crimson-headed sons who as typical boys, were obsessed with giving each other as much grief as they possibly could. Theirs was very much an idyllic American family: enthusiastic about sports, active in church and generous contributors to their community.

Not having children of our own, Gail and I enjoyed watching the four of them go through the transitions of life, sharing each benchmark of graduations, girlfriends and gridiron achievement.

The solidness of their family process gave me a sense that yes, this world was still a great place to be, with good people making every effort to make it better and enjoying themselves along the way. That for me was what Cathy and her family, the Nichols, were all about.

In February/March of '99 the Nichols took a trip to their timeshare on the big island of Hawaii. They had purchased it a few years before and loved spending time there, always returning with enviable stories of sun, fun, golf and lots of spontaneous family adventure.

Toward the end of this trip, however, Cathy became constipated. Not unusual on a vacation with lots of rich food, different water, flying, etc. So they weren't really worried until it didn't go away after returning home to Minnesota. Alarmingly, after only two days back, Cathy began vomiting bile.

It was frighteningly clear that this was something far more serious than simple constipation.

They ended up at the ER in St. Paul, about 25 minutes from their home. A GI study showed an ominous tumor intertwined amongst the tissues of Cathy's transverse colon, blocking anything from getting through. Her entire digestive system had been backing up for days with no way to purge the building pressure and toxicity except by throwing up.

She was immediately scheduled for emergency "dirty" surgery. Dirty surgery means that there was no time to clean out Cathy's colon and digestive tract, indicating not only the severity of the blockage, but the gravity of the situation.

Fortunately for Cathy, the surgeon on call was one of the top practitioners in his field for this type of operation.

Family and friends breathed a heavy sigh of relief when we were informed that the surgery had gone "very well" despite having to do it "dirty," and because the tumor had not broken the colon wall, there was a good chance that they "got it all." But for me, when I heard THOSE fateful words again, an uncontrollable shudder went through my suddenly brittle feeling bones. Randy's haunting, sunken eyed, pre-death visage staggered out of the vault where I thought I had locked it away forever.

Not again, not again, please God, not again.

Miraculously though, a biopsy of the lymph nodes in the area of the mass came out clean. Wow! Really? Cool! THAT is GOOD news! My cynical heart suddenly might have to eat some crow. I hoped so, and I had the ketchup ready!

They rated the mass itself on the cusp between a grade 2 and 3. Not the worst you can have, but certainly enough to lose sleep over and give serious cause for concern.

Because of the rating and extent of the mass, Cathy opted to follow-up with oral chemo, which hopefully would take care of any roaming cancer cells but be less grueling on her body. She would keep her hair, have less discomfort, etc., and her oncologist entered her in a study of a new med they both agreed would be appropriate.

Anything stronger at this point seemed unnecessary, especially because after surgery her tumor markers (indicators of tumors that show up in the bloodstream) were well within the normal range.

More good news. There WAS hope! OK black-eyed Randy

visage, time to shrink back in your vault and out of the forefront of my mind.

Cathy was upbeat after the surgery and relieved to have it over with. She felt good and enjoyed getting back to her work at the dental office, guiding her sons to manhood, and spending time with the love of her life, Bob.

As the months passed, friends and family remained upbeat and hoped for the best. The further Cathy got from surgery without any major problems, the easier it was to exhale, to let go of worries and fears. But, as with Randy, it was impossible not to keep at least a small part of one's soul braced for the worst, just out of self-defense.

At a family outing I mentioned the Gerson Therapy to her. Even though I knew it might be an awkward conversation, if I didn't take the risk and things turned out for the worse for Cathy, I would have second guessed myself for the rest of my life.

I posed it as an insurance policy, even though she was doing well, mentioning that it could help her body cleanse itself not only of any remaining cancer cells, but the toxicity from all the treatment she had been through to this point. She listened, but quickly and politely declined. As with Randy, it didn't resonate on any level.

I just prayed somehow, this time things would work out differently.

Unfortunately, in the fall of 2000 after a regular checkup, Cathy's tumor markers were elevated but doctors couldn't find anything. She felt OK though, and she and Bob went back to Hawaii.

But even the gentle fragrant breezes of the Big Island couldn't slow down her increasingly higher marker numbers. By March 2001 they were off the charts - but still her physicians found nothing.

It took two more months to isolate any specific tumors. They showed up finally in scans as potential ovarian masses and vague spots on her liver. They did a needle biopsy to see if it was recurring colon cancer or by some miracle something less threatening, but the results were inconclusive.

Suddenly the dam of possible recovery had broken and Cathy and her family were up to their necks in the river of confusion, ambivalence and mixed messages that seem to define cancer.

What is it? Why did it recur, if it even is a recurrence? What now? CAN'T WE JUST BE DONE WITH THIS AND MOVE THE HELL ON?

They decided to do surgery to find out exactly what was happening.

Gail had accompanied Cathy on many of her doctor's appointments, being an extra ear to help process the myriad of information she had to sort out, and to make sure she wouldn't be alone. Gail had reduced her hours at work just to help. It was during a conversation before this next surgery Cathy intimated her most chilling and painful fear, "I'm afraid they're going to open me up, and it'll be so bad they'll just close me up and send me home."

And that, in essence, is just what they did.

In addition to a good sized mass on one of her ovaries, necessitating a hysterectomy, and definite spots on her liver, only some of which the surgeon was able to remove, he said Cathy had a scattering of masses, "bird seed" he called them, throughout her abdominal cavity. Picking around at them would indeed be fruitless. Biopsies of the tissue showed it was recurrent colon cancer, a virulent, tenacious killer with a survival rate of only 10% after five years.[3,4]

Shit! Damn! Here we go again.

In August, after healing from surgery, Cathy started a different, stronger round of chemo. Ever the devoted sister, Gail found her several hats with faux hair sticking out to wear over her rapidly balding head.

But Cathy had a hard time with this new chemo. Her blood counts were so low she didn't even finish her first course (odd it should sound like a dinner party).

As she tried to continue the regimen in fits and starts, dehydration and diarrhea set in. Cathy bravely learned to inject herself with anti-diarrhea drugs and even with that, landed in the hospital at least once to get her fluid levels where they should be. Eventually though, she had to abandon the treatment altogether.

It had simply become untenable.

All of this, needless to say was incredibly tedious, complicated, and frustrating not only for her, but for her family and friends as well. It had been three and a half years of chaos and uncertainty with the basic overriding question always being, "Can she pull out of this?"

By spring of 2002 she had recovered from the grueling and seemingly cruel chemo regimen, and for a brief period of time her life, like her hair, had returned to normal, even though indicators showed she was definitely not out of the woods.

Her primary oncologist told her flat out there was nothing more he could do so she tried to get in some experimental studies. She was rejected from one because of a blood clot in her lung caused by the intensity of the chemo she had been taking.

On Mothers Day, she and Bob caught up with us at a great local restaurant, Me Gusta in St. Paul. We were there with her and Gail's mom and her boyfriend, Bill.

Cathy looked sharp in her blue workout suit and white pristine tennies. It was great to see her with hair, and we all enjoyed a normal family celebration replete with good food, good laughs and lots of giving each other grief. The mood was light and it was encouraging, whatever the realities, to see her looking so normal, enjoying one of the simple pleasures that makes it all worth it, Mother's Day.

It was the kind of holiday family meal where everyone feels at least a modicum of safety from the painful parts of their lives, be it cancer, jobs or fender benders. Cares are pushed away with laughter, fear dissolved by communion, faith bolstered by love.

We relished in that safety of shared experience for at least two hours and then parted company. In a few short months we would be brought together even closer as Cathy began to slip away from us.

On her 49th birthday, July 17th '02, she went to the hallowed Mayo Clinic, the Minnesota bastion of cutting edge medicine. They tested her from head to toe to see if there were any other possibilities for treatment.

One of the nurses took the bold step of making a suggestion that was in some of our minds, but we dared not utter. She said, "Have you considered doing nothing?" And although it's a logical statement to make, perhaps a merciful one, it also means you have given up, that's it, case closed. At 49, you can kiss your boys, your friends and your loving husband and family goodbye.

It changes everything from "if" to "when."

That was not for Cathy and Bob.

They had always encouraged their son, John, to win his football games, to play hard to the end no matter what the outcome. It wasn't their spirit, their outlook. In everything they did they brought joy, support and optimism, always being a welcome spark for friends, family and co-workers.

Quitting was not an option. Not only would it not be right for them, they didn't want to let down all the people who were pulling for them.

They would fight on.

They prayed that Mayo might come up with a miracle.

Indeed as they left the clinic their doctor had said there might be some possibilities for this or that study, a new med, a different approach.

But shortly after getting home they got the call that nothing at Mayo would pan out.

However, as that door shut, another one opened as Cathy's primary oncologist in St. Paul got her into a fresh study with a new experimental combo of meds. Ever hopeful and with literally nothing to lose, she signed up. Unfortunately it proved to be just more trauma on her already beaten down body and spirit. The new combo made her very sensitive to cold, so much so that on one trip to the hospital, her face and systems literally froze up in the parking ramp and she had to be ambulanced to the ER, less than 100 yards away.

So, she had to abandon that study too. Now there were no other doors, just a long hallway with no way out.

We saw her in early December. She'd had a big burst of energy and gotten a lot of things done for the holidays. We had a nice visit with her and her family as she lay reclined in the living room in her favorite easy chair. She kept up with the banter of Bob and the boys, who still gave her the verbal grief all boys, young and old, give their moms and spouses and girlfriends. At least that part of her life was still normal.

Although she was resting comfortably, she repeatedly mentioned a persistent pressure she felt in her abdomen. She had Gail feel the apparent cause, a hard spot in her belly lurking under her navy blue sweatshirt. While it alarmed Gail, it obviously helped Cathy feel not quite so alone in her suffering.

Unlike Mother's Day, where she looked healthy and it seemed anything was possible, this day you could tell she was a very ill person. She was a bit pale, and the fatigue of all her trials seeped softly but persistently out through the corners of her deep brown eyes.

As much as I hated it, in my own mind I had gone from "if" to "when." I got angry with myself for even having the thought. Who was I to mentally start putting someone in their grave? But looking back, it was just my own defense mechanisms making a preemptive strike, desperately trying to dodge at least some of the emotional bullets inevitably storming our way.

In early January of '03 she was back in the hospital with diarrhea and dehydration. She had been in a couple of times after we saw her in early December, but this time after being admitted, her bowels ceased pushing anything through. It didn't get caught right away, because no one had been monitoring her bowel output.

As the bile and toxins backed up inside her, she of course had increasing pain. They put her on two pain meds at once - six Fentanyl patches and Delaudid in a self administered pump. We still don't know if it was the combination or the quantity of these two meds, but shortly after they were applied Cathy went into a bizarre, hallucinogenic stupor where she lost all track of reality.

All she could say many days was, "I gotta go, I gotta go." Whether this meant home, to the toilet or to heaven was anyone's guess. Eventually an NG tube relieved some of her suffering and deflated her by now incredibly distended abdomen. When hearing about Cathy's state, a physician who was a friend of the family intervened in what seemed to be an incredibly poor lack of oversight by the hospital.

He was appalled at the combo and amount of pain meds being administered, and the Fentanyl patches were removed the same day. But despite his best efforts, she would never again be the same person or even have a modicum of the lucidity that defined her as Cathy.

While she was there, they found the cause of the backup - a tumor completely obstructing her bowel. In addition, the spots on her liver had now become a very large mass completely encompassing that organ, the apparent cause of the pressure she felt at Christmas. She also had a lot of fluid buildup that had to be removed via pericentisis.

It was time to let go.

As circumstances worked out, I was the only one able to go with her when the transport came to take her to hospice.

As I waited with Cathy for our ride, an idiot nurse, without reading Cathy's chart came in and said, "Well, aren't you lucky, you're going home today!"

Oh my God! Now, not only am I going to be the one accompanying Cathy to the last place she'll see on this earth, I had to reinforce that in her very confused mind.

Choking on my words, I agonizingly did my best to tell an understandably confused Cathy no, she wasn't going home, she was going to hospice, in essence saying, "You're going to die and will never see home again."

I then went outside and read that nurse the riot act.

How on earth could she be so callous working on an oncology ward? And how could she put me in such a devastatingly difficult position? It's trivial and petulant, but I wanted to make her feel guilty as hell for the rest of her natural life.

The best part of the day was that the hospice was a beautiful, peaceful place to die. Set up well for the patient, family and friends, it was a welcome relief from the bings and bongs and incessant hubbub of the hospital. The staff was caring, attentive and concerned for our welfare as well as Cathy's.

Dying here would be easier than the pretense of trying to make her well at the hospital.

I got Cathy settled in and Gail arrived within an hour, thank God. The stress of being alone on Cathy's journey to the last room she would ever see was more than I could get my little puppet boy head around. Bob had to work, the boys were in school, and her siblings had obligations.

I understood that. It was just so surreal, a situation I had never experienced. I just wanted to hug and hold her the whole way in the ambulance, but that would have been an inappropriate dramatization of the situation. So I sat and chatted with the driver as she was attended by a tech in the back. Still, mentally I held her in a protective bubble and had she cried out, I felt like I could have ripped through my seatbelt to help her. She was at arguably the most vulnerable moment of her life and whether God wanted me to be or not, I was steadfastly committed to being her guardian angel.

At the hospice, with Gail finally there, I could let go. It was a nice place to be. Gail could sign all the intake papers and I could finally leave Cathy's side.

My job of buffering her from the world and any other "You're going home!" nurses was done for the day. As I pulled up in front of Gail's and my little turn of the century spindle laden house that afternoon, I called my wonderful understanding parents on my cell phone . . . and began weeping uncontrollably. I hadn't planned to let go, but nestled in the emotional embrace of Mom and Dad, the floodgates just opened. And I full well realized that while many of the tears were for Cathy, some were still for Randy, and a hell of a lot were for me.

At the hospice, Cathy was never alone. Gail and her mother set up camp in her room and a steady stream of friends and family poured in.

Bonded by our grief, we couldn't help but become close. We all shared meals there, laughed there and wept there.

One afternoon the staff summoned us all into Cathy's room saying she might go anytime. About a dozen of us gathered around her bed as she lay there, eyes half shut, the click of her NG pump pulsing rhythmically in the background.

We all joined hands and waited. Someone said a prayer. We waited some more. 10 minutes passed. We waited some more. 20. Had it been any other circumstance I would have broken the tension with a joke. It was getting to the point where you could tell some folks were pretending to be focused, but were probably drifting off into thoughts of football or recipes. Suddenly Cathy's mom said "Look up!" What the hell for we didn't know, but we did it anyway.

25, 30, 35 minutes. We're all looking up and I was having serious trouble suppressing the giggles that were welling up inside me. If it had been a Monty Python movie, Cathy would have popped up and said "Hey, I'm not dead yet! Piss off!" As it was, a staff member or someone had the mercy to verbalize what we all by now knew, "Maybe this just isn't the time."

I had to go out the front door and laugh out loud, both to relieve the tension, and at the thought of all of us standing there for 45 minutes looking like idiots.

Although she didn't go then, different parts of Cathy gradually began shutting down, but her strong, loving heart just wouldn't let her pass for another three days. She slipped over to God late one evening with her mother in the room and Gail at her side, caressing her last breath with all their senses before letting it drift delicately to heaven along with Cathy's beautiful spirit.

Four years of hopes, doubts, dreams and suffering were over.

Gail spent the night at home for the first time in six days and began her own recovery.

Cathy was laid to rest on a grey, bitter, windy January

day. A couple hundred people attended her service, and I lost it when I saw that the church choir she had been such an integral part of had left her chair open. You could almost see her there, joining in enthusiastically, but not quite understanding that the service was for her.

I did have to chuckle at the reviewal when Cathy's son Nick asked me "Please, Uncle Jim, don't throw your voice into the casket," not knowing that as much as I loved Cathy, that was an honor reserved only for Randy.

Gail was exhausted physically and mentally from the ordeal. She, almost as much as Bob, had been there for Cathy during the entire saga.

I was so grateful that in a little over a month, Gail had a wonderful trip to France planned to attend the wedding of a girl for whom she had been an au pair just out of college.

She was very close to the family, and they would embrace and nurture her, take her beautiful places, and make her forget the ravages of cancer that had decimated her sister. It would be just what Gail needed most.

Except for one thing: two weeks later it would be my turn.

---

3. Yahoo!® Health, "Colon Cancer," http://health.yahoo.com/coloncancer-treatment/colorectal-cancer-metastatic-or-recurrent-treatment-overview/healthwise--tv7575.html.

4. American Society, "Colorectal Cancer Facts & Figures Special Edition 2005," http://www.cancer.org/Research/CancerFactsFigures/ColorectalCancerFactsFigures/colorectal-cancer-facts-figures-special-edition-2005.

Chapter Three

Well, your spleen is fine but . . .

The discovery of something amiss with my body had no warning signs, no out of place discomfort, no mysterious pains or ominous bleeding. It came after a show in Yankton, South Dakota. Yes, lovely Yankton, home of big belt buckles, Tom Brokaw and the Lewis and Clark Trail. In fact, it was near Yankton in 1804 that Lewis and Clark tried to flush a prairie dog out of its burrow for shipment back to President Thomas Jefferson as a sample of western wildlife.[5]

Prairie dogs aside, in February of '03, I was just glad to be getting back to the routine of making a living. The week after Cathy's death I had won the first round of a talent competition at Jackpot Junction Casino and was looking forward to the finals in April. I brought Gail's mom with me to give her a respite from the stress of losing her daughter, and she had a great time feeding the nickel slots and playing the flirtatious coquette with a couple of lonely widowers who chanced her way.

Doing gigs and the talent show was a totally different energy than Cathy's ordeal, and it helped purge a lot of the overriding sadness I was feeling by doing what I do best, making people laugh.

But I had a lot of trepidation about getting back to Yankton. Not because of performing, that part would be a piece of cake. By this time, I had been making a living playing with big wooden dolls for 15 years, and this gig was a fairly cut and dried affair.

I was getting anxious because the last time I was in Yankton I had rolled my Isuzu Trooper on ice coming into town.

It was a little more South Dakota adventure than I had bargained for, much more than your typical trip to the Black Hills, where the most exciting thing you do in the car is trying to figure out just how many obnoxious Wall Drug billboards actually exist, or playing "License Plates" for five hours straight.

Always up for taking the path less traveled, that day I had decided to take a back road into Yankton, thinking it might be more scenic than the monotony of the interstate I had been cruising down for hours. Unfortunately, it was one of the coldest winters of the decade with record snows, and I forgot that unlike safety-and-rust-loving Minnesota that dumps tons of salt on even the remotest highways, in root'n toot'n South Dakota, even if a glacier suddenly covers the state, they will not salt their roads.

Why? I don't know. Maybe if you need salt on your roads you're just not quite man enough to live in South Dakota. Or maybe they just can't stand to see their vehicles cannibalized by the stuff.

"Well, we may lose a family or two, but we'll save a lot of Silverado's and F-150's!"

Or just maybe it's a throwback to their Wild West heritage. "Hell, a good Appaloosa never needed salt and so, by God, neither should automobiles!"

Whatever the reason, I wasn't expecting any trouble

having just exited a relatively ice free I-29. It hadn't snowed for a few days and I thought even without salt, things should be fairly clear by now.

Silly me. About two miles down my country road, I hit a patch of glare ice going about 40 mph. My Trooper spun around 180 degrees, catapulted off the opposite side of the highway, and rolled one and a half times like a 3,000 pound Nadia Comaneci.

Far from bouncing back like Nadia, however, my poor Trooper looked like a skier who missed the end of the jump: crumpled, disfigured, dejected and half buried in a three foot deep snow bank.

The good news; thanks to the Lord watching out for fools and children, me being the former (because as much as I wanted to blame South Dakota, ultimately is was MY fault . . . . damn it!), and a sturdy seatbelt, I was fine.

It wasn't my day to become an odd and insignificant foot-note on the evening news: " . . . and we leave you with this tonight - ventriloquist James Wedgwood died in a car accident today. He is survived by his parents, his loving wife, and three now very quiet little wooden friends."

Five minutes after the roll, help arrived. Looming over the horizon and blocking out the sun with its immensity, came a four-wheel-drive-engaged, cylinders injected with tes-tosterone, mondo magnum pick-up truck. Two massive mounds of prairie beef in full hunting regalia thudded out of each cavernous door, steaming in the chill of the ten-degree air.

We couldn't have been more different. Me: 145 lbs. of puppet boy. Them: ¼ ton of predator looking to kill.

"Need a lift?" one of them grunted. I stood there elated to be saved, but trembling a bit at the sight of my saviors. Their names were something like Cletus and Rastis, and as I struggled up into the cab, "Rastis" had to move the Colt 45 revolver perched ominously in the middle of the bench seat.

He lovingly placed it under the Winchester rifle hanging in the window behind us. As I sat between them, I suddenly became the squashed middle of a living, breathing concertina. But at least I was saved, or so I thought until we turned the wrong way. I knew the nearest gas station was east and we headed back west. A feeling of foreboding permeated my body. Instantly the ugliest scenes from "Deliverance" and that incessant banjo music throbbed into my head. Would my remains be ravaged by starving coyotes, not to be found until next year's harvest, identified only by my most recent root canal?

"Our dog jumped out of the bed of the truck a couple of miles back; we gotta find 'im," Cletus blurted out. Right . . . now I was sure I was going to become some sort of Great Plains sacrifice to the hunting gods, a wink and a nod between two good ol' boys shared over beers for years to come. But sure enough, a little ways down the road, there was Lukey, or whatever the dog's name was, trotting down the side of the gravel shoulder.

I was never so glad to see an animal.

As promised, with Lukey now where he should be according to South Dakota standards, freezing in the open bed of the truck, Cletus and Rastis delivered me to a gas station. And one tow, five cans of Fix-a-Flat, and ten rolls of duct tape later, my Trooper and I were on our way to the show in Yankton two hours later, one more show in Sioux City the next night, and a six hour drive back to St. Paul with a crushed roof and bent front wheel the day after that.

Flushing out a little prairie dog? Lewis and Clark had nothing on me in the adventure department.

So, I was understandably a bit anxious to return to the site of this previous debacle. But I was looking forward to the show itself. South Dakota audiences are always great, not withstanding my initial trepidation about Cletus, Rastis and Lukey.

My shtick and their sensibilities are always a good fit. I'm not sure why. Maybe it's because my father was born there.

Or maybe it's just that I find all those jackalope so oddly appealing.

The show was for Lesterville Feed & Grain. Some of the people I admire most are American ag producers: Corn & bean growers, beef producers, pork producers, dairy folk. These people work hard, often make very little money and would give you the best Walmart shirt off their backs if you needed it. Even the one they'd bought on special.

I remember sitting next to a couple who were dairy farmers at one of these events in western Wisconsin. Because they had to tend their animals 24/7, the banquet was the first night out they'd had in seven years!

At the event in Yankton in '03, it was also Valentine's Day. Holidays are fun to gig on because you always have a couple of special jokes for the occasion, and people are usually in a better mood.

So, after a brief stop at the Lewis & Clark prairie dog historical marker, where I removed my hat and squeaked in homage, I pulled into the hotel, grateful to be on all four wheels and no Rastis or Cletus in sight.

The banquet room was nice, typical for this type of hotel with round tables and an 8'x16' riser for me. There was lighting already mounted in the ceiling which meant I didn't have to use my own spots, reducing my set up time by a good 20 minutes.

Things were plugging along well. The audience should be great, the weather the next day was scheduled to be a relatively warm 50 degrees, and I started feeling a little cocky. "Yeah, I'm back in Yankton but it ain't gonna get me THIS time. Nyeh, nyeh, nyeh. I'm gonna kick some South Dakota entertainment tail, and maybe even cruise my butt home for a little 3:00 A.M. Valentine snuggle with my woman!"

Another reason I felt this way was the act was the best it had ever been. My material was diverse and creative, my timing was great, and I knew how to handle almost any performance situation. Doing the show was the most fun part of the business. Onstage, I could leave behind the marketing, phone calls, driving and . . . union issues with my dummies (they keep demanding bathrooms in their suit-cases!).

But on another level, I somehow didn't have quite the physical oomph I used to. The shows were fine, where adrenaline would take over and let my midlife body catch up with my hopelessly adolescent spirit.

But in between, during setup or rest periods, I didn't recover like I used to.

It always kills me when I hear rock stars whine about being on the road. "Oh, it's sooo hard to be on tour! Like, we did 13 shows in two months in different towns. The worst was when I had to sleep on the same satin sheets on my luxury bus two nights in a row because my stupid staff couldn't find a laundry-mat. It was sooo ishy. I just don't think I could do THAT again! Thank God now I'm a recording artist."

In the year before this Valentine's gig, I did hundreds of separate shows all over the country and that included setup, teardown, driving, plus foot rubs for the dummies with Murphy Oil.

In the month of August alone that year I did 54 shows, 34 in July.

But rather than recovering like a Brittany Spears back-up dancer, bouncy and ready for more, I was starting to feel more like Keith Richards looks.

I arranged setups to minimize my load-in trips. Instead of exploring fairgrounds, I stayed in my car and slept. Instead of partying with a corporate client, I went back to my room and crashed.

It was the same in Yankton. I remember before the show, limiting the number of trips up and down the stage steps and feeling a little weary.

I just figured it was because I was pushing 50. I knew eventually I'd have to back off my workload, and that would be that; I just didn't know exactly when.

I perked up when I met the client though, and his friendliness got me looking forward to the show and pushed any concerns of fatigue aside. It was going to be a fun night with cattle raisin', corn and bean growin' Yanktonites, fatigue be damned! Yeee Hawwww!

And, adding to my newly found energy as I was setting up, I noticed the hotel had a couple of racquetball courts. I checked them out. When I saw the highly polished wood floor, the intimidating expanse of stark white walls and the countless blue rubber ball marks mutely testifying to innumerable sweat filled battles, I was immediately transported back to college at Indiana University.

In courts like this I had spent countless hours banging out school stress, a couple of bad relationships, and the post adolescent struggle to find out who the hell I really was.

I thought maybe I'd come back after the show and sneak in just a few volleys to relive those glory days, making a mental note to override any feelings of young man machismo that might be rekindled on the court with my midlife sensibilities, and thereby avoid any truly debilitating injury.

If you've ever played racquetball you know the feeling; it

happens the second that munchkin sized door slams with an echoey "bang" behind you, and your nostrils embrace the intoxicating fragrance of new Nikes, a freshly popped can of racquetballs and battle ripened tee shirts.

Your testosterone takes over and starts chanting, "Do something stupid to prove you're a man. C'me on, it's expected of you! You didn't watch all those hours of 'Rat Patrol' and 'Combat' in the 60's just to be a wimp, did you?"

"Chase a shot that in the long run means absolutely nothing and split your head open so we can be proud of you!"

While part of me thought that sounded like fun, I wouldn't give in this time. I would temper my ball smashing enthusiasm in the court just enough to be safe, but still have a little fun.

This was Yankton after all, and vivid memories of my rolled Trooper reinforced my catastrophic superstitions about being back here.

Anyway, before I could even think about putting a racquet in my middle aged hand, I had farmers to perform for. The show went great; they were very appreciative with many folks saying I was the best they'd ever seen. Of course when people say that, I have to take it with a grain of salt, full well knowing I'm probably the ONLY ventriloquist they've ever seen.

It does my heart good though knowing that somewhere, in the middle of a South Dakota cornfield, up on top of a combine the size of Mt. Rushmore, a little crackly grin will sneak across a farmer's sun dried face as something unforeseen sparks a memory of a chuckle he had this night.

Or that maybe over early morning coffee at the local Cenex Cooperative, with their coats still on so as not to seem too relaxed on a work day, voices young and old will tell those who weren't at the show how their best buddy so-and-so looked so stupid up there, talkin' to that damn piece of wood.

Riding the buzz from the performance, I was able to tear down quickly afterwards, and once the room had cleared of people, that ever-beckoning racquetball court began calling my name, almost insistently. With the dummies fed and watching Letterman, I changed, charged up to the front desk, gave the clerk a deposit on a racquet and balls, and suddenly I felt I was on my way to some nostalgic athletic nirvana. My senses were filled with collegiate memories of battles won and lost, studies avoided, and several enjoyable matches against a lovely blonde Swedish foreign exchange student who lived in my dorm. Her father had coached tennis legend Bjorn Borg and many days I didn't stand a chance, but with her being a very nubile 18-year-old, somehow that really wasn't the point. After corralling my junior-in-college libido, I drifted back to the present and the task at hand; can I even hit the ball?

I started slowly, a few gentle volleys against the wall's imposing white expanse. But there was no kidding myself. I knew after a few minutes I'd be embroiled in a fantastic fantasy game against the #1 player in the world, who only held that ranking because my racquet gripping fingers had been freakishly injured by an overzealous fan's crushing handshake, and now it was payback time.

I slowly increased my pace up and down the court, side-to-side blamming several missed kill shots with the cheap rental racquet. I was getting back into the swing of it. My pace picked up, the stiffness in my shoulders was fading, and my fantasy opponent was sucking serious wind.

But then it happened. The ball came high off the back wall. I rushed to the front of the court to crush it into the corner, when suddenly there was no traction under my feet. Snowmelt on the roof had leaked through and left a large slippery puddle about four feet from the front wall. My foot slid out from under me as I tried to plant it and I came down hard with my left elbow smashed under the left central part of my back.

For about the first thirty seconds, I was stunned. I couldn't figure out why I had lost traction so completely. Then I saw the large laconic drips rhythmically diving down from the ceiling like an old Esther Williams movie.

It was otherworldly, almost ethereal until I became aware of the PAIN! Excruciating pain engulfed my entire left side. I couldn't even imagine moving . . . anything! I didn't know what would happen next. Would I be able to rise and get help like a diminutive Spandex engulfed Phoenix, or would it be weeks before another racquetball playing guest registered at the hotel? By that time the roof leak would have filled the entire court and when the door opened, I would come gushing out like a drowned ant caught in the drain of some Godzillian cooler.

I knew the only thing that was going to move in the next few minutes were the neurons in my brain because my body was screaming, "Don't even think about lifting a pinky buster or we'll kill you," which is not a good thing for a body to be saying!

I couldn't remember ever experiencing such totally engulfing pain and being unable to right myself.

Then it hit me: The Yankton Curse was alive and well.

After five minutes of immobilization with the drip from the ceiling taunting me with each rhythmic splash, "Gotcha," I mustered the strength to roll over on my stomach and onto all fours. Owww! I waited some more, trying to fool my zinging nerves into thinking I was stopping in this position for the night. Once they were lulled into passivity, I made the final thrust to my feet. Fortunately the pain wasn't any worse, but I could only move at .5 mph. as I struggled not to twist my torso in any way.

I didn't have a water bottle in the court, which worried me, because it could be three days before I made it to the front desk.

As I oozed along the corridor of the hotel, I knew I needed an ER. Not just to be sure my spine hadn't been thrust through my liver, but for any liability issues that might arise later on.

When I finally schlumped into the lobby, the clerk had that "Oh you're hurt (I hope we're not screwed)" kind of look on her face. I told her what had happened, and I made sure someone got a look at the water still dripping dangerously onto the floor, just in case insurance and attorneys eventually got involved in my debacle.

The clerk got me a cab for the hospital and I was on my way. And of course, being Yankton, the cab smelled like a 50 year old ashtray as the driver puffed away and prattled on about her kids and grandkids. And then these words scraped past her nicotine laden vocal chords, "Do you mind, I have to pick up my son on the way?"

"Do I mind? DO I MIND? I am in some serious pain here and more than just a little freaked out but gee wiz, sure, pick up your son, take the longest route possible to the ER and while you're at it, let's go to frickin' Disney World!" I thought. But with her being the only cab in town, I reluctantly grunted "Sure," and off we went to get her boy.

What seemed like 14 hours, ended up being only a 10-minute cab ride, even though each bump was like a punch in the kidney. All I could do was stare out into the darkness at the last remnants of Valentine's Day and think, "Boy, does this suck." And at the risk of sounding very wimpy, I wanted more than anything to have my mother there, fretting and fussing over me and unashamedly encouraging my own self-pity.

The puffing cabby, and by now her puffing adult son, dropped me at the ER at Avera Sacred Heart Hospital. It was the first ER I'd been in where they actually acknowledged my agony when I hobbled through the door.

Smiling, concerned faces helped me through the blur of intake information, got me one of those stylish bracelets so if I passed out at least they could call one of my dummies for life and death decision making, and hustled me into an exam room.

They hooked me up to all kinds of monitors. Blood pressure, heart, and I think one wire was even DSL because I kept seeing flashes of "Google" in my eyes.

The nurse helping me was amazing. She was kind, validated my pain, and my not too well concealed fear. She even laughed at the couple of jokes I was able to eke out as much for my benefit as hers, and made a couple herself. But most importantly, she was from Minnesota. She could talk about home at a time when I most wanted to be there. I thanked God for her that night and do to this day.

She got me stabilized and 10 minutes later the doctor came in. Those 10 minutes of waiting were so strange. And why is it always at least 10 minutes? The Doc never comes right in. Is it just to get you jumping around in your own head enough that you'll believe anything the physician tells you? And you're alone, in a sterile room with odd instruments all around, wondering which ones are going to be used on you. "What DOES that piece of machinery do? What is that more-sterile-than-I'll-ever-be-in-my-life smell? Why do they shut the door? It's not like I'm going to try and escape. Are they all talking about my Mickey Mouse boxers out there? Have I finally been abducted by aliens?"

I always have the urge to touch or move or change things in those rooms just because everything always seems so sacred. I mean, wouldn't it be fun to surprise the Dr. with a "Whoopee" stethoscope?

What keeps us from doing that anyway? It's probably because our lives are in their hands. And paybacks are hell. I mean, I sure wouldn't want to be the recipient of a "Whoopee" hip replacement!

So I sat there in what I call 5th grade mode - hands folded, back straight, praying that the upcoming encounter with the surrogate principal won't be too intimidating.

Fortunately all my fears were mollified when Dr. Brad Hart walked in, a late 30's fellow in blue scrubs sporting neatly cropped sandy brown hair. He had an easy, approachable way about him similar to my Minnesota nurse, and a good blend of compassion and confidence.

As I told him my story, he did a lot of the classic, "Does it hurt here? How about here?" and when he got to the left middle part of my back, I beat him to the punch yelping, "Ow, yep it sure hurts there!"

Right away he said, "Well, I think for sure you've got a couple of broken ribs."

"OK," I thought, "I can deal with that. Some pain, a little immobility, no more mash pits, OK, no sweat."

"And I'm concerned you may have ruptured your spleen," he added.

"OK, this I CAN'T deal with," raced through my head.

What did this mean? A friend in high school had lost her spleen due to a car accident. Did this mean I was going into surgery right now? Was I hemorrhaging to death? Why did I even have a spleen anyway?

And worse, would I be stuck in Yankton for months?!?

"Let's run a CT and check," he said.

I thought, "CT, what the hell is that? Am I gonna be on cable?"

"James," he said, using my name to get me focused in like a new owner talking to a puppy, "we inject dye into your bloodstream then you go through a machine that looks like a big doughnut and it creates sliced images of your insides."

That didn't sound as much fun as cable.

As I watched with more than a little apprehension, the nurse wheeled in a cart on top of which, neatly laid out in what was apparently a specific order, were hypodermic needles and vials of mysterious fluids. Apparently this was some kind of serious procedure because there were now two nurses involved. Did they need two because of the extra equipment, or just to hold me down when I screamed?

I was starting to lose it a bit. I've always almost fainted when I gave blood to the Red Cross, and the last time my arm bruised up like an apple found in a five-year-old's lunch pail . . . after he's in college.

They graciously put the needle for the dye in my wrist in deference to my bruise potential. A couple of seconds later - I don't know if it was the stress, my back pain or the sight of that big needle itself; a giant of a thing for injecting contrast medium into my now trembling blood vessels - I began getting very light headed.

"Mr. Wedgwood, how are you feeling?" one of the nurses asked, suddenly peering intently into my eyes and at the same time assessing my skin tone.

'Well, part of me is very perky but the other part is having a very serious discussion with Jimmy Hendrix," is what I think came out at that point.

My blood pressure had dropped and I was fainting.

I don't recall how they pulled me back. I just remember saying goodbye to Jimmy and telling him his dentist wouldn't like him playing his guitar that way.

"There you go Mr. Wedgwood, you look a lot better now," the nurses chirped. I had to take their word for it because there weren't any mirrors in the little La La Land I had been visiting. "Now just relax, we're going to inject the dye and it's going to feel a little warm and tingly as it goes through your body."

Warm hell, I felt like I was getting a transplant from Three Mile Island! I could feel it coursing into the farthest reaches of my being. I discovered parts of me I didn't know I had. But I really noticed it when it hit the place where all those one-tailed guys hang out swimming laps to stay in shape, praying that someday, with a little luck, they might be "The One."

I glanced down to that region and I swear it was glowing with an eerie, "War of the Worlds" pulsation.

I had to restrain myself from asking if anyone wanted to roast marshmallows over my privates.

I breathed a sigh of relief as they told me this sensation wasn't permanent . . . although a sick part of me kind of wished it was.

Then they slid me into the big doughnut. It started whirring and buzzing and then an automated voice, like Hal from the original *2001: A Space Odyssey* articulated, "Hold your breath."

Several seconds later, "Breath out." Then again, "Hold your breath."

It really wasn't that bad and it proved to be a chance to just lay there. All that focus on breathing actually calmed me down a bit and as they sat me up upon completion, I felt ready for whatever came next. Heck, if they left me alone again, maybe I would play with the sacred gadgets in the exam room. A little super glue on a tongue depressor, some well placed rubber vomit, maybe a dribble specimen cup! Yes, this could be fun after all!

Interrupting my gadget musings I heard the Doctor's voice, "Mr. Wedgwood, would you come with me?"

His voice was still soothing, but there was an odd touch of intensity in it now. When I walked into the film imaging room, there were all my innards, broken down into nice neat seven millimeter slices.

It's humbling and intimidating to have the mystery of your guts splayed out like that. "As long as I can't see it, everything must be OK," had always been my philosophy.

But somehow, seeing my body like this, I felt very vulnerable, like all my personal secrets were on those films too, with nowhere safe to run if something embarrassing popped up.

"Well, your spleen is fine . . ." he started. "Whoo Hoo!" I thought. "I won't be stuck in Yankton! I'll have bitchin' pain for a couple of weeks, I can live with . . . "

"But . . ." he continued. A "but?" Uh oh, there's a "but." ". . . but this whitish blobby thing over here is a 1.8 centimeter mass on your left kidney.

Huh?

"Right here," he said pointing to the film, "half is in the kidney, half is out on the posterior, or back side."

No jokes for this one. With that one sentence, "a 1.8 centimeter mass on your left kidney," everything changed. That feeling you only get a few times in your life rushed over me. You get it when you move as a kid, when your spouse says she's leaving you, or when you lay your best friend to rest on a cold, dark, drizzly, December day.

Shit, damn!

Was I going to be Randy all over again?

He said he didn't know exactly what it was, not being a radiologist. He said "It could be a cyst, or benign . . ." in my head I finished his sentence ". . . or virulently malignant and in six months I'll have tumors popping out all over me!"

After "the news" I went back to the exam room and got dressed in a daze, the kind of daze you have when your brain has fallen and it can't get up.

It was Valentine's Day. I had missed being with my wife

on Valentine's Day and now I didn't know if I'd live to see the next one.

They gave me the scans to show to whomever the next step would be, called "the cab" for me and said, "Uh . . . Good Luck!"

There was compassion, helplessness and sincerity in their voices and I appreciated that, especially since they had just given me a possible death sentence.

The loneliest part came when I was waiting for the cab in the entryway. I just wanted to get somewhere, anywhere, just get things moving. I accidentally kept triggering the automatic door bringing unwanted attention to myself. It was cold. It was 1:00 A.M. I felt so damn alone. The only place to sit was a group of wheelchairs stationed against the wall, but I wouldn't let myself do it. It's one thing to sit in one of those things when you think you'll never need it, quite another when you might. It was an admission I couldn't acknowledge.

The last person I'd seen in a wheelchair was Cathy, just days before she died. It was not a role I was quite ready to understudy.

And of course, when I most wanted to be anywhere but where I was, the cab took forever to arrive.

While I was waiting I could feel the furtive glances of the hospital staff with each accidental opening of the automatic door. The phrase, "That poor son of a bitch" kept floating into my head. Was it from them? Did I imagine it? Hell, I didn't even care.

Finally the cab pulled up with Smokey and her son, the Bandit, bringing with them all the normalcy of life. Their conversation revolved around his girlfriend, errands at the grocery and the dog. My head overflowed with surgery, radiation disfigurement, and "What do you want on your tombstone?"

I had to hear a familiar voice. I suddenly wanted more than anything to get back to the room and call Gail, or better yet, to have her somehow magically be waiting for me there, to be embraced in her loving arms, to be held and comforted and have her be best friend, lover and surrogate "mom" all at once. To tuck me in, to bring me tea. To make it all better. Maybe if she could just hug me enough it would all go away.

But the click of my card key brought me back to Yankton and the empty, cold, dark, dispassionate room at the hotel.

As I fumbled in, I was just starting to get that intense post trauma pain that comes after serious injury. The kind you feel when the anesthetic effect of adrenalin has finally drained away and any movement whatsoever makes your body scream, "Oh, you thought that was funny Jack, huh? I got your pain right here! Now stop movin' around!"

I did. It took me what seemed like four days to get undressed and find some sort of position to lie in for the night. It was like that guy that guides planes into the gate, "Ok, OK, easy, LEFT, LEFT, LEFT, forward and - lock it!" And you are in the hangar for 8 hours.

Except I forgot to brush my teeth. "Screw it!" I thought. "If they rot in my head overnight, I can live with dentures."

But worse than the physical pain was the sudden realization that as much as I wanted to talk to Gail, to hear her sympathetic voice, part of me dreaded it. Why? Because if I called I would have to tell this beautiful woman, who two weeks earlier had been at her sister's deathbed after a four year cancer cataclysm, that her own husband might be starting down the same relentless, unforgiving road.

In the forefront of my mind was her 24/7 vigil at Cathy's hospice and her desperate need to recover from exhaustion. But oops, "Ding" she was possibly about to get an unwanted and undeserved round two.

I couldn't do this to her. The pain from Cathy was still fresh in her wonderful face, pooling under her deep brown eyes as they frantically searched for respite.

I was supposed to help HER recover. To make her relax. To take her out to dinner. To be her ear and listen to whatever she wanted to say about Cathy, the experience, fears, resentments, anger and celebration without judgment. To heal her torn spirit with the salve of sympathy and the steadfastness of my love.

If I went down too, could she even survive? Would she even want to?

Our street in St. Paul already had enough widows on it, five altogether, two of those under fifty, and the thought of her becoming number six saddened me greatly.

It just seemed so unbelievably cruel to put her through the whole process again so soon. What was wrong with the universe? Didn't it have compassion? A sense of fair play? She had put in four good quarters, 60 full minutes with Cathy and now it should be "Miller Time" damn it!

I dug out my cell phone, which I had brought to bed so I wouldn't have to torque my body off anymore, and pressed the speed dial marked "HOME."

I didn't want to tell her the whole story, about the mass, but we had spoken just before I went into the ER. She already knew I was in distress and would be anticipating an update.

"Hi baby," I blurted. "Hi Honey, how ya doin'?" she cheerfully replied. They're words many couples exchange, but that ritual verbiage floating across the frozen prairie of South Dakota and into my heart that night could've melted permafrost.

"Well, I like almost fainted, my spleen is OK and I spent some quality time with a gargantuan donut," I began. "Well, that sounds OK," she replied.

"Yeah, and . . ." gees, do I really have to do this? "They found a mass on my left kidney . . . so, how's the dog?"

"He's fiiinne," she stammered haltingly. "What did you say about your kidney?"

"They found a mass about 1.8 centimeters on the left one . . . uh . . . want to get take-out when I get home?"

I asked Gail months later how she took "The News." Her family, the Norwoods, are a very practical species and this mode apparently took over immediately. She thought, "Gee, am I going to have to go to Yankton and pick him up? He's got his van and show stuff so should I bus it? How about getting time off work? Mmm, and most importantly, is his life insurance paid up?"

Not quite the dramatically romantic vision I had pictured. Oh well.

We chatted for about another 10 minutes as I recounted my harrowing tale in the ER that I was sure was worthy of a special episode of the NBC hit by the same name.

She listened, sympathized, and reminded me practically, "We don't know what we're dealing with yet."

She said, "We just need more information. It could be benign, it could be a cyst, or it could be that rotten olive you swallowed last year."

She was right. And the soothing, sensible tone of her voice convinced me too, however temporarily, there was no reason to go nuts until we had the whole picture. We figured out logistics for the next couple of days, and gave each other copious verbal hugs and kisses. I finally drifted off into a comforted, if still very painful sleep.

Maybe it was nothing. The mass was a fluke, a glitch, nothing. And as I dozed off the realization hit me that whatever it was, the universe may have actually arranged for me a very precious, albeit challenging and painful, gift. The "mass" had been found early enough so that whatever it was it could be dealt with before it morphed into some kind of "Thing From Inner Space."

It seemed so obvious at that moment that this was no accident. I fell off to sleep thinking, "They ('they' being the gracious souls that watch over my paltry existence) wouldn't have shown me this now if it truly was my time to die. I was shown this for a reason, it was no fluke!"

Or maybe I was just blowing a lot of pain induced, hallucinatory smoke up my ass!

---

5. "A Timeline of the Trip," accessed June 18, 2010, www.pbs.org/lewisandclark/archive/idx_time.html.

Chapter Four

So, what is it?

I barely remember the next morning except that everything was stiffer. Sitting hurt. Standing hurt. Breathing hurt. Blinking was OK. I did a lot of that just to keep my morale up.

When I checked out, the clerk and I discussed who would be contacting me about the medical bills, etc. and I made a point to wince in agony ever so subtly several times during that discussion.

I was angry about the water in the racquetball court, but at the desk I tried not to get self-righteous about the whole thing, and put all those dumb "hot coffee in my lap at McDonalds" lawsuit stories out of my head.

On the other hand, if their insurance didn't at least pick up the trip to the ER, someone in their office was going to get a late night visit from my evil ventriloquist puppet, "Son of Chucky."

The drive home started out pretty well. It was a crisp sunny day; I found a position I could tolerate in my van and the Vicodan they gave me in the ER took a lot of the edge off. I could even take extra before a show if need be because I figured working a dummy didn't qualify as "operating heavy machinery."

My thoughts drifted about whom to tell when, calling my GP, but still trying to perpetuate a safe modicum of denial. Don't get anxious. It could be nothing. Think benign, think BENIGN!

But after about a half hour my diversionary tactics broke down and the worst insecurities of my new 1.8-cm-mass-reality welled to the surface bringing with it copious tears. "I could be dead in six months," I finally let myself admit. The tears gushed down my cheeks, onto my jeans and covered the complimentary hotel-lobby-toasted-bagel-and-cream-cheese sitting in my lap.

Randy was diagnosed in June, and residing in his poorly heated but cozy, subterranean-eternal-apartment-for-one by December.

More tears bubbled out. "Of course if I die, I'll get to see him." That thought cheered me up momentarily. Then I thought, "Screw that, he checked out first, let him come back to me!" Of course how that would happen exactly, I still haven't figured out.

It's cliché, but I drifted into all the things I hadn't done yet with my life: The TV show, the charitable foundation, the trip to Australia, the Botox.

Had I made a difference (Kleenexes were now starting to pile up on the floor of the van like sand in an hour glass)?

Well, I had made a lot of sick kids at the children's hospital laugh hosting their in-house cable show for several years. And I had brought some much needed respite to downtrodden pork producers when the bottom fell out of their pricing. And Patrick, my leprechaun dummy and I had a lot of fun when he got put through airport X-Ray machines. Not only did the security officer see a body in my carry on, he then heard it screaming, "Hey loser, let me outta here!" (Of course that little bit of fun ended after 9/11).

But was that enough to make it a life?

Had I done enough good to make up for the girlfriends I dumped, money lost in day trading, and the fifth grade Gerbil cage I never cleaned?

The Kleenexes were up to the edge of the seat now.

Shame mixed with regret, fear and a deep sense of loss as the tears flowed from deeper parts of my being. At first they were made up of that morning's coffee, then went to CT scan dye from the night before and were now flushing up the most ancient debris of my now possibly tenuous life.

It just seemed such a waste. Everything was all set up; my marriage, job, and studio were all great. The house was almost paid for. The doors to a long and prosperous and reasonably fun life were right in front of me and I was finally mature enough to know how to turn the key.

Except now, suddenly, some joker had gone and changed the damn lock.

I knew I was going to have to pull over soon because the van looked like the inside of a trash can at a 'Brian's Song' film festival (which, by the way, is possibly the only movie it's OK for a guy to cry at).

When I pulled off at the Blue Earth rest stop I was going

to empty out the Kleenexes, but decided at the last moment to leave most of them in the van. Why? I have to shamefully admit I got caught up in the drama of the moment, and somehow having Gail see all those tissues when I got home would give me emotional validation. Something along the lines of "No, I'm not making this shit all up!"

My thoughts continued like this the entire way home until eventually my head was like the Indy 500, with everything screaming around inside at 200 mph. A few times the thoughts careened out of control and a caution light came on behind my somewhat glazed eyes. I'd feel my pulse slow down and my breathing return to normal, but when the wreckage of that thought cleared it was back to the races.

Gratefully, my brain slowed down at least temporarily when I finally pulled up in front of our little 1904 gingerbread and brick house on Superior Street.

I was never so glad to see Gail. She was waiting at the door like some 50's June Cleaver tableau with our dog, Merle and Foxy, our cat. Merle barked his greeting bark, Gail hugged me a little harder and longer than usual and the cat meowed, although I think that was only because I hadn't changed his litter box in a week.

Gail listened attentively as I spilled the story of my travails in Yankton, the drive home, etc. Her attitude was great. She was calm, practical and kept repeating, "Well, we don't know what we're dealing with. Once we do, we take it from there." And indeed, a kidney mass was not necessarily the kiss of death. My own father had a small, totally encapsulated mass in his right kidney for years which they removed Halloween day 2001, and he was doing fine two years later at the ripe old age of 79.

Gail's approach was the best. I felt stronger just observing her pragmatic, logical attitude. She was my rock, my bit of unemotional rationality in the chaos, my Superwoman . . . until she helped me unload the van. Bingo! The Everest of Kleenexes between the front seats got her. Shame on me, shame, shame. That prompted more hugs, but this time she shed some tears too. Some for me, some for herself, and I'm sure some residual tears for Cathy.

We went to bed that night resolving to take it one step at a time as she suggested, because that was all we could do. Whether that first step would head us to surgery, recovery, or the beginning of my end only time would tell.

Where would I be in a year? Still holding my honey, albeit listing to starboard a bit having ballasted a kidney, or up with Randy raising hell in heaven, my dummies languishing forlornly on E-bay, or out on their own trying to find work in department store holiday window displays.

The next morning feelings of introspection had to be tabled. It was time to get the ball rolling. Everything had to be started and fast. I was highly motivated, like a home seller with a job waiting in his favorite city. Having your own mortality knock hard on the door will do that to you.

The first order of business was to see my GP. She could make initial assessments, referrals, etc., and hopefully give me more of what Gail had the night before; rational perspective.

I called her office and said with some urgency, "I have a mass on my left kidney and need to see Dr. Taylor." In an icy, dispassionate voice that gave no affirmation of my situation the receptionist said, "Oh, you need scheduling, I'll transfer you." Click. Buzz. Static. "Scheduling, who do you want to see?" this even colder voice asked. Someone had to understand my urgency, so I was damned if I was just going to say Dr. Taylor's name. "I have a mass on my left kidney and I need to see Dr. Taylor." "Just a moment," the now disembodied seeming voice said. It sounded annoyed that I had even dared to tell it what was ailing me - after all, this is "SCHEDULING," and anyone who crosses the line of actually looking for empathy in the midst of a frightening situation will be punished! The now Terminatoresque voice came back "Dr. Taylor's first appointment available is March 21. And who will this be for?" "What?" I thought. "Are you frickin' crazy!? Are you deaf and dumb (as in stupid)? I could have a tumor the size of Pluto by then, more than a month away! I could be one big pustulous mass with little stubs of hands poking out, rolling and bouncing into oblivion by then!"

Trying hard to suppress my outrage, I curtly stated, "I don't think you understand, I have a mass on my left kidney and time is critical here." Of course I didn't know that for sure. I didn't know a damn thing yet, but at this early stage of the game I had let my dramatic-theatre-major-side run amock, and didn't really want to stop it. By God, if she wouldn't give me validation, I'd give it to myself!

"That's all we have and the next one is on the 24th." The voice was so emotionally dead now it was descending into a fast food drive-through crackle.

"Well, . . .that just won't do," I somewhat impotently mustered and hung up.

It wasn't so much that she couldn't have cared less about a possibly fatal condition. It was that these were the first health care "professionals" I had contacted. It was their business, no matter what their job, to show even a modicum of compassion, to offer alternatives, to be frickin' human at the very least.

It brought up memories of waiting three hours in an ER a few years earlier to get stitches in a sliced and bleeding hand without so much as an offer of a Band-Aid or cleansing until the doctor walked in.

It also reminded me of a pre-op nurse asking my semi-anesthetized 78-year-old father to mark with a Sharpie where his kidney surgery incision should be.

And most painfully, it brought back images of Cathy's "You're going home!" debacle.

Well, I don't take this crap. My self-righteous, angry, "OK, this is a battle" mode kicked in and I called the office back.

I said I did not want scheduling. Fortunately Dr. Taylor's personal assistant had picked up the phone, and after she heard my story, graciously and with all the compassion I had expected but didn't get with the first call, got me in the next day.

What a difference one caring person exercising common courtesy can make.

I had an appointment, I felt validated and I greatly appreciated it. But from here on in when dealing with the Western Medical Machine, I would keep my guard up.

The next day Dr. Taylor somewhat restored my faith in traditional medicine when Gail and I entered her office. She greeted us with a cheerful smile beaming out of her blonde, all American face. She showed concern yet no sense of panic. She, like Gail, wasn't jumping to conclusions without all the facts.

She put my CTs from the Yankton ER on her viewing board, and as she carefully contemplated their implications, I was suddenly overcome with that sense of drama that I had seen in countless TV shows, when the doctor is about to tell the family wonderful or devastating news. It's never in the middle.

I could feel the background music swelling up. The tympani were rolling. I had to admit the actor part of me was even enjoying it a bit.

"Well, I'm not sure, it could be a lot of things," Dr. Taylor said calmly.

The tympani stopped abruptly, and the TV show cut to a Snuggles commercial.

It was in the middle.

"It's a bit beyond my expertise to diagnose but I wouldn't worry just yet. I want to refer you to a specialist," she said still calm and even a little upbeat.

Well, OK. That sounded very pragmatic and coming from her, somehow the world still seemed like a happy place. Gail and I felt a little better.

We got an appointment to see the urologist Dr. Taylor recommended, Dr. Hampton, two days later (at least his office understood the urgency of the situation right off the bat!) and went home to try and relax a bit till then, and pretend it wasn't necessarily the end of the known universe for us. And if we couldn't believe that in our hearts, at least we would try and fake it for 48 hours.

Throughout all this Gerson had been in the back of my mind. It was one thing to believe in it and try to get others on it when your own body is healthy. I discovered it was quite another to seriously contemplate it for yourself.

Thirteen organic juices, four of them made from fresh calf's liver, B-12 injections, organic saltless food and yes . . . five coffee enemas a day . . . just seemed totally overwhelming, if not downright disgusting and humiliating. Latté with friends is one thing. Latté from a bucket on a cold bathroom floor via personal reverse osmosis is quite another.

I would have to stop work, cancel shows, and give up my main social venue, eating out. And liver juice! Bleeccchhh. Couldn't I at least mix it with Häagen Dazs or something? "Hey kids, it's our new flavor, Peanut Butter Crunch with Raw Liver! MMMM!"

But on the other hand if it worked, if I had the courage to go through everything Jaquie Davison did, if it really rejuvenated every system, every vein, every nerve – it would be incredible.

It could supposedly clear out the steadily clogging, cholesterol laden arteries I inherited from my sextuple bypass father, and rid my body of years of convenience store road food residue. Skin absorbed motor oil, paint, BGH, agricultural pesticides, and water born fluoride buried deep in my tissues over the decades would be shown the nearest exit like a streaker at the Super Bowl. And hopefully the mysterious orb plopped in my kidney would be tossed out too.

I knew it would not be easy. The process of not only getting rid of the cancer but also of completely detoxifying the body so it wouldn't return took at least a year and a half. And I figured almost everyone close to me would be against it, thinking I was some kind of earthy-alternative-anal-fixated freak. I didn't care. I would feel like such a hypocrite for pushing this on others if I didn't at least explore it for myself.

It was time to step up. Plus, contemplating Randy's fate with conventional treatment was a VERY strong motivator.

The image of his hollow, Auschwitz-like features saying goodbye for the last time, and the effect his and Cathy's un-Godly process had on all of us scared me a hell of a lot more than coffee in my ass.

I called the Gerson Institute in San Diego the day after seeing Dr. Taylor and left a message. They have a small budget and can't get calls 24/7. They did return my call the next day as promised and we began exchanging information. "How healthy was I? Was I ambulatory? Could I feed myself?" Well, yeah! Of course! Why not? I'm still doing shows for goodness sake.

Then they explained. For most folks, Gerson is seen as their last ditch effort after rounds and rounds of chemo have failed and left a hairless, green-skinned shell in their wake, and repeated surgeries have not "gotten it all." It seemed so like a sick, Hitchcockian cat and mouse game to me.

I guess many people can't even walk when they get there. I felt lucky, very lucky. I now really believed someone on the other side had put together my little accident so I did have "time." I just prayed I would make the right choice and prove worthy of this arranged resurrection.

They gave me the names of three men who had done very well on the therapy whom I could call, and said they'd mail me a packet that had more information and an application. If I decided to go to the clinic, they wanted to be sure I was in good enough shape to have a reasonable hope of survival. While I knew this would not be an issue for me at all, I think they didn't want to give folks too far along with their illness false hopes.

So, with an appointment to see the urologist and Gerson information on the way, I got a much needed sense of control, however tenuous. I was taking action, empowering myself with information, and it felt good.

Gail went with me to Dr. Hampton's office. He was a tall late 50's early 60's man who did his surgeries at Abbott Northwestern Hospital where I used to work as a graphic artist. If I needed surgery, it would be comfortable there. I still knew some staff and I might even be able to bag a tape of the surgery to gross out my friends over pizza.

He looked at the scans from Avera, said he wanted to get another, more thorough series done and then described options.

He did not want to biopsy the mass for fear of spreading cells. Well, I liked this guy already. I would not have let him biopsy it anyway for the same reason. He said even though the needles for that procedure were very thin there was too much risk. And as I knew from Randy, when this spreads, it's like a killer bee attack seeking to obliterate three vital parts of your body - your liver, your lungs and your brain.

Not that my brain was that valuable anyway, but I did like breathing and I figured my liver must do something important.

A biopsy was out for another reason, rational or not. Four weeks earlier, the kind, joking elevator operator in the building where I rented my studio, a friend that taught me dirty words in Spanish and was one of those people that always gave a nice, friendly "Hi, how are you, how's the weather?" kind of regularity to your day, had died from a liver biopsy gone bad. He had the surgery, it got infected and three days later it was "Hasta la vista amigo."

Added to that, Randy's father, suffering from prostate cancer had almost gone the same way after a botched bladder biopsy went into infection overdrive. Either they got the infection under control just in the nick of time, or more likely, Randy was having too much fun on the other side without parental supervision, and kicked his old man right back into his body.

To put it in words Randy might have used, "God was 30 seconds away from beeping Dad's barcode."

For all those reasons and Dr. Hampton's apprehension, a biopsy would not be in my future.

Also, chemo and radiation were not an option. They don't work on kidney cancer - if indeed it was malignant.

And of course that was the $64,000 question, even though I really didn't want to verbalize it and give it validity. But it had to be asked, even though I knew without a biopsy it was impossible to know exactly. Did Dr. Hampton think this "thing" was malignant?

He said from his experience, it was 95% sure to be the big M, the nasty one, the word that even now is hard to write. "Well like, are you positive? Couldn't it be damage from an injury or a genetic aberration, or a lower percentage or maybe . . . ?" I queried.

"Nope, 95% sure," he said without batting an eye or indulging my insecurity.

C'mon, throw me a bone here buddy, "Are you sure?" I pleaded.

"Yes." was the simple reply.

"OK then," I thought, "no fudge room. I can't linger in the illusion of 'benign' and have to move on."

"Well, what are the options?" I asked.

Without chemo or radiation, surgery was it. Gee, like father, like son. If only Dad had saved his kidney after it was removed, we could have had them bronzed, and the matched set could sit on my parent's mantel in between the Hummel monk feeding birds, and the tried and true Seth Thomas clock.

"We'll either do a V section or take out the whole kidney," he said.

You know, when it's someone else getting surgery I have no problem. I even get cocky about it, with a little superiority complex, like I'm above it happening to me. Yes, my body will remain pristine because, by God, I'm James Wedgwood, and I'll never have one of those scars that look like the unfurled sides of a baseball left to rot in the outfield at the end of summer. Oh, I'll be there for you, because that's my role. But I'll never be the "sick" one.

Why the hell did I think that?! Was I nuts? No, just scared to death and vain, and the thought of putting myself so totally in someone else's hands to hack me up made my tenaciously independent and self reliant soul cringe like Napoleon at Waterloo. It wasn't just surgery, it would be a defeat of sorts. Something I couldn't get out my Dremel tool and duct tape and fix . . . damn!

And Dr. Hampton, reasonable up to this point didn't help matters when he took his index finger, put it on my left side, ran it around to my back in a two foot long swoop and said, "And I will cut you from here to here."

I swear the spirit of Bella Lugosi somehow possessed him right then, if only for an instant.

I freaked! Cutting people was nothing to him, I know, but I felt incredibly violated. It was as if there was glory in the power he would have over me in the operating room. "Go cut your own ass buddy," were words that fortunately never made it to my lips as he continued, "and I'd like to do a bone scan." Bone scan? What the hell is that? He answered, "They inject you with a radioactive . . . " the rest turned into traffic noise in my head. "Do I look like I want to be frickin' Three Mile Island to you?" I thought. "Radioactive goop in my bones? Are you crazy?"

And he was so nonchalant, almost cavalier about it all, as though this was all as normal as brushing your teeth. He insisted it was all safe, but to me there was no way radioactive material could go into my marrow and be "safe." If I didn't have cancer yet, I sure thought I would by the end of the diagnostics!

I mean honestly, radioactivity in my bones? I could just see myself the rest of my life trying not to be conspicuous in theatres, my skeleton glowing like a Bulova watch face, or friends pretending to have power outages at parties just to experience the "Incandescent Ventriloquist."

It was time to go, before I said something stupid to the good Doctor I would regret later. But we did have one all-important question that had to be asked, even in my teapot-about-to-boil-over state of mind: "If we did nothing, how long would I have?" "I'd estimate about five years," he stated, again in his very matter of fact tone of voice.

Fine. I had a number and I would digest its implications later. I agreed to a new CT, (that seemed prudent), declined becoming a human Luminaria with a bone scan, grabbed Gail and got the heck out of there!

Through Dr. Hampton, the seductive door of traditional medicine was beckoning, but that day it wore a Cheshire grin.

I had seen so many people start just this way. Hack, cut, radiate, poison, cut again and again with no guarantees. Forget that. Sure, it had worked for my father, but somehow I felt that for me it would be the beginning of the end.

I was jaded and I knew it. For Gail's sake I couldn't just run away. And due to my own hyper state of reality, I probably was overreacting. So, what would be the next step? The prudent choice would be get a different perspective, the proverbial second opinion.

Gail's brother Paul knew another urologist who had done his vasectomy, Dr. Swenson.

Dr. Swenson was a prominent urologist at a regional medical center. Again, the call for an appointment lead to a three-week delay. The fact that so many doctors are so busy got me thinking there is certainly something wrong with health in America. How can that many people be so desperately ill? Maybe my journey would help me find out why.

In this case we played the "Who you know" card. Paul knew Dr. Swenson' staff well and before you could say, "I hope my health insurance is paid up!" we had an appointment for two days later. Maybe this guy would be more of the Marcus Welby I was looking for.

In the interim, I went back to Gerson explorations. I made what was to be by far the most important call of this entire process. I phoned Rodney, a patient who had recovered from kidney cancer on the Gerson therapy. He lives on the east coast and was eager to tell me his experience. Over ten years before he had been diagnosed with a tennis ball sized tumor in his left kidney. At that time Rodney had been a smoker and he attributed his mass to this. The National Cancer Institute[6] confirms that this is one of the causes. As with me, his doctor prescribed surgery.

While they were operating, Rodney said they found another, cherry sized growth on his other kidney (How? I don't know. I had trouble figuring out the logistics of that one).

Rodney was screwed. They left his right kidney in because to remove it would mean dialysis (artificial filtering of the blood) typically three times a week, four hours per session.[7]

And at this point Rodney's right kidney despite its mass, was still functioning normally.

After recovery from surgery, Rodney was scared, but wanted to keep his remaining kidney at all costs. And while dialysis is a miracle, that big multi-million-dollar machine still can't approach the efficiency of one little fist sized kidney!

Why? Well, kidneys are amazing organs. In the kidney,

blood flows through narrow vessels lining tiny bulbs that act like sieves. Water, salts and some sugars pass out of the blood, collecting as fluids in the bulbs. This fluid flows along looping tubes where most of the water returns to the bloodstream along with valuable salts. Waste products continue to filter out of the blood and into the fluid which becomes urine.

Urine then flows into a cone shaped area of tissue filled with tiny channels. These merge into larger ducts channeling urine into a collecting chamber at the kidney's center where it eventually flows on to the bladder for storage . . . until intermission.[8] Your body has to go through this cleansing process or the blood will become too toxic, much like a charcoal filter taking poisons out of drinking water.

Understandably Rodney wanted to hang onto an important little organ like this. There had to be some way he could fight back and keep his remaining kidney, even with its mass.

In his search for alternatives Rodney came across a book written by Beata Bishop called *A Time to Heal - Triumph Over Cancer,* where she chronicles her journey on the Gerson Therapy. After reading it thoroughly and with few other alternatives, he decided this was the course he should take.

He went to Gerson clinic in Mexico and stayed at a hotel, visiting the clinic every day, learning the therapy, studying all it's ins and outs and complexities. After about ten days and several inspirational conversations with Charlotte Gerson, Dr. Gerson's previously mentioned daughter, who now spearheads Gerson therapy promotion throughout the world, Rodney bought a juicer, packed himself up and headed to his native Columbia for four months of retreat, reflection and intense treatment.

He did it all himself which is amazing. The cooking and shopping alone is enough work for one person, let alone hand pressing the juices, preparing and administering coffee breaks, and taking time for much needed rest.

But Rodney persevered. He also used the time for an overall life assessment and spiritual renewal. After the four months, and feeling much better, he came back to the States, continued the therapy and went back to work. He even tried doing the enemas at the office for a while.

He also got scanned.

When he went to the doctor's office to get the results of this follow-up scan, his new doctor (his original one had left the practice) said his original doctor must have made a mistake . . . there was no tumor in his remaining kidney. It was gone!

New Doc said old Doc must have misread the original set of scans (which had mysteriously disappeared) but Rodney knew better. Gerson had worked and worked well.

Rodney was elated. He'd been given a second chance. But then he was angry. He told me passionately that if he knew then what he knows now, he never would have had his FIRST kidney removed. He regretted it deeply, and lamented that he lost feeling in areas where they had clipped nerves during the procedure.

He emphatically praised Charlotte Gerson and the therapy. He also wanted his doctor to give him his kidney back and repeatedly emphasized "I wish I had done Gerson first."

Wow! Well. I was invigorated. Maybe this was the way to go! Keeping my kidney sounded good to me.

I was pumped. This was the first actual validation I'd had for going Gerson, even though I still felt insecure about it.

Yes, Gerson was a very different treatment than typical western medicine, but the impact Jaquie Davison's book had on me was still strong, and some part of me has always been drawn to the non-traditional. And quite honestly, surgery scared me a lot more than this did.

Feeling like I might have a viable alternative to "slice and dice," I was buoyant.

I wanted to share my joy so I rushed in to tell Gail. As I conveyed Rodney's unbridled success on the therapy, I could see her face fill with doubt, concern, and fear. Her mouth went into this funny little position it always does when she's torqued off but doesn't want to verbalize it. But as anyone who's married knows, you can't hide emotions from a spouse you've known for 17 years, there's no faking it, they just know you too damn well.

I didn't know whether to call her on it and open what I knew would be a can of worms, hell probably a whole bait shop, or try and let it slide.

I couldn't. I craved her support in what for me felt like a desperate hour. I wanted her to share my joy and hope and optimism about what Rodney told me and make it bigger.

But she hadn't read Jaquie's book. She hadn't studied the simple logic of the Gerson Therapy. She hadn't embraced the concepts.

She had just buried her sister, watched cancer ravage her, and been at her side for her final breath.

Doing something far out, and what I'm sure seemed flakey as hell, especially when my mass had been found so early, probably seemed like lunacy and no doubt terrified her.

So we stood there enveloped in one of the worst spousal juxtapositions imaginable; craving comfort but attacked by alienation, both of us so deep in fear it would have taken the Hubble telescope to see anything clearly.

I got upset. She withdrew. And there was no Dr. Phil to sort it all out.

I don't even recall if we resolved it that night. It was the first of many such moments as we tried to muddle our way through the confusion, choices and overwhelming new reality of the weeks to come. For God's sake, this is when Gail should have been recovering from the stress of taking Cathy to chemo, going to her doctor's visits and ultimately, laying her to rest.

Despite my own neediness of the moment, I felt a lot worse for her than for me.

When the Gerson packet arrived things were still a bit edgy between Gail and I, but I plowed ahead and filled out the application anyway. Rodney's experience and passion gave me a lot of psychological momentum, and reinforced the choice I was starting to embrace in my gut.

The application asked for medical history and a blood workup which I got from Dr. Taylor, and I sent the reports from my visit with Dr. Hampton too. Looking at the questions about bleeding, vomiting, other treatments, etc., it was obvious they frequently dealt with patients in pretty bad shape.

It was now becoming a habit to thank God for my episode in Yankton.

Before I definitively made up my mind though, as to which course of action to take, I wanted to see what our second urologist had to say.

Again Gail graciously went with me and fortunately by the time we got to Dr.Swensons' office, things were a lot calmer between us.

A few good nights' sleep, petting the dog, those simple things can diffuse a lot of tension. Especially the dog. One look at our dog Merle's face during stressful times and you can tell he has taken the whole conflict upon himself, like he's thinking, "I know you're angry and sad, but really, I don't think I pooped anywhere I shouldn't have. And I really do try to hold in the pee while you're gone but sometimes when you're gone too long, a little just slips and I . . . oh, I'll just go sulk in the corner."

And then you have to reassure him because he's just so genetically insecure that way, and by the time you've gotten him peppy again by singing stupid dog songs in silly voices, your own emotions can't help but mellow out like butter on a steaming baked potato.

We would do a lot of silly singing over the next few months. We were lucky it was winter so the neighbors wouldn't hear it and talk more about us. Living across the street from a ventriloquist and watching him parade in and out with his dummies, occasionally talking a bit too well to himself, I'm sure causes more than a little snickering.

When Dr. Swenson entered the room at our appointment and stuck out a large friendly hand, I liked him immediately. He went above and beyond the call of duty to explain everything to us. If he did the surgery, he would pull the whole kidney leaving a good "field" or buffer zone around it so as not to disturb the tumor.

I knew after that half hour that if I went this route, he would be our man. I mean, he had done my brother-in-law Paul's vasectomy, and Paul still had just two kids and a low voice. Paul described Dr. Swenson as "a craftsman" which made me wonder, "Was Paul watching somehow when Dr. Swenson closed the family faucet permanently?" Just the logistics of that were more than I could ponder and I put it out of my mind, in the same place I put, "How do cats mate?," and "What really goes into head cheese?"

Dr. Swenson did alarm me though because he WANTED to do a biopsy even though he said results might not be conclusive. He said, "We would do it under a CT scanner to make sure the long, narrow needle . . ." again, as I had in Dr. Hampton's office, I just mentally checked out. My body was sitting there but the thought of more CT radiation and a long needle puncturing the mass sent my brain back into La La Land. I knew if we did that I'd be dead in six months. And even with the biopsy, he said they couldn't be 100% sure as to the nature of the thing.

I was confused then, trying to figure out, "Why even do the biopsy?" Maybe it was his standard procedure, I don't know. Besides, his radiologist after viewing the Yankton scans, like Dr. Hampton, also said it was 95% certain to be malignant and that was good enough for me.

Despite my confusion over the biopsy, Gail and I both liked Dr. Swenson and his gracious approach, and Gail's brother even offered to show off Dr. Swenson' incision marks to check the quality. Well, no, not really, but my Dad does this with every surgery he has.

"Hey, check out this baby from my bypass!" or, "This sucker is where they yanked the artery out of my leg! Whoo Hooo! Jim, you look a little pale . . . Jim, Jim . . . JIM!" So it has become kind of a joke in our family.

Anyway, in Dr. Swenson we had a "guy," a nice guy who listened and cared and that was reassuring. Chalk one up in the "The surgery option might be OK" column.

---

6. National Cancer Institute, "What You Need To Know About™ Kidney Cancer," accessed June 18, 2010, www.cancer.gov/cancertopics/wyntk/kidney/page4.

7. American Kidney Fund, "Hemodialysis," accessed June 18, 2010, www.kidneyfund.org.kidney-health/treatment/hemodialysis.html.

8. Richard Platt, *Stephen Biesty's Incredible Body* (New York: DK Publishing, 1998).

Chapter Five

Decision Made

In all of this, I began the task of telling people what was going on, and while at first it was nice to touch in with family and friends, it soon became tedious. I'd start with the rekindled college machismo racquetball story. We'd be joking because they'd probably been there too - OK, then the fall and the chatty cabby, still light but painful - that set the stage - then the five words that blindsided everyone: Mass On My Left Kidney.

It got harder as I went through my Rolodex because I had to put people in what is arguably the most awkward conversational position possible, over and over, "Hi, how's it going? How 'bout them Vikings? Say, I can't make 'er to the game Friday 'cause a . . . I got cancer . . . OK?"

Then as they stuttered, "What!?" I just wanted to close, "but don't worry, you can still borrow my binoculars. Bye." and avoid all the follow up shock and sympathy. But of course I couldn't. I had to stay on the line, give more details, and in many cases help them with their own grief process.

After eight or nine calls to our inner circle of family and friends, it was too hard to go through it again and again, answering all the questions and hearing the awkward pain in their voices, so I asked Gail to call folks more on the periphery.

Anyway, I had processed the whole damn thing already

and telling people about it repeatedly kept drawing me back into that Kleenex-between-the-seats-self-pity state of mind, and I really didn't want to be there anymore. Enough of being maudlin. I was ready to act. Let's go! Let's move! Researching and pondering my options brought a sense of control I desperately needed, even as my body was trying to sneak it away from me.

A day or so after seeing Dr. Swenson, the Gerson Institute called. The physicians at the clinic had reviewed my information and I was accepted. Now it was for real. I had to make the decision in the next day or so. There were schedules to rearrange, set up at the house to do if I went to Gerson, and either way, money to find.

I wanted to do Gerson in my heart because I knew if I didn't, I would always look back and wonder, "What if?" And Gerson would go after EVERYTHING. Not just the symptom - the booger on my kidney - but the cause too. If it performed as billed, it would clean out my body like backhoes at a Hazmat site, and if I was a good boy and lived clean after that, I hopefully could avoid many of the degenerative diseases that plague our Dorito and Coke loving nation.

I just needed another push to be sure.

I called two more recovered Gerson patients. Over ten years ago Bob had been sent home to die with severe lung cancer. His docs had done all they could. He did Gerson and a year later went back to these same docs and they thought they'd seen a ghost. His lungs were clear and he was living happily retired with his wife down south.

Another fellow had malignant melanoma over a decade ago. He is paraplegic and couldn't even do the coffee enemas. He is now cured of the melanoma completely.

Both men said it would be a ton of work. Both men, like Rodney, said if they had to do it over, they'd do Gerson first.

That was it. After those last two calls it was a no-brainer.

I was healthy, the mass was small, and my schedule could be worked out. I didn't have a body compromised by chemotherapy and radiation. And, by God, I was funny too. Let's give it a shot. If I get scanned in six months and the thing is bigger, I've got Dr. Swenson. If it's smaller, whoopee! I get to be the next Rodney!

From that moment, we were off and running on the Gerson Highway. Why do I say "we" were off and running? Because although I hadn't told Gail of my final decision yet, I couldn't do the Therapy without her. At the very least for the first few months, I wouldn't even be able to shop for groceries.

I figured I'd be able to make the juices and handle the coffee breaks, but the rest would be up to her: Cooking special soup, vegetarian organic meals, trips to the coop and Whole Foods, and hopefully a modicum of emotional encouragement.

I didn't expect anyone, friends or family, to support the process. I was sure they'd all think it was flaky as hell, that I was signing my own death warrant. I planned on being laughed at and seeing written in people's faces, "Oh, I thought he was at least smarter than that. The puppet thing was weird enough, but this? Oh Gail, that poor woman. I must have her over for tea."

Much to my surprise and delight, in a lot of cases quite the opposite happened. More people than I can recall said things like, "You know, my uncle got cancer and he did such and such alternative thing and it went away."

Or, "You know, I watched chemo tear up my mother and if I were in your shoes I'd do the same thing. 'They' don't have all the answers." Or, "I saw a thing on Oprah about this one therapy, it sounded great! Something about finding a gene."

Of course I also got, "You know, a friend of ours had his kidney out 35 years ago and he's doing fine," or "Yeah kid, I got one kidney and I still ride the missus like Richard Petty at Daytona."

The latter statements made it tempting to do a 180°. VERY tempting. With surgery, I'd be done with the whole process in about eight weeks. And maybe I'd be that guy 35 years down the road telling some young buck the same thing.

Or maybe I'd be Randy.

Of course why not do both? Have it taken out and do Gerson too.

I thought a lot about that. But if I had it out, I'd have no empirical indication the therapy was working. And people would really wonder why I was still doing all this if everything was fine.

Most importantly, surgery treated only the symptom, not the cause.

Do we cut off our ear because it aches? Our hands because they're riddled with arthritis? If I have a fungus do I lop off my foot? We treat the cause of the earache, the pain in our hand and the itch in our foot.

Plus one of the doctors said the growth is my own cells gone wacko. It's not a foreign invader. So I figured if my body made it, with help it can fix it too.

To my surprise, most everyone I talked with during my decision making process had been touched by cancer in one way or another, and realized the ambivalence of treating it. And maybe, just maybe, if this weird-juice-organic-coffee-butt thing worked for me they could do it if their time came.

I think a lot of people have that dread of getting cancer buried deep in their psyches. I saw it in their eyes, "God, he's skinny, doesn't eat much meat, exercises and HE got it. Gees, maybe I should rethink my pizza, beer and potato chip existence."

From my mother I got, "Well, Jim you're a grownup, and I can't tell you what to do," which told me she really wanted to. But the tone in her voice also had a bit of curiosity about the whole process, and she did encourage me to follow my heart.

My main agent, Gary, kind of scowled when I mentioned alternative treatment, but still was amazingly supportive and emphasized having "backup."

I was most surprised that no one said, "You idiot." And as the process progressed, most skepticism gave way to fascinated curiosity and intrigue. I quickly realized giving friends and family as much information as possible would be the best way to quell any fears they might have. I gave everyone I could Charlotte's booklets describing the therapy and highlighting successful cases.

I sent my mother Beata Bishop's book knowing she would devour it in just a few of her regular late night smoking sessions.

Not only did my little PR jobs give those around me a more articulate understanding of what I was doing, it gave the whole process more validity in my mind.

To my surprise though, one of my toughest sells was Gail. Not that she wouldn't help. Not at all. Gail is that wonderful type of person who once committed will do her part 1000%. As we got ready to go to the clinic she was reading the "How-to" books, buying things we needed and checking her schedule. But deep inside she was scared to death and probably mad too. Angry at two strikes back to back. Angry at no reprieve. Petrified of being a widow at 43 with one less sister's shoulder to cry on.

I suggested she read Jaquie Davison's book, the one that had such a big impact on me so many years ago. She kept making excuses. She told me later she was in too much pain to get hopeful and consequently kept pushing it away. And while I understood that when we discussed it months later, at the time I didn't know what was going on and it made me feel a little more insecure about the whole thing, a little betrayed, even though I knew she would be there by my side no matter what.

I would have to remember Rodney whenever I had doubts. He made it, so can I . . . damn it!

I got things arranged with the institute: paperwork, a physical from my GP, blood tests, plane tickets, etc. We would start March 19th - three weeks away.

Everything would change after that, more dramatically than I could ever imagine.

I'd be out of work for at least four months, so I met with my two agents and good friends, Gary, the owner of G. L. Berg Entertainment, whom I mentioned earlier and Tim, one of his key agents and another close friend. We had all been through a lot together over the years. Countless county fair conventions, chamber banquets, basketball weekends and my national appearance on "The Statler Brothers" TV show. We had all grown a lot personally and professionally together and they, apart from Randy are the closest thing to brothers I have, even though they both stand over six feet and I'm a wee munchkin at 5'6" on a good day.

I remember we were at a national fair convention in Vegas one year and feeling cocky. Gary came back to our booth at the trade show after surveying the competition and stated, "Our agency could kick their ass."

Tim came back a little bit later, a talented performer in his own right, after seeing an act showcase and stated, "I could kick their ass."

Then I, having seen another ventriloquist standing all of

4'11" an aisle over in another agency's booth stated, "Yeah, and I could kick his AND his dummy's little ass!"

We were to meet at a coffee shop in Minneapolis to adjust my schedule. On that particular day, the magnitude of everything had made me a bit flighty. Driving over, I was sure I had left a teapot boiling on the stove, went back home to check it out and of course, it was off and I ended up being 20 minutes late.

I brought my CT scans to show them and you could see in their eyes the physical manifestation of what I had heard in their voice on the phone, "Shit, this is for real." They kept their game faces on pretty well, but their own fear and trepidation oozed out of the cracks a bit.

During the CT showing I lost it a little, choked up, and dripped a tear in my latté diluting that beautiful froth. Why then? Because I was with two friends, two noble individuals who pick up what I can't handle as friends are supposed to do, for whom years of trust and mutual life experience mean something, a commodity worth more than all the gigs I'd ever done. And facing a totally new life or potential lack thereof, the honesty of their compassion just made me let go.

We cleared the calendar for four months and thinned it to six. Just like that. And in this business that is huge. I've done shows with diarrhea, heat stroke, in rain, snow and 10 minutes after learning my cat died. It pained me incredibly to actually wipe out that much work, a few thousand dollars worth. Oh, for some shows they could get subs, but others would be lost forever.

When I started out in 1982 each gig was precious and that psychology was still strong. I had to perform or there would be no mortgage payment, no car, no spiritual retreats with the dummies!

But Gary and Tim took care of it all. Just like that. And they never complained about what I knew was a major hassle for them, not to mention the financial loss. Not one word.

Noble friends indeed.

Other friends came up to help me close down my studio. It wasn't that expensive, but the extra $300 a month would help during my down time.

Plus if I croaked, Gail wouldn't have to deal with it.

One of my best non-entertainer friends, Ralph, came up and facilitated what I could not, getting everything ready to move home: packing, organizing, deciding what to throw out. Twenty one years of my life as a puppet boy was strewn all over the floor waiting to be loaded into boxes: Luanda, my cabaret diva's original hands, scripts taped to my wall of rehearsal mirrors for Betty the dancing, talking broom, joke books, old magic tricks and anvil cases for dummies not yet conceived intermingled with oddities like "Alien Gonzales," a head shop statue of a "Grey" I once contemplated giving ventriloquial life to.

Packing all this up and closing the studio down would prove to be more emotional than I had anticipated. It was 510 sq. feet of pure creative space. Twelve foot ceilings terminated at nine foot southern facing windows out of which I spent many an hour brainstorming comedy ideas, contemplating the lives transpiring like so many busy ants on the sidewalk five stories down, or just feeling downtown warehousey cool. And this space was all mine - my colors, a faux tree in the middle with expansive fabric branches laced with sparkling mini lights inhabited by watchful paper mache' tropical birds. I built it as my own visual and psychic retreat from the dark days of the interminable Minnesota winter.

Shutting it down was a symbolic death, an acknowledgement that I had to deal with my disease, and that it could be the beginning of the end of everything. It sucked to lock those big industrial double doors for the last time and listen to the slam echo so hollow in that long, now so stark, room.

Ralph had even painted a cartoon mural of me and Patrick, my leprechaun dummy, as circus performers on one of the walls. I loved it. We'd had several nights of pizza, beer and laughs as he created it.

Now it stood alone, the last silent testament of what that wonderful space had been.

To make room for my studio stuff at home, I had to sell one of my Triumph sports cars, a TR3B. Now on the surface, it's a very desirable car. Only 2500 or so were imported, and it looks cool as all get out with its bug-eyed headlights and grinning grille smiling right out of 1963.

But to restore it would take years and thousands of dollars and as anyone who has owned a Triumph will tell you, you don't really own it, it owns you.

Doing a full restoration on a '76 Spitfire had more than taught me that. There was a fellow in the Triumph club more than eager to buy it and although it was sad to see it go, I also felt an incredible sense of relief. Years, possibly decades of potential automotive and financial suffering had just rolled out of my garage, and I had made money on the deal! Maybe cancer wasn't so bad after all.

We arranged for a house sitter, another wonderful friend named Mary who loves our cat. She was between jobs, and our house would serve as a respite from her apartment as she contemplated the next step in her life.

She and another friend, Nancy, who I would swear is a lost sister separated at birth because of her love of humor and irreverent wit, would shop so there would be food ready when we got back.

Nancy and Ralph helped me in another very important way; they are both cancer survivors of very serious manifestations of the disease, ovarian and colon respectively. Ralph was stricken in his early 20s due most likely to a genetic predisposition - there was a strong history of colon cancer in his family. Gratefully, he had fully recovered after surgery and was living a productive life working with the developmentally disabled, not to mention bringing me to near tears with his hilarious impressions.

Nancy was at first diagnosed with a benign mass in her abdomen, which when seen during surgery proved to be a large ovarian tumor that had spread over to her uterus. But, after a hysterectomy and follow up chemo she, too, was doing well working as a graphic artist, designing my brochures and lifting my spirits with her ever optimistic outlook.

Their success and ability to move on, without dwelling on what they had been through, provided an invaluable model for my attitude. I wasn't always able to live up to it, but I was very grateful to have them as a first hand resource for what this process would be like, and I would draw on their experience and support frequently over the next two years.

With the help of these friends and many others, almost everything was in place for my return from the clinic. When I got back, my life would center around the special juicer which arrived from California not long before we were scheduled to depart for Mexico. The UPS guy staggered a bit as he dropped off a 60 lb. mass of All American stainless steel straight out of "Robocop", called a Norwalk.

Chapter Six

Mr. Jalapeno!

This Norwalk looked like it could not only juice any fruit or vegetable know to man, but oak trees, granite and small Toyotas as well. It didn't come with a helmet or goggles, but I did add some Kevlar to my favorite kitchen apron just because it looked so darned intimidating.

After hiring 14 pro wrestlers to haul it to our upstairs kitchen (our home had been duplexed at one point, so the second kitchen would soon become "Juice Central"), we had to build a special pedestal for it anchored deep in the earth's mantle.

All comedic exaggeration aside, this thing was the real deal, which was comforting to know since it would be the main tool in what I hoped would be my miraculous recovery. We experimented with a couple of trial juices, but failed to insert the carrots into the grinder properly and spewed bright orange carrot bits all over the kitchen. But the juice tasted like no other, fresh and alive, and it was nice to know at least that part of the treatment I could probably handle.

We had reverse osmosis water installed . . . twice. The first time, after plunking down $1000, the thing put out a dribble, and when I called to complain the water production wasn't anywhere near what had been promised, the sphinctorially challenged sales guy said, "Well, to get the output you're looking for, we can upgrade you to a better producing machine for another $250."

I was pissed. It was the only time I remember playing what I call the "C" card.

I said, "Look, I want what you promised at the price you promised, or you can uninstall the whole thing. I have cancer and I don't have time to screw around." Although I promised not to use the big "C" for evil purposes ever again, the next day I was on the schedule for a new, better system at no additional charge that put out the quantity of water I had been promised in the first place.

It was the start of an attitude I would keep throughout the therapy: an intense intolerance for BS. When I seemed to be facing my possible demise, I just didn't have time or patience for it.

We had one more issue to sort out, arguably the most major one. Who would go with me to Mexico? The clinic wanted you to have a companion, preferably the person who would be doing most of the extra work day in, day out over the next two years.

Gail was the obvious choice, but there were complications. As I mentioned earlier, she was scheduled to go to the wedding, in Paris no less, of a young woman for whom she had been a governess just out of college.

She was very close to the family. When Gail's father died of melanoma at 52, they had taken care of everything to get her back to the United States. She had lived with them as part of their family for a year, and the bond with them was vibrant.

She also desperately needed a vacation. Her life and

Cathy's had been inextricably entwined from her diagnosis to her last breath four years later. In between, Gail had been there for countless doctors' consultations, chemo treatments, helping her nephews, and maintaining her vigil at the hospice.

This woman had just finished one big helping of heartache and desperately needed this long, leisurely junket to "Gay Paree," but the universe was force feeding her seconds whether she wanted any or not.

In many ways I was far more concerned for her than me.

We discussed having my mother go for part of the time and have Gail come later, but the logistics were just too complicated.

But I didn't want Gail to feel like she had no choice.

The last thing I wanted her to do was cancel her trip. Damn it, she had been so looking forward to going and France would be the perfect respite for her wounded spirit. Unfortunately, after agonizing contemplation, she decided an unknown clinic in Mexico would replace Paris. It would be saltless oatmeal instead of croissant, more sick people instead of vibrant youth starting a new life together.

Boy, did I resent cancer that day.

I had a few gigs on the books between diagnosis and our departure. I was nervous about the strain and various friends became my roadies. Glen, a wonderfully talented musician/comedian, helped me at the oil refinery fireman's gig. My longtime buddy Dave, a newspaper circulation manager, sojourned up north for a hard drinkin,' hard smokin' manufacturing plant gig, and Gail went on my last pre-therapy show for the St. Patty's Day bash at a parish in Faribault. The highlight of that affair was my leprechaun dummy Patrick McWiggins, looking for his long lost brother, Father Flannigan, the priest there.

A typical week in the life of a regional entertainer.

I felt a bit tired, but the gigs went well and it was good to end on a high note, not knowing if that parish show would be my last. I took posters from it with me, just in case, and left that room with a bittersweet feeling of nostalgia tempered with more than a little fear.

That night a cold brought on by fatigue and stress was starting to manifest in Gail. She had spent the show in the car sleeping, which was probably the best thing she could do for herself. The rest of our time at home was spent in last minute preparations.

For our house sitter, Mary, living in St. Paul for a couple of weeks would be a good change of venue for her. She would lavish attention on our ever petulant cat, Foxy, or as I sometimes call him, "Old Piss 'n' Boots," and take the time to clear her own head between jobs. She is another one of those saints who was able to step in at just the right time.

I felt extremely blessed because a lot of things worked out that way, and I was so impressed by so many people's generosity. I wondered if I could be so magnanimous if the situation were reversed.

During these days of preparation I tried to do the therapy

as best I could "half time," to break myself in. I fumbled with trying a French Roast enema or two, not knowing I was preparing the coffee all wrong and not realizing it would be much easier with a plastic enema bucket, rather than the hot water bottle I got at Walgreens. I tried to eat all vegetarian organic and continued trying to get the hang of the Norwalk juicer, managing to gulp down at least a few juices each day. The actual therapy would prove to be far more intense, but these practice rounds at least helped soften the shock.

And then we were off to San Diego for what would be my last days of a "normal" lifestyle.

Our flight was uneventful and our hotel was near a charming part of the city called Old Town. After settling in, we decided to walk over there. It was full of old time shops, restaurants, bars and bustling tourists with anxious kids tugging on their parents sleeves, insistently declaring they couldn't live without this or that trinket.

As pleasant as it was, ever present in my mind was the lump in my kidney, just kind of hanging there like a buzzing fly trying hard to spoil a picnic.

But the weather was beautiful, and by this point with all the preparation done, the house in good hands and despite our reason for being there, this evening was a welcome transitional oasis. Not in Minnesota, not yet submerged in what would be an entirely new reality, we could breathe easy, if just for an evening.

One of our major focuses was where to eat my last "real" meal.

Food was such a wonderful social event for Gail and me, and I had not let myself think too much about giving that up for what would end up being two years. No restaurants, no pie, no wonderful Indian Samosas, no salt, no refined sugar, no (one of my staples on the road) tuna fish sandwiches, no convenience store cranberry juice full of high fructose corn syrup, no Sun Chips, no Ding Dongs, and, Oh My God, no TWINKIES!

Arrrrgggghhh!. HOW WOULD I SURVIVE???

One of my favorite things to do, after being on the road, was to take Gail out to eat, relax, see how her days had gone and recount my show adventures and debacles.

Gail, a children's librarian, shared tales of storytime kids not quite making it to the bathroom, outlandish patrons and funding politics. I brought tales of dummies limbs falling off during shows, and audience volunteers trying to hand me their false teeth. It was important bonding time, important out of the house time, easy, comfortable time.

Could that still happen over carrot juice and the major Gerson staple, Special Soup? I hoped so.

I would now be eating virtually everything at home and she would be making much of it. It would be a huge change for us; little did we dream how huge.

But that night we let ourselves relax in the temperate southern California air and soak up the ambience.

We checked out the menus at several places, but they looked too hectic inside, or there weren't any vegetarian items for Gail.

Finally we wandered by a small Mexican walk-up place with an approachable local feel about it. They had delicious looking veggie burritos, quesadillas and of course, standard meat filled Mexican-American fare.

I got a black bean burrito stuffed with onions, diced tomatoes, and other veggies served with two kinds of salsa, and just as important, my last Coke. I mean damn, Coke rots my teeth, hurts my stomach and gets me hyper . . . and I do love it so, especially over ice on a boiling hot day. Mmm, mmm, mmm.

It was all so good, an hour later walking by the place again, we got more to take with us to the hotel. It was salty and cheesy and spicy and gooey, and the Coke was super sweet and fizzy and just as wonderfully decadent as it should be. A stark contrast to what we would experience the next day.

Embraced in the afterglow of sunset, our walk back to the room was peaceful and soothing to our anxious spirits. We had lingered quite awhile and by that time had Old Town practically to ourselves. It almost felt like many of our vacations together. A bit exotic, unburdened and almost frivolous, as though you know a storm is coming but you know there is nothing you can do about it, so you become inexplicably giddy. Back at the hotel we sat on the bed, relished our seconds from the Mexican place, and dozed off shortly thereafter. Our last day of typical American lifestyle was over.

At 8:00 a.m., our driver arrived to take us across the border to the clinic in Mexico. He picked up a buddy of his along the way and their playful banter was a welcome distraction from my own anxiety. I would be out of the country for two weeks, trusting my life to foreign doctors and doing unspeakable things with coffee.

But there would be plenty of time to think about that. Right now their friendly, jabbing exchanges kept me in the moment and there were no delays at the border, for which I was grateful. An inspection by curious Mexican agents would have only heightened my feelings of insecurity about what was to come in the ensuing days.

Lucky for us, our Gerson chauffer seemed to know everyone on both sides of the line, and crossing was more like ordering a Big Mac from a high school friend at the drive through window, official but refreshingly casual.

Now in Mexico, we eventually we turned off a main artery and meandered into a well kept neighborhood of very nice, tidy homes, eventually stopping in front of what looked like a large, rambling, white stucco house or small mom and pop hotel. After paying the shuttle fee, we entered through the front black cast iron gate. It opened into a small, simple, well kept courtyard accented with blooming fruit trees and a softly gurgling fountain.

There were rooms above, rooms below, a kitchen area off to the right and the medical office directly ahead under the staircase. Another narrow passage led, as we would find out later, to the dining area, a recreational meeting room and a Gerson friendly, chemical free pool.

We were met by a cordial young man named Anthony who had been expecting us and greeted us by name, which I thought was a nice touch. After his gracious welcome, he beckoned us into his modest office. As we crossed the courtyard, I saw a few faces I would come to know well in the ensuing days, other patients from all over the world. They had come here looking for an alternative to chemo, radiation and surgery . . . or to recovery from it, and for several of them, this was their last hope. Each had a unique story but with a similar theme, and it would be fascinating to watch this chapter in their sagas and mine unfold.

To my surprise, while we were meeting with Anthony, my first juice arrived served by one of the ever cordial kitchen staff in an 8 oz. clear plastic solo cup. It had a lid with our room number written on it in orange wax pencil.

Wow, my first official classic Gerson apple carrot juice. It went down easily as Anthony described the different procedures, etc., that would take place over the next two weeks: How things operated, that there was medical staff on duty 24/7, and how to use their internet.

His professional but friendly demeanor created a good first impression and his perfect English was comforting to hear. At the very least, I wouldn't have to rely on my Jr. High Spanish if I ended up having some unforeseen medical catastrophe.

We went up to our room at the top of the stairs just to the left to settle in, and no sooner had we set our bags down than there was a knock at the door. "Mr. Wedgwood, jugo!" Apparently, I would need that junior high Spanish. Fortunately I knew what jugo meant - juice. I was caught off guard that it came so close on the heels of the first one, just 30 minutes, but soon I would know the jugo routine by heart. This was another apple carrot, mixed with four teaspoons of potassium powder and two drops of Lugol's (iodine) solution. Again, it tasted great, smooth and sweet, and down it went.

I knew from studying the Gerson handbook that it was important to drink the juices immediately because the live enzymes in them that do so much of the healing work, deteriorate quickly once the juice is made. And with what we were paying for them per day, I didn't want to waste a single one.

Our room was not hospital-like at all. It was more like a simple budget rate motel: two twin beds, TV and a bathroom with shower. The only hints indicating you weren't there for a beach vacation were the air purifier in the corner, and the aqua vinyl-covered bench with an IV pole standing dutifully at attention next to it. And although I quickly would discover what THAT was for, and basically already knew, I didn't want to put it in the forefront of my mind just yet. I was scheduled for my intake interview at 10:30 with my Gerson Doctor, or as I would come to call her, my GD.

I had already sent a lot of medical history, but there was still some paperwork to fill out as we waited in the open lobby of the Doctor's office. The entry was a sliding glass door right off the courtyard and in the foyer was a basic desk, chairs and a scale.

I have to confess a bit of American arrogance at this point but also a great fondness for the simplicity of this place. I had just come from the world of big CT scanners, enormous hospitals, and physicians in multi-suite highrise offices.

This by comparison seemed quaint, but at the same time the approachability and straight forwardness of it all made the prospect of undertaking the Gerson therapy a bit less intimidating.

When we entered the office we were greeted at the door by my cordial, yet very professional Gerson Doctor. I would refer to her as that, or GD for short, throughout our stay. It wasn't that she didn't have a lovely name, I just liked that I finally had an actual, real live licensed physician who practiced Dr. Gerson's Therapy. It was like coming in from the Western Medical wilderness, and there by the fireplace was my GD with warm soup, a glass of juice and bedtime stories about amazing cancer recoveries.

She had thick dark hair cut shoulder length, the traditional white lab coat, and invited us to sit as she worked her way behind her slate grey metal, industrial looking desk. Also in the office, observing the intake was another doctor, who was in the process of becoming a certified Gerson practitioner, a GD in training. Her glasses and pulled back hair gave her a Marion Librarian style, but something about her made it seem that after hours, she just might transform into something else altogether - maybe Carmen Miranda with a lab coat and stethoscope.

Gail and I sat down; she was feeling more and more miserable by the minute with Kleenexes bourgeoning from every available pocket and sleeve. The cold she had at my last show was still dogging her with a vengeance. I handed my new GD my CT scans and prepared to listen intently as she gave us an orientation for the clinic.

Gail had certainly been there and done this. She had made a point of accompanying Cathy on as many doctor appointments as possible. Between the two of them they remembered things much better and it was an immense help to Cathy and Bob in their decision making process.

Gail even ended up being the one to sign Cathy's "Do Not Resuscitate" authorization at the hospice. It was a sobering moment, signing off on someone else's life, and she had been a bit shocked by it.

I kept wondering if she had anything left for this. Maybe she should just be up in the room sleeping, pretending she was actually in Cancun, and would be having Margaritas any moment brought in by a friendly Cabana Boy.

In contrast to Gail's voracious cold and emotional baggage, I was doing pretty well. The relaxed, low-tech atmosphere put me at ease and my choice of path had been made. Sorting through what seemed like a thousand opinions, worrying about being a burden to so many people had been confusing, taxing and frightening. But now, with tasks to accomplish and skills to learn, that was all behind me and across the border in another country. And given the simplicity of the surroundings, it almost seemed to be in another time too, like some 60's era road trip movie I'd seen years before.

My GD started by doing what most physicians do on intake: Going over the form with my history, allergies, etc. She stopped at heart health and my family history. I mentioned my father's heart attack, pacemaker and sextuple bypass, and that I was a prime candidate for heart disease with a cholesterol level of 217.

She said matter of factly, "The Gerson Therapy will clear that out."

What? I hadn't expected this and part of me wouldn't let me believe it, but if it did, hey what the hell, great!

She seemed peculiarly unalarmed by my kidney mass. Maybe it was the small size, my overall good health, I don't know. I asked her point blank about my prognosis and again in a voice that had not an ounce of worry she said, "Very good."

While this sounded wonderful, I wasn't ready to let myself totally believe it or let down my guard. I kind of tucked her statements away in the same drawer with the "They got it all" statements I had heard about other cancer patients who were no longer on the planet.

But I also kept an open and hopeful mind. I mean, that's why I was here, to make the miracle happen, and it was a relief to actually hear it from a medical professional, one who didn't think carrot juice and enemas were medicinal heresy.

It was then time for the physical exam. I was asked to go into an adjoining exam room and disrobe down to my, as my Marine Corp father would put it, skivvies (to this day I don't know the etymology of that word, but it sure is fun to say).

The trouble was, I didn't have any "skivvies" on. I chuckled and apologetically explained to the nurse that I would be right back. He was actually entertained by this and very tolerant. It was our first encounter with Marco, and over the next two weeks we would come to appreciate his jokes and infectious friendly energy. He would become part of what we came to consider our Gerson family.

But for the task at hand I needed "skivvies." I quickly ran to the room, put on a pair of boxers Gail had given me that were black with bright red jalapeno peppers on them, pulled up my jeans and bolted back down the stairs.

By the time my GD entered the room, I was back on the exam table in an open back gown and the jalapeno boxers, mildly panting from my sprint and speed change. She asked, "Now, you are decent?" I dug out that Jr. High Spanish and replied, "Si, claro, yo tengo jalapenos!" (Yes, of course, I have jalapenos!)

She cracked a smile, Marco laughed and from then on I became "Mr. Jalapeno!!!," and they knew at that point I would not be their typical patient.

The main thing I recall about the exam itself was her thumping my back over the kidney. She said, "Any pain?" I replied, "Just a dull ache."

"That's normal. You usually don't have pain with this." Indeed, my only symptom of anything had been fatigue. Heart and lungs and everything else for that matter seemed fine, and after the exam she told us, almost with surprise, "We're going to put you on the full therapy."

Why the surprise in her tone? Was there any other way? It was what I had been expecting.

She continued, "13 juices, 5 coffee enemas a day, plus injections of B-12 with liver and oral supplements."

While all of that sounded daunting, I still didn't understand why it was anything unusual here at the clinic.

Just then, my next juice arrived from the kitchen. Somehow their staff must have secretly rigged me with a GPS locator, because it was obvious they always knew where I was.

This one was a deep forest green color. As I drank it down, I didn't think I could ever get used to this taste. Earthy in a nasty kind of way, it left a heavy aftertaste and made me a bit queasy. I had the reaction similar to someone having hard liquor for the first time: A pucker, a squint, a swallow and an "Eeeewwwe boy!"

Made up of lettuce, red cabbage, green peppers, green apples and other "green" stuff, it would be a good six months before I actually found this juice palatable.

But as to why being on the full therapy was communicated with a bit of surprise, I would come to find out most of the people there weren't on it!

In fact, of the 11 or so patients at the clinic, I would be the only one doing 13/5. Most others were drinking 10 juices, doing three "coffee breaks" as we would come to call them, and none of the intensive castor oil treatments (more on that joyful procedure momentarily).

Why? Because the Gerson therapy doesn't just go after the cancer. It is an intensive detoxification of the entire physical system. Decades of poisons from pesticides, air pollution, smoking, etc. trapped in our tissues are extracted and pulled into the bloodstream. The coffee enemas then open up the bile ducts and other elimination systems in the liver and pancreas to expunge these toxins from the body via the colon. It all works together. Without the detoxifying effects of the coffee enemas, patients run the risk of hepatic coma, due to the failure of getting the freshly freed poisons out of their bodies and blood stream.

For the patients who had been on chemo, their livers were just too toxic to cleanse on a 13 juice, five enema level.

And the reason many of them don't even do the castor oil treatments prescribed by Dr. Gerson? It would pull too much toxin too fast into their bloodstream and they could not eliminate it efficiently enough.

When taking the castor oil, the patient drinks 2 tbls. of that truly nasty goop followed 5 hours later by a coffee enema laced with more castor oil. This puts the detox mechanism into overdrive.

And lucky me, because I was so darn healthy otherwise, I would be doing these every other day for the next six weeks!

It was odd and intimidating but at the same time energizing. By this time, Gail and I were totally intrigued and listened intently to what else the therapy would hopefully do. In addition to the afore mentioned cleaning of my arteries and of course hopefully taking care of my kidney, there could be other benefits.

My weight - which I had been trying to maintain at a steady 140-145 pounds would first go down and then plateau to quote my Gerson Doc., "Where my body thinks it should be."

Other ailments, that I'd had for years, might clear up too. My eyes should lose the yellow cast they had below the lower lid line, and I should end up with plenty of energy. One thing I was embarrassed to ask but was curious about, "Would my hair thicken back up?" It was vain but what the heck. Rodney, my friend in New Jersey, said that his gray hair turned dark again, as did Jaquie Davison's. While I wasn't gray, I had a good start on a male pattern five head (one step above a forehead).

Gerson Doc replied she had a couple of patients where that had happened, but no guarantees. Well . . . OK. I guess just staying alive and keeping my kidney would have to do.

One thing about the exam I will always remember was when my GD examined my throat with a tongue depressor. As I opened wide and said "Aaahhh," her first comment was, "Oh! Metal."

She was referring to the six gold crowns in my mouth.

She didn't elaborate and continued on with the exam, but months later I would come to understand her response.

At that time I liked my shiny gold crowns. I had been told by my dentist they were very pure gold and the best restoration possible. He loved them and so did I. I don't wear necklaces, bracelets and rarely rings, but for me these were kind of a kosher substitute. I mean it's gold, the metal that caused the "rush," that backed our country's currency for well over a century, that everything should be "good as." And for me it had a definite cool factor. But her reaction to my glistening molars sparked a little warning blinker in my head that wouldn't go out easily, like the "check engine" light flashing intermittently from the dashboard. Although I didn't know it then, that little comment "Oh!, Metal" from my GD would bourgeon into reams of research and hours in the dentist's chair once we got home.

But all that was in the future. For now, we had a therapy to learn.

My new Gerson Doctor wrapped up the exam with a few more thumps on my torso and "breathe ins" after which Gail and I returned to our room, kind of looking at each other with a "Well, here we go" expression.

Soon, another knock on the door. Another juice. "Ola', jugo," said the always cheerful voice. This one was straight carrot - easily palatable, no sweat.

Knock knock again - this time a different nurse. She brought up my supplements for the day to be taken with each of the juices.

Even though I had read about them in Dr. Gerson's book, seeing them all neatly tucked in their long blue pill box with a compartment for each dose was totally different. Yellow capsules, light beige capsules, dark beige capsules, big white pills, medium white pills, small white pills.

I couldn't even think about what they were all for at that

juncture. I just had to trust that all the staff knew what they were doing. At least they had idiot labels, so I would know exactly when to take what.

Knock knock - it was Marco again. He was here for my introduction to . . . OK, the enema bucket. Issshhhh. It had been sitting on the countertop in our room. You could tell this plastic apparatus with a long tube projecting from it rather enjoyed the intimidating effect it had on people. "Yep, I'm goin' where the sun don't shine, whether you like it or not boy, so git used to it," I could almost hear it gloating. Ewwwwe, am I really going to do this 5 times a day? Oh Man! At least my rehearsals in the tub made it somewhat conceivable.

And here at the clinic they did have that great aqua bench to lay on and an IV pole for the bucket. Ah, maybe this wouldn't be so bad.

Marco brought with him a thermos of warm coffee and a thermos of warm water. He described the proper ratio of coffee to water, how to lubricate the vaguely phallic looking red tip of the tube coming out of the bucket with Vaseline, how long to hold the fluid in the colon (10 minutes), and how to clean up afterward.

I was with him on all of this until he said the amount of coffee/water solution that was to go into my poor little colon would be 32 ounces. 32 ounces?! That's 2 pop cans full! The bucket was now openly laughing at me, and I could hear its plasticy, hollow twang resonating in my head. "Can you take all this sucka? C'mon, let's see what you're made of puppet boy!"

And according to the schedule, I would have to do this soon . . . in the next half hour. What a trial by latté!

Oh, and did I mention this whole "coffee break" class took place without Marco speaking English and me faking it with my pigeon Spanish? The gesticulating used to describe tube placement and my questions about how far it should go in was right out of a bad SNL skit.

"Aqui?" "No, aqui." "Y quanto?" "Trente dos." "Trente dos!! No es possible!" "Si." "No!" "Es muy mucho!" "Si!"

"Tu tienes leche para este?" "No, . . . yo tengo expresso!"

It was nice to hear him joke back so quickly. His sense of humor would lighten our spirits many times over the next two weeks.

He also showed us the little sign we could Velcro to the door to indicate "Don't come in, coffee break."

It seemed odd to announce it to the world, but it was becoming obvious the Gerson Clinic was definitely an alternate reality.

With this visit, Marco also gave me a shot of liver extract and B-12. Both are VERY important on the therapy and administered in the upper outside part of the butt cheek. The location has to be precise or you can hit the sciatic nerve. I had read about these injections in the handbook and been dreading this daily shot more than any other part of the therapy because, I HATE NEEDLES! While this would be nothing like Yankton and the CT dye injection, the anticipation of any needle prick makes me batty. And this one did hurt mostly, as I was to figure out later, because of the speed with which Marco injected the 3cc of fluid. But at least it was done, and I wouldn't have to worry about it for another 24 hours.

In addition, I would eventually have to administer the shots myself, which was a bit intimidating, but for now I had plenty of other things to think about.

Apparently Marco was already feeling comfortable with me, because when I asked him what position he wanted me in for the shot, he had me put my hands against the wall, legs spread and then he backed up like he was going to hurl the syringe into my derriere like a javelin in the Olympics. It was a great joke, distracted me from my shot anxiety, and I appreciated his taking the risk at humor.

When Marco left, the bucket started beckoning, "Are you ready? You want a piece of me puppet boy, huh? Bring it on!" But I decided I could squeak in some lunch before answering it's haughty challenge.

And so, with B-12 in my derriere, jugo in my veins, jalapenos on my boxers and a belligerent bucket beckoning, our new Gerson lifestyle was officially underway.

Chapter Seven

Coffee . . . the Wrong Way

Due to her cold, Gail could not join me for lunch and remained in the room. Many Gerson patients are so ill, their immune systems so compromised, that contact with a cold virus would be like a close encounter with Typhoid Mary.

So, I ventured down the stairs and negotiated the narrow corridor to the dining room. A few patients and companions had already arrived and there was a sense of instant camaraderie because we were all at the clinic for the same reason.

They were seated across three tables that held about six people each. The room had one glass wall with a door that led out to the chilly but "Gerson safe" (no chlorine, fluoride, etc.) pool.

On the other side of the small courtyard was a recreational room, which I later discovered had a widescreen TV, exercise equipment, and some very comfy couches.

Laid out to my left as I stepped into the dining room was lunch, buffet style with green salad, vinegar and flaxseed oil dressing, fresh fruit, baked potato halves, other mixed veggies and the ever present Gerson soup.

For companions there was nonfat plain yogurt too.

Conspicuously missing were butter, salt, pepper and refined sugar. Apparently tumors like sodium, refined sugar and most fats, so these are eliminated from the diet. The black pepper was gone because in some patients their digestive systems are so delicate it's too irritating.

Green peppers and fresh onions and garlic were OK though. Go figure. And I would come to eat them in abundance just to get some spices.

Also there was a tray with everyone's lunchtime juice on it. Mine was another apple carrot with my room number once again scrawled in orange on the top.

I filled my plates and sat with two couples, Fred & Julie and Nick & Jodie. Nick and Jodie were from Washington State, where Nick was an apple grower. He had been through the mill with his advanced lung cancer having undergone surgery, chemo, the works. He looked gaunt and tired, but he and his wife were very upbeat and enthusiastic about Gerson.

In my work as an entertainer I had performed for countless agriculture groups made up of folks like Nick and Jodie.

Just as in Yankton, banquets for corn and bean producers, cattlemen, poultry and pork producers were a mainstay of my business, and as such I had developed a special affinity for this special breed of American that these days seems harder and harder to find. They work their tails off, often for very low profit margins and yet are the kindest, most gracious and generous folks you would ever want to know.

I found it easy to talk and relate to them although looking at Nick was tough.

It wasn't him personally, but with all he'd been through it was the face of his disease staring hard back at me, taunting me through that pale skin, those sallow cheeks and turmoil sunken eyes.

I had just met Nick, but unlike Cathy and Randy I had no personal connection with him so why was I being affected this way? What was going on?

The difference was I had now been diagnosed myself, and I couldn't help but wonder if that would be me in two years, despite my best efforts. My Gerson Doctor's confidence not withstanding, there were no guarantees, no matter how dedicated I would end up being to the therapy.

Gratefully, a large booming voice interceded to pull me from my introspection. It was a Fred Lung, a mountain of a retired machinist from Maine. He is Ralph Kramden incarnate and, as I would later discover, had a penchant for hanging out in the courtyard in a tank style t-shirt, boxers, black sox and dress shoes. He had a friendly echoing voice, backed up with an east coast directness as evidenced by his first bellowed words to me, "So, what you in here for kid?!"

After I described my situation, he told me he didn't have cancer, but was suffering from a severe and somewhat mysterious deterioration of his liver.

His doctor had given him six months to live and told him to get his affairs in order (as I write this nearly 18 months later, he is very much alive and doing well).

He, unlike my apple growing tablemates, who had been at the clinic over two weeks already, had gotten in just a day or two before us. His wife was also very sociable, readily chirping in her version of Fred's situation.

Also at that lunch were a gracious man with a gentle southern drawl named John, the daughter of a Canadian man who was too ill to come to the dining room, and a sandy haired woman sitting alone. I would get to know all three at subsequent meals, each with their own unique and fascinating stories.

But for today, it was enough getting acquainted with the Lungs and the Handcocks, trying to warm up to the food, and taking a tray up to Gail.

Being a vegetarian for many years, she of course was in hog heaven. Consequently, the lunch I brought up looked great to her, and she would have no difficulties eating the same food as me and the rest of the patients. Other patient helpers didn't have it quite so easy. They didn't have cancer but were not allowed to bring in any outside food so as not to corrupt the patient's healing process. While they may have been craving a "Big Mac," a plain baked potato would have to do.

Gail was just digging in when, knock, knock "jugo," was the call from the open doorway. Another green juice. I thanked the kitchen person and gulped it down. Whew, these bad boys were something. And right after lunch. Any pleasant aftertaste I was relishing from my tasty vegetables was quickly obliterated.

It was like finishing off a meal of filet mignon with a dirt chaser.

But Gail's happiness with her food made me feel better. She was so sick by this point any bright spot in her day was welcome.

We finally had a moment while she ate to relax a bit. I still had a little time before my first "coffee break." I fell asleep as Gail munched happily, intrigued with the creativity the kitchen staff had used for her meal, and making mental notes for things to prepare at home. She got in a little pleasure reading too.

.

And then it was time. I could no longer delay my date with "The Bucket." As I looked at it sitting there, gradated, with that weird tube and red tip hanging out I wondered, "Why is it medical stuff so often looks like that, so foreboding and devoid of anything remotely comforting, so clinically dispassionate? I mean, can't they design it in plaid or paisley, or at least put a Smurf sticker on it?"

The bucket was silent now, maybe a bit chagrined that I had called it's bluff. Anyway, per Marco's instructions I put in just the right amount of coffee and then added the warm water from the thermos and room temperature water to get it as close to 98.6 degrees as possible, and of course, filling it to that oh so intimidating 32 ounce demarcation.

With everything primed and ready to go, Gail graciously agreed to take a walk so I wouldn't feel self conscious.

Let's face it. It's humiliating enough to be sticking a tube up your butt, much less having your spouse observe. Although she said it wouldn't bother her, I just didn't want her to see me like that. It was too dehumanizing. So, book, hat, and sunscreen in hand, she was off.

With the room empty and consequently my dignity intact, I picked up the bucket by the handles, corralled the flailing tube, and addressed the aqua bench. It all looked easy enough, but I was still apprehensive. Hanging the bucket on the IV pole would help, but to really get over any weird feelings I had about doing a coffee enema, I just had to jump in with both cheeks. Oops, and don't forget to put a little Vaseline on the tip of the strange red tube - very important!

I lay down and it was time for business. Now I heard the bucket chuckle ever so slightly. It knew what was coming and that there's something so strange about getting so incredibly personal with that part of your anatomy. We have been taught for so many years to be totally disgusted with it and now "it" and I would be on a meet and greet basis. Kind of like the relatives you knew you had, but because they were so peculiar you never wanted to be involved with them, and really didn't want to shake their hand because you couldn't even begin to guess where it had been.

Anyway, in went the red tip and I opened the plastic clamp on the long clear tube connecting it to the bucket. As the coffee flowed in, the warmth was actually quite comforting as it gradually, gently filled my abdomen, and my system was accepting it more readily than the hot-water-bottle-infused French Roast combo I had attempted back in St. Paul. At the clinic, they use an organic Mexican blend that my confused but curious colon seemed to like just fine.

I watched the level in the bucket get lower and lower. With about 12 oz. left I began to feel pretty full, but Marco said 32 oz. so I hung in there. 25, 28, 30, 32!! OK. I closed the clamp on the tube and delicately extracted the now somewhat less frightening red tip, grateful I would never have to see this process from any other angle. Gail and I would later nick name the tip "Mr. Pinky." We tend to nick name many things, and in this case it helped to diffuse the frankly disgusting reality of this flopping medical implement.

I was holding my own, a bit proud at getting this part of the procedure done without a hitch, but suddenly, with 32 oz. in there, that warm comforting feeling morphed into "over-loaded-water-balloon-waiting-to-burst!" I heard the bucket mutter "Told you so!" I imagined the headlines the next day, "Ventriloquist explodes and rains down on San Diego. Laughing bucket claims responsibility."

This was really a lot of pressure. Yikes! And I was supposed to hold it for 10-12 minutes!

Well, I knew almost immediately THAT wasn't gonna happen. After five minutes Mr. Sphincter called on the lower GI hotline screaming it was time to let go, and off to the bathroom I obediently went.

Expelling that much fluid from my then uninitiated colon created such a Vesuvian pressure that it almost lifted me off the seat.

I heard voices from Houston chiming in "Apollo, we have ignition." Honestly, it felt like a seven on the Richter scale. Whew doggies. I would never need Ex-Lax again!

And then, as I sat there in the bathroom, feeling like a washcloth that has been wrung out by Superman . . . Knock Knock. "Jugo!"

Crap, so to speak. I hadn't put the sign out. "Please just leave it on the ledge by the door, gracias," I yelled in a voice that tried to conceal the incredible awkwardness of talking to a stranger while evacuating coffee from one's hindquarters.

Ah well, it just added more texture to the moment.

I had some aftershocks following the initial blast, and then it was time to clean up. In Mexico, their septic systems often don't handle toilet paper, so there is a trash can by the stool expressly for this purpose. Fortunately, this one had a swinging lid to hide the carnage, and the bathroom had its own window for ventilation.

I rinsed out the still somewhat smug feeling bucket, tube and Mr. Pinky tip with castile soap, hydrogen peroxide and lots of hot water. OK, one coffee break done. That hurdle has been jumped, albeit with jet propulsion. Now if I could just stay on the track. I opened the door to look for Gail and there was my juice waiting for me, a carrot, perched as I had asked, on the ledge. With this one I took two liver capsules.

In Dr. Gerson's original therapy, as I mentioned, patients drank raw calves' liver juice. Jaquie Davison had done that. But by the time I came to the clinic the use of raw calves liver had been discontinued because even very young livers from all sources had become contaminated with campylobacter, a bacterium that can cause diarrhea, abdominal pain, fever, nausea and vomiting.[9] So, because they could no longer get pure enough calves liver, that part of the therapy was discontinued and replaced by capsules containing desiccated calves liver, three times a day. Part of me was relieved. Drinking raw liver juice sounded horrendously awful. On the other hand, I couldn't help but wonder how much effectiveness I was losing. Would my treatment work without it? Was I wasting my time?

Then I remembered; Rodney told me he got well without it, and if he did, then by God so could I!

The rest of that first day continued in a similar fashion: More juices, another coffee break, trying to help Gail get some rest and generally settling in.

At dinner, I sat with the gracious man with the gentle southern drawl, John Bachman. He had melanoma and was 18 months into the treatment by then. He had rented an apartment near the clinic and came by for meals and juices. It was more affordable that way, since he was doing most of his entire Gerson treatment in Mexico.

To me, he seemed to be sent by the universe as an emissary of good will and encouragement to all who were fortunate enough to come in contact with him. Whenever you engaged him in conversation, he listened intently and always offered supportive words.

He too had been through the traditional cancer mill taking something called "bio chemo" and having surgery. He still had masses that were palpable under the skin in his arm and elsewhere, and seeing them frankly sent a chill down my spine.

A mass hidden deep in my back was one thing, but a walnut sized lump staring you in the face every day from your forearm was quite another. While John had "stabilized," his masses weren't disappearing either. Despite this, he was very upbeat, energetic and impassioned. It was almost as if his mission was not as much to get well, but to minister to the others at the clinic.

His gracious, calming southern drawl and openness certainly went a long way in achieving that. He was very encouraging to me, since I was virtually the only one there who had come with so little involvement with traditional medicine. Based on the many cases he had seen come and go at the clinic, he felt my prospects were very good.

As he and I chatted, I noticed the sandy haired woman sitting off by herself again, saying cursory "hellos" and "goodbyes" to people as they came and went.

I made a mental note to engage her at some point too.

I took dinner up to Gail who was still dog tired and busy filling waste cans with snotty Kleenexes. I think she was trying to break my Yankton van record and was well on her way to doing so. I had not stayed too long at dinner so I could spend more time with her, bringing most of my food up with me. As we ate, I was trying to figure out ways to make the ever present soup more palatable. This night I put raw onions in it. For some reason when I had read about "The Soup" in the Gerson handbook, it sounded so delicious, so full of wonderful things: tomatoes, leeks, potatoes, celery root, garlic, onions and parsley. And according to Dr. Gerson, it was imperative for cleaning out impurities in the kidneys so in my case, it especially had to be eaten on a regular basis.

But without seasonings of any kind and ground down to a greenish brown mush, it reminded me more of an Oliveresque gruel than a healing miracle.

I had two more coffee breaks that night and by the last one I knew I couldn't stand another bout with 32 oz., so I made an executive decision and just put in 24, the bucket be damned. I felt a bit guilty, but the thought of bits of me raining down on Qualcomm Stadium was too vivid an image to ignore.

We tried to sleep, each in our single beds, mine being a hospital type.

Being in the hospital bed did not make me happy and on the surface it should have. It tilted up and down and other ways I never imagined. It had a very comfortable mattress on it. But to me it said, "Hey, you're the guy who is sick! The one who is infirm, who needs help, who can't do it all anymore, who might die." Images of Cathy in her hospital and hospice beds, full of tubes keeping her alive and meds making her loopy, streamed through my already overloaded head.

But after some calming self talk, I regained perspective. Bottom line? It was just a damn bed.

I mean really, it wasn't a big issue considering everything else going on but admittedly, I would never completely shake what it represented - my self imposed stigma of being the needy one.

Sleeping was tough that night. We were both restless being in a new environment, a very different routine - Knock Knock, "jugo" - almost every hour, new food and regular Gerson style "coffee breaks." Plus, God love her, Gail's snoring was keeping me awake and making her self-conscious. She is a wonderful woman and I love her dearly, but when she conks out she could keep a ship full of drunken sailors from getting any rest with her nocturnal nasal rattle.

It seemed I had just drifted off once Gail turned over on her side, silencing her cacophanous sinuses, when at 6 A.M. sharp, there was a knock bringing the morning coffee and hot water for the first of what that day would be five "coffee breaks."

Despite feeling a bit groggy, the day itself went pretty well. No big surprises, I ate a couple of meals with Gail in the room and we even took a short walk around the neighborhood.

We were getting familiar with the rhythms of the place, the timing of the therapy, etc. Apart from the four earthy green juices, which still tasted like dirt to me, I had no problems with the carrot, carrot/apple and fresh squeezed organic orange juice. I was getting to know the other patients better, and the spiceless organic vegetarian food was . . . well, what it was.

One thing I did do was talk to the physician on duty, the GD-in-training, about my concern for feeling like a Remax Balloon on steroids each time I took a bucketful of coffee for team Gerson. I said, in broken Spanish and as disarmingly as possible, "Yo poquito chico. Treinta y dos es malo para mi. Por favor solamente veinte y dos." (I am just a little guy, 32 is bad for me, please just 24!) I used my second grade sounding Spanish, even though she spoke perfect English to add some levity to the conversation and hopefully charm her into letting me do just 24 oz.

It worked. With a smile like a teacher who has just let a cute kid get away with more than she knows she should, she said that 24 oz. would be OK. I and my munchkin colon were greatly relieved.

Again, even though the day went well, sleep was difficult. I ended up sneaking off into one of the unoccupied rooms to avoid Gail's serenading sinuses, setting my alarm early and coming back with hopefully no one the wiser. I took all my bedding in with me and packed it back out when the alarm went off and finally got a decent night's rest.

I desperately didn't want to make Gail feel self-conscious about her nasal rumblings, but if I couldn't sleep I would go nuts.

It wasn't by any means just her snoring either. It was tough to rest during the day with the juice deliveries, B-12 shots, coffee breaks, housekeepers, etc. And at all hours there was street noise, some from what we came to call the "roof dogs." Many of the roofs in the area were flat and all of them seemed to have not one, but several short haired, scruffy, slovenly dogs just hanging out on them and barking aggressively at the least provocation.

How did they get up there and why? Were they guarding the shingles? Instead of cars, were they trying to chase low flying aircraft? Did they prefer rooftop sprinkler systems over fire hydrants?

And then there was the propane man. Every day, he would drive his truck through the neighborhood, broadcasting his service over his tinny, but oh so loud PA. The Spanish equivalent of "Propane, refill your old propane,'" would be the incessant chant from 7-11 A.M.

Apparently in our Mexican hamlet, no one calls for this, that or other services. They just wait for the truck to drive by and flag the guy down, like the ice cream man when I was growing up. "Hi, give me a fudgesicle, a bomb pop, and 5 gallons of LP on a waffle cone."

So, I continued with my clandestine nocturnal Great Escape, bedding and all, for two more nights until the empty room was filled with a new patient. I did actually sleep, but the stress of it all was taking a toll.

And then came my first castor oil day.

Marco showed up at 6:00 A.M., with a pill cup almost filled to the brim with a milky slightly yellow oil and, lo and behold, a 2/3 full cup of coffee. Coffee? To drink? Really, to drink? Hot damn, I would be in hog heaven! I hadn't had coffee that way in two weeks, and I was craving not just the beverage, but the ritual. I could fantasize about being in the bagel shop at home, totally relaxed after a great show the night before, the newspaper splayed out in front of me, savoring every rich, dark, caffeinated sip. Ooooh baby.

Why was a simple cup of coffee such a big deal? On Gerson oral coffee is strictly forbidden except for ½ cup to help the castor oil work through your stomach so you won't feel nauseated. For me it was like the most forbidden fruit made all the more desirable because you're already addicted to it.

And why castor oil? It's like a Roto Rooter for your liver. It grabs a lot of nasties hanging out in there and pulls them through with the help of a special enema five hours after drinking it.

Trouble is, it is awfully nasty itself, as I was about to find out. "Of course," I thought as I sized up the small cup of viscous ooze, "how bad can this be? It's not much, just one little cup, two tablespoons, let's just go for it."

I picked up the pill cup, put it to my lips and down the hatch it went. It was slimy and goopy, and the tenacious after taste clung to my mouth and throat like time delayed nausea.

I thought, "Well, at least I have some luscious fresh coffee to wash it down."

I gratefully pulled my first cup of java in two weeks to my mouth, anticipating the steaming aroma and . . . it was whimpily brewed, disgustingly tepid, church basement junk! Damn!

Of course it just magnified what a yuppie I was, hopelessly spoiled by my designer hazelnut back home.

But to the wussy stuff's credit, it got the slimy taste out of my mouth, and we were off to the races on my inaugural Castor Oil Day. Oh boy!

It didn't hit right away, but an hour and a half after sucking down those slippery two tablespoons, the time delayed blecchh feeling kicked in. The nurses gave me lots of organic peppermint tea which calmed my stomach, but then my emotions went ballistic. It was terrible and sudden. For seemingly no reason I was weeping, totally on edge and paranoid, interpreting innocuous comments as deeply personal slights.

It upset Gail terribly, and I felt bad that I couldn't control it. She ended up just leaving the room for several hours and I didn't come out of it until my third enema of the day finally cleaned out most of the castor oil and the toxins it had pulled from my tissues.

Gail took lots of long walks on subsequent castor oil days as a matter of self preservation.

We came to refer to my castor oil reaction as male PMS. It would totally wring me out. Charlotte said this was caused by the oil pulling out so many toxins from my bodily systems. That much poison being released is what was making me crazy. It was so bad, at breakfast and lunch I didn't want to talk with or see anyone.

Frank asked me to do a little show for everyone on one of these days and I remember resenting the hell out of him for even making the request.

The climax of castor oil day is the follow-up enema - a particularly devilish concoction of coffee, oxbile powder and, oh joy, more castor oil! Putting this where the sun don't shine pulls the initial oral dose and the poisons it has collected through and out of your system.

Uh, are we in the *Twilight Zone* yet?

The sickest part is you come to look forward to the follow-up enema because you know it will bring much needed relief. And the castor oil enema is like no other. It is so intense they don't even ask you to hold it for 10-12 minutes. In and out. And it's some kinda out!

Think of a day in Yellowstone watching Old Faithful, or Mt. Saint Helen's erupting to the soundtrack of *2001: A Space Odyssey* - doubled!!!

It almost levitated me off the seat. And the aroma! Well, to be discreet, the handbook mentions having to repaint rooms after some particularly toxic therapy patients have been in them, and now I know why.

The horrific thing was that all this nastiness coming out had been in my body! Possibly for decades! Permeating my tissues, my organs and my bones.

It was only many months later when my body actually started to feel clean that I realized just how toxed out I had been.

As they say in Minnesota, "Issssshhhhh!"

I really wished I could flush the toilet paper after the castor oil enema. Somehow putting paper with that disgusting stench in a plastic wastebasket, even covered, just didn't cut it. I wanted that stuff booked on a one way ocean voyage as soon a possible, but here in Mexico it would have to wait for the housekeeper.

I sure hope they paid her a lot!

The good thing was that once the castor oil enema was

over with, and I had recomposed myself to as close to normal as possible, and even given the bizarreness of what I had just done, I did feel better . . . wrung out yes, but better. All nausea had disappeared and emotional rationality had returned. Gail could now come back to the room without fearing male PMS.

The next coffee break four hours later was intense too, even though it was a normal one, as if anything on this therapy is normal. This coffee break seemed to get the residual castor oil out that was still rummaging in my guts. It wasn't really painful, just an awareness of bits of this slippery slime sliding through my systems.

By evening things had mellowed out completely, thanks to lots organic herbal mint tea, rest and reconciliation with Gail.

That night at dinner everyone seemed to understand my inhospitable demeanor earlier in the day and I was grateful.

It was kind of a tacit acknowledgement, "Ahhh, castor oil day, say no more." And for those who couldn't take it because their livers were too full of chemo, I detected just the slightest bit of envy, regretting they couldn't partake in this powerful part of the therapy, unpleasant as it was.

---

9. Charlotte Gerson, "The Evolution of the Gerson Therapy: Changes and Updates to the Therapy," www.thefreelibrary.com/The+evolution+of+the+Gerson+Therapy%3a+changes+and+updates+to+the...-a191308302.

Chapter Eight

New Lifestyle, New Friends

Back in the room, sleeping continued to be difficult. Gail moved to the rec room when she discovered my clandestine extra room excursions. I felt very bad, but she was too self-conscious about her snoring to rest comfortably in our room with me. Fortunately near the end of the week, I talked her back in after I assured her I could sleep fine with the new earplugs the clinic had provided.

Also, Nick and Jodie were going home to Washington. Nick was feeling better and they had been there quite awhile. Their room was bigger and a bit more off the beaten path, so I asked Anthony if we could move once it was available. This helped my comfort level at the clinic immensely. Being at the end of the upper balcony, no one got as far as our room unless they were there to see us. So all pass by traffic was eliminated along with conversations outside our door, carts rolling by, etc., and the extra space gave each of us some breathing room.

I was glad Nick and Jodie were going home with Nick looking and feeling better. I truly did like them. We'd had several good conversations over our breakfast oatmeal and luncheon baked potatoes. But there were many variables they would have to overcome once they got back to Washington. One was Nick, being a traditional American ag producer most of his life, didn't believe in the benefit of organic produce. He had sprayed his crops throughout his career and wouldn't even consider that this might diminish his apple's food value or worse, make them toxic. So, when they got back, they told me they would use cheaper, traditionally grown produce.

But in *A Cancer Therapy,* Dr. Gerson repeatedly emphasizes the importance of using only organics for nutritional value and freedom from pesticides and herbicides in all the juices and foods. Charlotte and the doctors at the clinic reiterated "only organics" to all the patients, but with the Hancocks, it fell on deaf ears.

Personally, though I would never express it to him or Jodie, I wondered if all those sprays weren't the cause of his lung cancer in the first place. But, maybe in their case the therapy would work without organics . . . maybe.

In the meantime, I decided the day after my castor oil initiation to befriend the sandy haired woman who often sat alone at the far table. There was something about her that intrigued me. So at lunch I sat with her and, being my unshy entertainer self, started a conversation.

It turned out she was from Holland and was here with her partner, Helena. Helena was very ill with cancer on one of her adrenal glands and in both lungs. She was too ill to come to many meals and when she did, she was withdrawn and only stayed a few minutes.

At this lunch Lilo, as her name turned out to be, was alone and after the cursory "Where are you froms?" etc., something started to click. She was 40-something with a European casual flair to her dress. It was easy to picture her communing with a friend at a sidewalk café, or hiking on holiday in the Alps.

The first hint at a connection between her and me came after an intriguing political discussion about the pending invasion of Iraq by U.S. forces. Her attitude and that of many of the non-American patients and staff at the clinic was that if the U.S. can just waltz into that country arguably unprovoked, what's to stop them in other countries? They saw it as imperialistic and a very dangerous precedent.

I found her intensity intriguing. Many Europeans are far more politically engaged than we are here in the insular heartland of America.

But, after that bit of intense discourse, it was time to lighten up. The conversation turned to food and as we went through the line for seconds, she cracked, "Oh, potato, such a surprise!" referring to the omnipresent potatoes that appeared at every lunch and dinner. With the wryness and twinkle that sarcastic comment engendered in her eyes, I knew I had a comrade in arms. I joked back, "and soup too, oh my!"

At subsequent meals we would chuckle about everything from the coffee breaks to the roof dogs and the propane man, interlaced with our histories, frustrations with the disease that brought all of us together, our high points, lows, and fears.

When Gail recovered enough to come to the dining room for meals she hit it off with Lilo too. Because of her year in France after college working as a governess, she loves Europe and for both of us conversations with our new Dutch friend were a welcome change of pace from the reality of why we were all there, cancer.

Understandably, for many of the patients the focus of their conversations was their illness: what they had been through, their prognosis, their discovery of the therapy and how they were coping with it. After all, it was the one thing we all had in common. But with Lilo, and eventually Helena as she felt better, sure there was some talk of our mutual disease, but usually our discourse was more like a party with everything but the cocktails. It was almost like being with friends at the college dorm, and I was grateful for it.

I wanted distraction from the travails of cancer, not to be further victimized by having it dominate my every word too.

Thanks to the earplugs, things got better with Gail back in the room. Although at one point when she was obviously distraught I asked her what was wrong, and after much prodding she said, "I don't know why I'm here."

I was astounded. She had no idea how lost I would have been without her and how much her support and presence meant. She felt without physical tasks to accomplish, she was doing nothing and might as well be back in St. Paul. She apparently saw me as coping far better than I let on.

I hugged her profusely and told her over and over again how much she meant to me, and how important her presence was.

After tears were shed, partly from stress, partly from relief and understanding, she realized how needed she was, even if it just meant reading a book in the same room with me.

She is not a person to just sit and lounge about, so the affirmation that a taskless existence for two weeks was OK was important. Plus she would be going to seminars on cooking, the meds, the juicer etc. that would prove invaluable when we got home.

On the third day at the clinic two important things happened. The first was they drew my blood to check on liver function, lymphocytes, white blood cells, etc. Much of it I didn't understand, but the cholesterol I did. It had dropped from 217 at my last check up at home to an incredible 155! That's right, 155! Well, by God something was going on!

That was amazing, and it was the first empirical thing I could tell my friends and family about. A 60+ point drop. I had struggled with cholesterol for years. My grandfather had died of arteriosclerosis at 62, and my own father had a heart attack at 67 and sextuple bypass (that's right, six arteries changed out) a few years later. And this in a man who was running mini marathons at age 65! Genetically, we Wedgwoods are just an arterial Drano disaster waiting to happen, which made the cholesterol numbers all the more impressive.

Other indications from the blood draw were normal for the therapy. Kidney function was fine as was everything else the Doctors look for. So we were off to a good start . . . apart from my urine taking on an odd greenish cast from the intake of all the juices. I made a mental note when I got home to write a special song, "It Ain't Easy Peein' Green," and sing it at talks about the therapy.

The other thing that happened was a visit from Charlotte Gerson, whom I have mentioned, the daughter of Dr. Max Gerson who created the therapy and the reigning matriarch of all things Gerson. As Gail and I sat in the room waiting for Charlotte's rounds to get to us, I almost felt like a third grader waiting in the principal's office after committing some grievous offence.

Why? It was like seeing a Hollywood star on film and TV for years and then meeting them in person. They could be the kindest person in the world, but you still are intimidated just by their presence. And Charlotte's presence definitely preceded her. It was palpable in all the rooms as she made her way through the clinic.

She herself had been cured of bone tuberculosis in her father's New York clinic more than 60 years earlier, so she knew first hand what we were going through. This therapy is her life and she promotes it tirelessly with newsletters, books, the Gerson Institute and countless seminars and public appearances. Not to mention making herself available to patients for advice and support. Rodney had nothing but wonderful things to say about her.

Even knowing her obviously magnanimous nature, I was still intimidated as her shadow went past our window and her impressive countenance crossed our threshold.

A few days shy of 82, the first thing I noticed was the brilliant, piercing blue eyes. It was as though they were illuminated from within by the pure energy of her being, beaming out from the wisdom of a face tinted with a beta-carotene (she drinks a quart of carrot juice every day), southern California tan. Her arctic white hair shone just as brilliantly, surrounding her face with an angelic glow, backlit by the afternoon sun.

She strode in confidently, commanding the attention of everyone and everything in the room. Honestly, I think I even saw the bucket cower and the IV pole stand up just a little straighter as she went past.

My GD and GD-in-training, usually animated when encountered alone, seeped in silently in her wake. Charlotte sat down on the bed opposite me, making a point to greet Gail, then looked me dead in the eye and said firmly, "Why do you have cancer?"

Well . . .uh . . . what the hell do I say to that? "Uh, er, a duh, gee Mr. Wizard, I dunno," I thought. It crossed my mind to be a smart ass and go for a joke, but honestly I was sure that with one piercing glare from those penetrating blue orbs she could strike me dead on the spot.

"Uh, maybe from eating too much tuna?" I lamely fumbled.

"Uh, huh," she replied.

"Or maybe from bad diet or stress and lifestyle." I was definitely in third grade mode now. It was like I hadn't done my homework but I didn't recall being given an assignment!

I would have said about anything right then just to get off the hot seat.

I was in such a daze from the surprise of her question that when she went into what was probably her standard stump speech about the therapy, all I could do was plaster on one of those blank, prom queen smiles.

I remember something about toxins and "typical American diet," and me being too young for all this, and "How is your wife doing?"

One thing I did get when I regained a bit of composure was her statement, "If they cut out a kidney tumor, it always comes back!" That stuck out because this woman had seen thousands of cancer patients in her day and probably knew what she was talking about.

Well, at least I had done something right in not being hasty about my surgery decision.

She then asked what I did for a living, and when I said I was an entertainer, a look of "Ah ha!" crossed her face. I'm sure she had images of me performing in a Lenny Bruce-smoky-nightclub-bar with tars and nicotine filling every cell of my body. But I quickly explained that I didn't work clubs - I usually work outside at fairs or in clean, non-smoking banquet rooms.

When we discussed diet, there was no smoking gun there either, since I was about 75% vegetarian. We moved on, a bit perplexed and she discussed treating the cause, not the symptom and paid a lot of attention to Gail's upcoming role in all of this. She in essence said that without her . . . I would die.

As melodramatic as it sounded then, how true that would prove to be.

She did seem to think that my prognosis, however, was very good. As she left, she almost dismissively referred to my mass as "your little tumor" in a tone that implied, "Well, of course yours will vanish! You're in good shape, you have support, no problem!"

I sure hoped so, but I would not and could not let myself be so absolute. Randy's "The Scream" like visage from his last days hung over me constantly, taunting my grasp on mortality. It was encouraging, however, to just see Charlotte. Her crystal lucidity and articulate interaction were as sharp as a twenty year old's. She had pointed out that she had no liver or age spots on her face or hands, didn't wear glasses, and was as nimble as someone 30 years younger.

And I had to remind myself again, she had recovered from bone TB on the therapy. She said she ate a vegetarian diet, no soy, and as I mentioned before drank a quart of carrot juice each day, and did one coffee enema.

I really didn't let the image of that last one sink in too far, but it was obvious from her living example that if I stayed with this process it could pay benefits for the rest of my hopefully long life.

After she left, Gail and I sat for a few minutes, a bit awe struck and unable to sort it all out. We were pulled back into reality by the omnipresent "jugo!," and it was off to the juicing/coffee break races again.

Over the next week and a half we settled into the routine. Being in Nick and Jodie's quieter, larger room helped our nerves calm down and made life easier. We also began a ritual of watching the sunset over the Pacific each night.

The oceanfront was just a couple of blocks from the clinic

and a walkway above the beach afforded a beautiful view to the west. Up the beach a few miles to our right were the glistening lights of San Diego and our home country. The U.S. had bestowed upon Gail and me so many blessings and opportunities that the families playing on the beach below most likely could only dream about. I often contemplated how many of them could afford the out of pocket expense for the possibly life saving treatment I was getting at the clinic.

Straight out was the endlessly undulating Pacific Ocean, marking hours, days and eons with each successive soothing wave. To the southwest, mysterious monster islands that no one seemed to know much about rose majestically from the sea, beckoning us to come out and explore their hidden lairs.

There was always activity in the evenings - soccer players on the beach, a surfing class, lovers among the craggy rocks, and always an odd looking canine or two.

Because of the rigors of the therapy and my uncertain future, we had to take each day one at a time. That made these moments all the more special, like an ice cream cone you want to lick leisurely forever, but you know eventually it has to melt.

We got to know Lilo and Helena very well and looked forward to our encounters with them. Helena improved substantially over the course of our two-week stay and began reading in the courtyard and making longer appearances at meals. We all laughed about our surreal circumstances, the eventually tasty to us but admittedly odd food and of course, the coffee breaks. We also engaged in many intriguing political discussions. We promised ourselves when all this was over, we would rendezvous in some exotic locale and stuff our by then cleaned out systems with highly toxic beer and pizza.

I still was on an emotional roller coaster on castor oil days, and some days just out of the blue, for no apparent reason. But our understanding of what caused these episodes helped. Gail could take excursions when I was loopy, and I would try to protect the rest of the planet from my irrational outbursts by hiding in the room.

I learned how to inject myself with the liver extract/B-12 combination, which I had been dreading. It felt so odd to be the one administering the shot. I had never done that before, and I had to twist around at a weird angle to reach my behind. I tried using a mirror, but seeing myself from that direction tended to make me lose my appetite.

I would also have to come to grips with the self inflicted stigma of the injections. In my head, anyone who had to take a shot every day was not a major invalid, but at least a minor one, as arrogant and condescending as that sounds. I held that thought even though a good friend of mine is diabetic and injects insulin every day. Of course, that was one of the benefits of having cancer, and yes I did say benefits. It forced me to examine some ridiculous prejudices I didn't even know I had. I could either let go of them altogether, or beat myself up with them since I was now the one who was ill.

With the shot, doing it myself made that choice for me.

When I started, it instantly was more comfortable because

the nurses always seemed to inject it so fast, the rapid expansion of tissue was painful. I did it nice and slowly and it quickly became routine; this task that I had been so dreading now had no power over me whatsoever. And it consequently removed any shot taking stigmas I had toward anyone else, especially my diabetic friend.

Invalid my ass! If you can put a shot in it damn it, you can do anything.

Learning to do the B-12 shot also forced me to recognize the power I had given something that I didn't need to fear at all. I began to look at other things in my life I feared - rejection, poverty, some types of success and death. I wouldn't resolve all of them instantly, but "the shot" had taught me that with determination I could.

Although we joked about the meals, they were painstakingly prepared to make the Gerson diet as flavorful as possible. Still, I pined for bagels and cream cheese, not just because of the flavor, but because it had been part of my morning routine for several years. As I mentioned, it was a particularly delightful respite after performing out of town for several days, a grounding ritual that meant I was back home, taking a morning off to relax.

I would have to let go of many things that gave my life a sense of regularity. Would I find something healthier to replace them? Only time would tell.

My GD came by each day to see how we were doing. They all knew, even more than Gail or I imagined, how much stress it would be on both of us once we were home. They were trying to prepare us for that with bits of advice and mentions of what would have to be done, and the time it would all take.

Some of it sank in, but as I would learn all too well in the coming months, most of it we would just have to experience first hand and muddle through. It ended up being a lot like a 40-something parent trying to tell a teenager how not to screw up, but there's really no way you can. We had no real concept of the magnitude of our undertaking and maybe that was better anyway. We might have been scared off otherwise.

And fortunately we had a good role model at the clinic to encourage us. Like Lilo and Helena, John Bachman had become a welcome dinner companion. He was a great listener and always encouraged each person's individual process. In his comforting, gentle voice he freely shared his own life story as it related to the conversation at hand, both the successes and mistakes.

Unlike most of us who were just starting Gerson, he was 18 months in on a three-year protocol. To actually see someone who had been on the therapy that long was awe inspiring, and made completing it seem at least plausible.

And was the therapy working for him? As I mentioned before, his masses weren't going away, but they weren't multiplying or getting bigger either. I was a bit scared for him, but couldn't help admiring his perseverance.

And it was also good to see someone that far along so full of energy and vitality. He walked every day, his skin had great color, and in different circumstances, it would be easy to picture him knocking off 18 holes a couple of times a week. If I was doing that well after a year and a half, if I could just stick with the therapy that long without emotionally imploding or causing a divorce, I would be ecstatic!

So, John's living example, along with Rodney and the other patients I had spoken with, kept the light brightly burning at the end of the tunnel which was important, since I had just entered the dark, foreboding front end.

I was beginning to feel it too, the effects of the toxins being pulled into my bloodstream and tissues being healed. My body was getting very busy, spurred on by the super nutrition it was getting from 13 daily juices and being put into overdrive with thyroid meds and niacin.

While I was able to go on walks, my pace had slowed and my endurance was greatly reduced. My whole body was changing on a cellular level. I imagined it would be how you feel in the later years of life, a total consumption of energy, in my case due to intense healing processes, different from any athletic, illness or stress exhaustion.

I kept waiting for the burst of feeling better that some patients describe early on, but for me an instant miracle remained illusive. Over our stay at the clinic, my progress seemed just slow and steady. Three steps forward, some days one back . . . some days four.

After roughly a week and a half I had my first "flare-up." All patients react differently to these. Dr. Gerson described them as "the reaction period."[10] Different parts of the body may become inflamed, the patient may get nauseas, reject food and/or juices or suffer cold-like symptoms.

The latter was my scenario. It started coming on in the evening and lasted through the next day and night. I felt EXTREMELY tired and had body aches like a virus that just wouldn't quite commit itself. I'd had another blood test the day before and my white blood count was up, meaning my body was fighting something. I retreated from everything except Gail that day, eating in the room and lying low. The staff were used to that. The great thing was I had been told there was usually a great surge of energy after flare-ups, and for me that was definitely the case. The day afterward I felt GREAT! Like I hadn't felt in years! I took a long walk and imagined that if this was how I would feel at the end of it all, it would certainly be worth it.

It really was amazing. Like I had my high school body back again.

The staff was encouraged because this meant things were on track. It was a lift for me as much emotionally as physically, and in the absence of doing shows, a good substitute for a performance high.

I hoped Gail would share the buzz, but her enthusiasm was decidedly measured at best. As was the case earlier after my amazing conversation with Rodney, she had to leave an emotional shield in place, just in case I ended up like Cathy and Randy.

I imagine for Gail her existence was becoming almost dreamlike, like being caught in a weird cancer infested Oz, where it's entirely possible everything WON'T turn out all right. Dorothy will never see Kansas again and the Wicked Witch wins the day. And no matter how many times she clicks her heals together, she just can't wake up from this bizarre, swirling surreality.

Not seeing the hope in her wonderful face was very hard for me, because I HAD to believe and have faith or I would be lost. We couldn't always work it out and when we couldn't she would take a walk, or I would lose myself in TV, or try to relish in the enthusiasm and hope of the other patients.

We weren't the only ones with struggles, of course. Fred and Julie were having some tough times because on top of Fred doing Gerson, Julie was trying to quit smoking while they were there. Many nights she didn't make it to dinner because the nicotine withdrawal was too intense.

With our room next to theirs, the occasional raised voices that seeped through from the other side of the wall bore testament that the road they were on had as many bumps and potholes as ours.

At least we weren't alone.

We also heard several surgical horror stories over the two weeks we were there. One person had multiple surgeries, but the tumors kept coming back. Another's surgeon in Canada had operated on his back for a spinal mass, but mistakenly removed normal tissue instead of his cancerous tumor.

Others at the clinic described the ravages of intense chemotherapy as they slouched at dinner with their hair all but gone, peering out through melancholy yellow eyes, surrounded by sagging sallow faces.

It was at these times I felt VERY fortunate indeed, because not only had they been through hell and back, but for them Gerson was their last hope.

Thank God for me it was my first.

The second week was easier because at least we knew the routine and were comfortable in our surroundings. Helena felt better, and our enjoyable friendship with her and Lilo continued.

Charlotte came by again, this time with her 60-year-old son, Howard. He was tall, robust and handsome with a full head of the same arctic white hair, beta carotene southern California tan, and of course those same intensely penetrating blue eyes.

During this visit I wasn't nearly as intimidated, feeling like an old veteran at 10 days in. Charlotte again mentioned that with kidney cancer, when they do surgery it always comes back. While I was still glad I had passed on that option, I had thought about that statement since her last visit and this time took it with a grain of salt. My parents had told me about more than one friend who had one kidney and were doing great - some as many as 35 years later. And as I mentioned earlier, my own father, who had a cancerous kidney removed Halloween of 2002 was doing just fine.

That's what made all of this so hard, there were no absolutes, even from experts for whom I had the utmost respect and admiration. I just had to sort through the myriad of information that had been thrown at me in the past six weeks and take my best shot.

God willing I would hit the target.

As our visit continued, Howard told us he had tried to open a Gerson clinic in Sedona, Arizona but for a variety of reasons it hadn't worked out. You could hear the frustration in his voice when he talked about it. It was obvious during our entire conversation that Charlotte and Howard were passionate about Dr. Gerson's work, and its continuance was of the utmost concern to them.

When they came, it was a good day for me physically, and I was able to kick in at least some of my entertainer's confidence. It gives me, after thousands of shows in hundreds of different circumstances, the ability to deal with almost anyone in any situation, regardless of their social, business, or economic status.

Consequently, I was able to joke and banter with them to some degree and diffuse the highly focused intensity that had defined Charlotte's previous visit. Why? Because I wanted to move beyond intensity and change the ratio of cancer talk from 100% to say, 30%. After six weeks of being diagnosed and 10 clinic days, I was weary of defining myself as a cancer patient. I wasn't. I was James Wedgwood - fun, goofy guy who happens to have a mass on his kidney and now let's move the hell on!

Joking with them instead of listening like an awestruck lemming was part of that redefinition process, although I don't think I was quite conscious of it just yet.

And they took it well too. I think it was actually a pleasant surprise. I'm sure some days they don't want to talk about cancer either, but since it's their "thing," they have to. I imagine sometimes they'd love to walk in and say, "Whoa, how 'bout those Chargers last night. Boy, did number 56 blow it! Oh, by the way, how's your melanoma? It's tolerable? Great. Do you think Jerry Rice will win 'Dancing with the Stars?"

I also remember telling them at that meeting that because of my ease in being in front of people, and assuming that the therapy lived up to its billing, I could be a great spokesperson for it. I don't think they really took me seriously, perhaps because the image of a dummy describing the wonders of coffee enemas just didn't ring as very effective to them, and frankly it might be a bit scary.

But of course, none of my wooden associates would be involved (unless of course they wanted to be). I would use my performance, improv and comedy gifts to bring Dr. Gerson's message in a different way, packaged with entertainment and some levity so folks wouldn't be scared off by another droll cancer speech.

I didn't press the point but hoped, someday, I could make that happen.

The redefinition of my own self image drew me more towards Helena and Lilo, because they didn't want to talk about cancer all the time either. At dinner, it was often understandably the focus, but we didn't want to dwell there. It was ever present in the room anyway, whether we discussed it or not, but we just weren't willing to surrender our spirits to it as well as our bodies. At least that was a battle WE had control over.

And we chose to control it with laughter. Jokes flew about

our table in broken English and bad Dutch translations. We were often the loudest table in the dining room, and often the last to leave. Our fun spilled out into the courtyard between coffee breaks, the enemas themselves brewing ample opportunity for levity.

As one of my good entertainer friends says on his business cards, "To Laugh Is to Live," and if that is true, Helena, Gail and I and Lilo would be reminiscing about these days at least three decades from now.

The daily routine continued. 3 Juices at meals, 10 "Jugos" delivered, a daily shot in the ass of B-12/liver, 5 enemas, a cornucopia of supplements and castor oil every 48 hours. The daily propane man, the roof dogs and the ever-present "Soup" just added to the ambiance.

Maybe it was really just some odd cruise I had stumbled onto or a weird night in Vegas, and soon I would wake up back in St. Paul trying to figure out how I had gotten there and where I'd been.

But no, it was real and most days I felt fortunate to be able to be part of it.

We had continual menu surprises such as occasional corn on the cob and amazingly flavorful oat cookies made without sugar, butter or salt.

One memorable lunch we even had a Mariachi band come and serenade us. Another day we had a party for Charlotte's 82nd birthday which in addition to being fun, punctuated the benefits of the Gerson therapy as she stood there celebrating with the energy of a 40-year-old. We also got to meet more new patients, each with different stories but the unfortunately common theme of having to give up on traditional approaches to healing.

Toward the end of our stay, we arranged with Anthony to take home a three month supply of meds. We'd had all the classes we'd need to do the therapy at home, and although the prospect of going it alone was daunting, we were as ready as we would ever be. I figured in our two week stay I consumed 182 juices, did 72 enemas, and hadn't had even one Coke, Dorito or chocolate chip cookie.

If I could stand the regimen for two years the juice/enema numbers would be roughly 9,464 juices and 3,640 enemas.

It was then I realized that like marathoners in the Olympics, I had to take this race one step, one day at a time. Otherwise the magnitude of the task would surely overwhelm me well before the finish line. And this was a race I couldn't afford to lose.

I still yearned for my peanut butter bagel and a cup of Hazelnut coffee, but cheating when we got home would not be an option. There was just too much at stake.

The last days at the clinic rolled by, and although it wasn't exactly a vacation, I relished this time because all too soon Gail and I would be on our own. Our stay, despite its travails, had brought us closer. Those nightly sunsets were the moments you recall throughout the rest of your lives together, and with the vendors, roof dogs, Helena and Lilo and jalapeno underwear, we had managed to have some fun too.

The morning we were to leave, Anthony arranged for our

shuttle. He wanted a picture of us because we were "special." He made a point to tell us he didn't take pictures of everyone, and exactly how we were different, I really didn't know, but it made me feel good. Hopefully, we had given something to the patients and staff there, as they had given so much to us.

We hugged Helena, Lilo, and John Bachman and thanked Marco, my GD, and Charlotte who was visiting that day.

We also said goodbye to the other patients we didn't know as well, but still meant so much just knowing what they were going through. It was bittersweet because some of them I knew probably wouldn't make it, despite theirs and the clinic's best efforts.

And then it was done. The gate shut behind us, and we were off to San Diego.

I got in the shuttle looking and feeling much different than the burrito stuffed man that had gotten out of it two weeks earlier. I was about 10 pounds lighter, a bit gaunt and short on stamina. My skin was more sensitive to direct sunlight and my other senses were starting to jump into hyper alert mode. At the same time, I felt not only physically lighter, but spiritually as well, as though my soul had noticed I was rinsing out its vessel.

How I would respond to my old environment with my new physicality, only time would tell.

---

10. Max Gerson M.D., *A Cancer Therapy: Results of Fifty Cases and The Cure of Advanced Cancer by Diet Therapy* (San Diego, Gerson Institute), 201.

Chapter Nine

Home to Our New Reality

At the border, partly because of the medical transport sign on the side of our van and partly, I think, because I looked so wrung out, they let us back into the States without a hitch. I had been very worried my bag full of supplements, needles for injecting B-12 with liver and four enema buckets would be an issue, one I could barely stand to deal with at this juncture. I could just see myself trying to explain the buckets to Customs, "No, it's an enema bucket, not a bong, and you certainly don't want to be sucking smoke through it!"

We also had thermoses of juice and Gerson lunches for the trip, graciously put together for us by the kitchen staff. It was comforting to have these treats on the plane, a bit of the clinic womb coming with us, especially since I was halfway through a therapy day. There was salad, greens and fruit, the ever present soup and of course - potato. Everyone else's ham sandwiches accompanied by peanuts and Moist Towelettes didn't even look good to me by this point. I couldn't even drink the water because of fluoride and chlorine, but I had my thermos full of carrot juice so I was in good shape.

After landing we were met by Mary who had been so gracious taking care of our home. Her time at the house had been good for her - visiting friends, indulging in her favorite St. Paul eateries and relishing her between jobs respite.

It was truly a testament to the concept of synchronicity. She and Nancy had shopped for us so the house was full of produce. It was like coming home to family after a long journey and we appreciated it so much.

We chatted, caught up on how Merle and Foxy had done, Foxy having the night before consumed from the top of the table no less than half of Mary's take-out Chinese. Ah, the wonders of a 13 pound cat!

It would have been nice to just collapse after Mary went back to her real home in St. Louis Park, but Gail and I knew the truth - we still had a lot of work to do yet that night. I had five juices still to grind and press and two coffee breaks to prepare. Gail immediately started making soup and we barely spoke as we each went to our respective tasks. I camped out in my upstairs juice kitchen, and she headquartered downstairs in soup and veggies central.

I think we were each up until at least 2:00 a.m. that night as we did our best to become faithful practitioners of my . . . OUR new Gerson regimen.

Those first weeks I was in a daze.

Even with the pre-Mexico practice runs, I didn't have the hang of the juicer yet and that resulted in several carrot eruptions out the top of the feed tube. If you don't slide the carrots into the tube at the correct angle, it spits carrot bits back out the top, flinging them throughout the kitchen, up to the ceiling and all over the cabinets like a mini Krakatoa.

I also had to learn the eccentricities of the pulp pressing process. Once you get the angle of your carrots right, or whatever produce you're using, the Norwalk grinds them into a mushy pulp which is then placed into a cloth bag and pressed hydraulically to extract the juice. When everything works like it should, the juice flows steadily and evenly into a stainless steel tray that channels it into a waiting glass or pitcher.

Unfortunately, there are some variables that have to be accounted for or you can get surprises. When the bags get beyond their prime the pores of the fabric get clogged and they begin to squirt streams of juice, almost willfully, at the operator of the machine. This can happen even if you think you have rinsed them religiously after each use, especially if you're making lots of green juices, which tend to gum things up more than the carrot concoctions.

I got nailed numerous times before I wised up and either wore an apron or no shirt at all. Gail and I bought a few orange colored ensembles just so our accidents wouldn't show.

Occasionally, the bags would explode under the juicer’s pressure because I got lazy and tried to use them too many times. Well, not exactly explode, but the open end would slip out suddenly and forcefully eject its contents.

One time a green pulp eruption (looks like mashed spinach) covered a window 10 feet away from the juicer, like some odd mush bomb hurled from a medieval catapult.

Eventually, some of these issues were resolved when I changed from using bags to simple squares of cloth. For me they were easier to keep rinsed out and I was less tempted to overfill them. I simply folded one over the fruit and veggie pulps and put it in the press. When I was done it was easier to just flip out the now almost dry pulp for compost, whereas with the bags I had to dink around turning them inside out.

In addition to learning bag and feed tube skills, the Norwalk had to be cleaned after each juicing session. This involved dismantling several pieces, cleaning them in hot tap water then rinsing them with our reverse osmosis set-up . . . twelve times a day!

In addition, to get the organic produce ready for the juicer, it had to be thoroughly washed and trimmed to fit down the feed tube. I used a large stainless steel bowl filled with distilled water and a touch of hydrogen peroxide for this job, and it was soaking some sort of produce almost 12 hours a day.

The only juice that didn't require quite as much effort was the first of the day, a hand squeezed organic orange juice done on an old fashioned glass citrus juicer. My Aunt Margie made orange juice this way till her dying day. I remember thinking that was a lot of work for a glass of orange juice, and why didn't she just join the 20th century and get frozen.

I was quickly learning the older, simpler, less processed ways were much better. I could hear her spirit occasionally over my shoulder saying, "See Jimmy, I told you so."

In addition to the juices, I had five enemas to prepare. I soon realized how spoiled I had been at the clinic where everything but the actual procedure was done for you. At home I had to prepare the organic coffee by boiling it for five minutes to remove the oils, then simmering it covered for another twenty minutes. When coffee break time came, I would heat up distilled water and mix it with room temperature water to get the blend to body temperature, put it in my plastic bucket and head to our upstairs bathroom.

I was grateful I had remodeled this room a few months before my diagnosis because I would be spending a lot of quality time in it over the upcoming months. As bathrooms go it is good sized, about 7'x12' tucked above our downstairs kitchen at the south end of our house. The solitary window allows lots of soothing sunlight, and the original claw foot tub, pedestal sink and vintage nickel plated and white porcelain fixtures create a relaxing ambience.

We didn't have an aqua vinyl bench, but the floral hooked rug with a towel or two placed on it proved very comfortable to lay on. Actually, I would put my upper torso over the rug and hang my derriere off the end on its own towel, just in case there were accidents.

I also was in charge of making sure my pills were laid out in the correct quantities and taken at the right times, which was painstaking at best, even with the very specific chart my GD had provided.

I had thyroïd to boost my metabolism, niacin to open up my blood vessels (both to aid in the efficient removal of toxins), liver tablets to compensate for the lack of raw liver juices, pancreatin to help with digestion, something called Inflazyme, that I didn't really remember what the hell they told me it was for, and COQ10 for my heart.

In addition, many juices had Lugol's (iodine) solution and dissolved potassium powder added to them.

Some of the meds had to be taken before meals, some couldn't be taken when there were apples in the juice, and with the thyroid, if I accidentally took too much, it could play havoc with my heart rate.

Again, I realized how spoiled I had been at the clinic. I just took whatever they laid out in the long blocky pillbox and didn't think about it. Now, I had to make sure it was right, and with Gail preoccupied by cooking, the buck stopped with me - no backup.

I eventually developed a system where I would fill seven boxes on Monday so I would be set for the week and could eliminate at least one daily task.

I also did the shots. I had gotten them down pretty well by the end of our stay in Mexico. All I had to do differently was fill the syringe with the correct ration of B-12 and liver extract. I still wasn't very fond of them mind you, and never got completely comfortable with it. And who the heck would? It's a shot! But at least it was manageable and no longer had any fearful power over my psyche.

Gail had also learned to do the procedure, and on more than one difficult or particularly tiring day, I remember asking her to do the actual injecting.

With me doing juices, coffee breaks and meds, and Gail cooking everything but my morning oatmeal, we had all the bases covered, but it was still very difficult doing it ourselves. Many days in those first weeks, I would start at 7:00 A.M. and not finish until midnight because I had to rest frequently during the day from the fatigue of it all. I would drink a juice at say 8:00 A.M., lay down and not be able to get up till 11:00, getting behind three hours. I would then stay on schedule for another three hours, but lose an additional hour later in the afternoon.

And castor oil days continued to be brutal, with high emotion, nauseous stomach and incredible fatigue. I would have to continue consuming that little pill cup of gooey delight every other day for another six weeks. Mmmmm, mmmmm good!

To cope with all this, I had to keep in my mind that the way I felt meant good things were happening. My whole body was changing. Slowly but surely it was addressing poisons and toxins accumulated over 47 years of a typical contaminated American diet and lifestyle, which was no minor feat.

I would have to be patient. There were just no short cuts.

But at least because I was home, I could start the day with a simple, but infinitely pleasant ritual that helped establish a regularity to my days, a small but important comfort zone.

It was having my oats and reading the paper. I would get up, make my orange juice, take my castor oil if needed with its requisite cup of coffee, do my first coffee break, start my oats on the stove and then venture down to the corner to get a paper from the newspaper box. The trouble was, in the first few weeks, I was so tired I could barely walk the half block to the box. Each step was labored, my pace like that of an 80 year-old man. I usually took our dog, Merle, with me and he would glance back at me repeatedly, surprised at my lethargic pace. He was far more accustomed to our zooming, multi-mile rollerblading adventures. But as animals do, I think he had a sense that there was something wrong with his alpha male, and he usually had a great deal of patience.

He would help me toddle back to the house, protectively escorting me the entire half block. I would then sit at the little red-topped table next to the western facing window in our upstairs kitchen, serve up my now perfectly done oats laced with organic banana slices (but no milk, butter, sugar or even raisins!) open my paper, thank the dog for his assistance and eat my breakfast.

It was simple, pleasant and predictable. And oatmeal was a food I understood. It at least, even without any added seasoning, was something I had consumed all my life, and because my father used to make it for us on a regular basis, also bought back many comforting, nurturing memories.

Most days the newspaper walk went off without a hitch. Even in drizzle, Merle would drag me down to the corner. It was almost as though he tacitly understood the importance of our new ritual.

And it was good he was with me, because on occasion the newspaper walk could be fraught with emotional hazards.

At the end of our block is a church and many mornings that spring and summer they had funerals. I don't know why they had so many that year, maybe '03 was a bumper crop for the grim reaper. The folks dressed in black always set my mind wondering if my own service was imminent, and would I even be remembered a couple of months later. "Oh James, yea, he was kinda funny. Short though, and really spacey. Want another beer?"

But the worst part was the hearses, parked impatiently out front wanting to get this or that decedent in the ground so they could get back to the garage for a wash. Their idling motors spit out a taunting tone, daring me to walk by just close enough so they could suck me and the rest of my life inside.

And if they didn't get me on the way to the corner, I knew they would try again on the way back, when I was distracted with perusing the front page of my newly purchased paper. It was as though they knew, like a wolf sniffing out wounded prey, that I was in a state of physical and emotional limbo, and if they were patient, they just might get their chance to pounce and whisk away another victim, laughing about it later over oil changes.

It may have been my imagination, but I think Merle tugged us along just a bit quicker every time he saw those salivating black and chrome station wagons lurking in front of St. Stanislaus Church.

I often felt halfway between life and death in those weeks, and lack of sensitivity in that direction drove me nuts.

I bumped into a friend who does carpentry work on our house one day on my paper walk, and when I told him about my situation he started droning on and on about his sister who had cancer and didn't make it even after battling every way she could.

The seemingly uncaring monotone of his voice and continued repetition of the mantra of death and hopelessness drove me crazy. How can another human being be so callous? I wanted to smack him and say, "Are you a fricking idiot? Why don't you shut the hell up?! I need hope and encouragement here, not this crap!" but being raised to be overly polite, I couldn't let myself do it.

But I stewed about it all day. At that time, it was like there were none of the protective emotional layers around my body that most people have, as though every nerve was just hanging outside of my skin, begging to be irritated.

I made myself cool down, but did go over to his place that night and told him how deeply what he said had affected me. How I felt I was barely clinging to life by a tenuous string of carrot juice and rectal coffee, and his comments had crushed my spirit like a tormented sparrow withering in a cat's mouth.

He may very well have thought I was nuts, bipolar, manic-depressive or worse, but I didn't care. I just had no time for people who could so divorce their brains from even a modicum of human compassion and tact.

Fortunately, my rantings hit some nerve in him; he apologized and we are still friends. Maybe he tolerated my tirade because I had brought him food when he fell off a roof and broke his hip in three places - or maybe it was the best way to get me out of his apartment.

When I got back home, I realized I might be at risk on any venture outside what Gail and I would eventually call my Gerson cocoon. That cozy upstairs kitchen with its sunny west window and broken-in couch would become my healing womb, shielding me from any unforeseen contacts that might intrude on my vulnerable mental and physical state. It would have to be a sort of nurturing fortress, a place where I could feel safe, where I could battle cancer without battling the world too.

Was I being selfish to cloister myself away like that? Possibly. But there are times in one's life when you have to do what you have to do, and you can't give a damn about what other people think. On Gerson, nasty junk was being pulled out of my tissues, putting all my nerves on hyper alert. Any sensory input - sound, touch, anything - was magnified twofold. That combined with a severe lack of energy and the stress of dealing with mortality issues made me feel vulnerable on a purely instinctual level, like a wild animal searching for a safe cave or hole to die in after being wounded by a not so accurate hunter.

Unless you have felt this way it is hard to imagine. I know people who saw me at that time had little inkling of what I felt inside. None of them had watched anyone do this before. Apart from losing weight, I looked normal enough. My hair wasn't falling out, I wasn't green, I still had all my parts and they didn't have to visit me in the hospital. I was keenly aware of that fact and hence my intense self-protectiveness. I would have to respect what I was feeling and take every precaution to care for myself physically and mentally because it would not be innate for other folks to do so.

I'm sure some of them thought, "He's just drinkin' a bunch of juice. How frickin' hard can THAT be?"

How frickin' hard indeed!

And so, with our systems in place, a womb to run to and Whole Foods and the co-op close by, we were on our way. Gail and I knew there would be unforeseen bumps in the road, things we had no way of predicting, but at least after the first few weeks things were settling into some kind of manageable routine. A tough routine, but manageable.

What made me persevere? Most folks would have said "The hell with this, cut the little 1.8 cm bastard out of your kidney and be done with it." But when I looked at Cathy's picture on our wall, and remembered Randy's agony, and the pain in all of us who watched them die and love them to this day, that was all the motivation I needed. They had tried the traditional path and checked out anyway, miserably. I had to give this my best shot, for me, for them, and for the thousands that sadly will follow us.

Maybe, just maybe, me going through this could make a difference.

I kept in touch via e-mail with my Gerson buddies. The Hancocks went back to Washington and Julie was fond of sending funny animal pictures. Her daughter was helping them, and they too were struggling to keep up the pace. She once wrote something like, "Gerson can heal the patient, if it doesn't kill the caregiver first!"

I also kept up with John Bachman, who always had gracious words of encouragement, and our friend and her daughter up in Canada.

I also e-mailed Fred Lung ("Hey kid, we're doing great!" was his usual reply) and called the clinic to see how our favorite friends, Helena and Lilo were doing. In addition to all the other meds I was taking, I wanted a regular dose of their fun, witty energy in my life. I needed it to keep me from dwelling too much in my own self-absorbed introspection.

As I have mentioned, our conversations at the clinic kept us tenuously floating above the viscous quicksand of cancer emotions that threatened to suck us all down.

We all knew we were ill. We all knew we could die. But who the hell wanted to give power to it by continually verbalizing it? It reminds me of the main character in *All Quiet on the Western Front* saying (and I paraphrase) as he lay in a trench with an enemy soldier dying next to him by his hand, "To think of this man and his family, his life away from the war would be madness, and I cannot allow such thoughts to enter my head. I cannot survive if I do."

And so they would laugh and drink and carouse. And God willing, survive.

As would we . . . God willing, God willing.

On occasion I did wonder why I had been given this gift of finding the mass so early, in such a freak fashion. Why me?

I certainly was no holier than Randy or Cathy or Helena or my father or John Bachman or the millions of others who hear "You have a mass," from their doctor each year. Why me? Why goofy "Puppet Boy" me?

But I couldn't let thoughts like that dominate my thinking either. There was too much work to do to succeed, too many juices to make, too many coffee breaks to prepare and administer.

I had to accept this gift and assume that someone far smarter than I and for reasons I really couldn't fathom, wanted me to go through this.

I prayed I was up to the task.

Chapter Ten

Making Peace with Mr. Bucket

While after a few weeks making the juices became almost routine, the "coffee breaks" were a totally different matter. At first it was wonderful to be in my own bathroom, free from interruptions, far less self conscious than having everyone in the clinic knowing what you were doing when you had that little sign on your doorknob like a neon beacon blaring, "Yep, I'm in here with a caffeinated tube up mine." And even with her assurances that my special time with "Mr. Bucket" didn't faze her, I was always nervous about Gail inadvertently barging in after her Jim-needs-some-special-privacy walks. It was just too humiliating. It's one thing to see your spouse getting out of the shower dripping and naked, but quite another to see them mainlining Mrs. Olson's favorite brew backwards.

So, as I have said, my big old 1904 bathroom with its original claw foot tub, pedestal sink with antique nickel-plated fixtures and sunny southern window was extremely comforting.

And the enemas went smoothly for about the first week. Then my colon began rejecting them like a Paris Hilton boyfriend. I would put the tube in and only be able to hold it for two or three minutes. Then my body would loudly declare, "Out, out damn coffee," and it was all I could do to make it to the toilet in time. I tried smaller quantities, which helped temporarily, but eventually I could barely get them going at all. But I had to detoxify!! Gerson recommends when the colon is tender to make the enemas from

Chamomile tea and doing that a couple of times a day helped. But I knew I would need the real thing sooner or later, so I thought changing coffee might be beneficial.

It was. I went to Whole Foods and got a robust French roast with a lovely bouquet that made my sphinctoral interludes almost as pleasant as a petit déjeuner on the Champs-Élysées.

For about two weeks.

Then the early evacuations returned with a vengeance. I went back to the Mexican brew we had brought with us from the clinic and the switch brought relief - again temporarily. I called Charlotte and she said sometimes the trouble is due to toxic pressure. In other words, so many poisons are pouring out that your colon just can't wait to get rid of them.

That made sense. But I also did a couple of other things. I only took as much volume as I could handle. At its worst, that was 16 ounces. I also tried other coffees. Eventually I found a great organic Mexican brew at Whole Foods (24191). The beans are a lighter brown color than most whole beans and far less oily. I would use this coffee for the duration of the therapy. And, on castor oil days it was damn tasty - out of a cup of course. Whenever we had friends over in the months to come, I always felt very Martha Stewartesque when they would comment, "MMMMM, that's good coffee." I never told them what other parts of me relished it too.

The other thing I did was to reduce the quantity from five enemas a day to four. Oh, sometimes if I felt particularly bad, or when I was doing Castor Oil, I would indulge in all five, but just the time and effort involved was so all consuming on a day-to-day basis I couldn't handle it. It was the one thing on the Therapy I did not think I could do completely.

As I have mentioned, you have to make the coffee by boiling, simmering then straining it. It has to be mixed with the proper proportion of water and brought to body temperature, then when you have finished, clean up yourself and your new best friend, Mr. bucket. It usually took at least 30 minutes to complete the entire procedure and often more than 45.

Many times I would think I was done sitting on my porcelain throne, get up and be almost dressed when I would get a San Andreas style aftershock. Yep, my innards wanted to erupt again, which meant another 5-15 minutes doing my best impression of "The Thinker."

It could be a real pain in the ass . . . so doing just four enemas a day was almost Nirvana.

After several weeks and all the adjustments, life in "Starbutts," as Nancy christened my bathroom, gradually mellowed. My daily dance of the derrière became almost second nature, and I was eventually able to easily hold the requisite 32 ounces prescribed on the therapy for 10, even 15 minutes. Marco would have been proud! I felt good about doing my blood cleansing cycles. When I was feeling cocky, I would even sneak in 42 ounces, just to see what kind of man I really was!

And, as odd as it sounds to someone who has never done this, they always made me feel better. For any discomfort, from dizziness, pain or headaches, there was consistent relief in a well placed bucket of java.

Indeed, if I went even an hour beyond the normal four-hour rotation, I knew it. A toxic, light-headedness would consume me. Focus would go and I could even become disoriented. The 13 juices were constantly cleaning my cells, pushing nasty junk into my bloodstream for ready rectal removal, and to block that process was uncomfortable at the least and potentially very dangerous at worst.

Dr. Gerson, in *A CANCER THERAPY* writes, "This detoxication of the whole body has to be carried out over a long period of time, until all the tumors are absorbed and the essential organs of the body are so far restored that they can take over this important 'cleaning function' by themselves. If that is not effected to the necessary degree, the entire body becomes the victim of a continuously increasing poisoning with dire consequences (coma hepaticum)."[11]

And that is how the four dollar plastic bucket that taunted me in Mexico and it's ever present three feet of tubing and quirky red tip, quickly became my best friends, meeting for coffee four times a day and spending lots of quality time together.

And I was grateful for every minute of it.

---

11. Max Gerson M.D., *A Cancer Therapy: Results of Fifty Cases, and the Cure of Advanced Cancer by Diet Therapy*, 6th ed. (San Diego, Gerson Institute, 2002), 16.

Chapter Eleven

Saint Gail

Even though Gail had initial trepidation about my choice of treatment, once the decision was made to go Gerson, she immersed herself in the process. From the start, it was obvious she felt incredibly responsible for me, as though my mortality rested completely on her lithe shoulders. The moment we got back from Mexico, she religiously made sure I had everything I needed to make this arduous process a success. And for the first several months her duties were enormous, even though we had a pseudo division of labor.

As I have mentioned, we set it up so that I would make and purchase everything for the juices and breakfast and administer my meds, while Gail would cook the other meals and keep us stocked with distilled water.

But I say "pseudo" division because all this was predicated on how I felt. In the beginning, I was only able to make one junket outside the house each day. Anything more tired me out completely and on many occasions, especially when taking castor oil, I was just too physically spent to go out at all and it fell to Gail to pick up the slack.

She has always been a very involved and busy person. Even though she had already cut back her hours at work to care for Cathy, she still taught classes, worked out regularly, did Pilates, frequently volunteered for this committee or that, in addition to hosting the same in-house TV show once a week at Minneapolis Children's Hospital that I had been part of a few years before.

And now she would be shopping, cooking and bending over backwards to make two meals a day palatable to a semi-invalid without salt, meat or processed sugar and bear the burden of being his primary human contact each day, dealing with his hopes and insecurities, fears and triumphs, while facing the very real prospect of soon being without him forever.

She had to do all this while tucking the grief of Cathy's death away in a tightly sealed emotional lock box to only be opened when she had a big enough spiritual reservoir to absorb the shock.

And that reservoir would be running close to empty for at least the next 10 months.

Given all this, she did a yeoman's job. She studied and prepared, with exacting precision, almost every recipe in the Gerson cookbook. Most were very tasty, although very different from anything on the traditional American diet.

Roasted root vegetables, countless variations of potatoes (rosemary potatoes quickly became one of our favorites), stuffed peppers, and even several odd but welcome varieties of sweet desserts. Baking a banana with a unique Mexican sugar cane from the clinic was especially tasty.

We also thought up a few of our own. One we enjoy to this day is baked pepper strips with slices of garlic and tomato on top.

And of course there was the soup. Every three days the patient is supposed to have a fresh batch of Gerson soup and eat it at lunch and dinner. Taken from Hippocrates himself and designed to cleanse just about everything that needs cleansing in one's body, it is a wholesome mix of onions, leeks, tomatoes, celery root, parsley, garlic and potatoes, cooked slowly with purified water and ground to a mushy sage green for easy digestion and efficient nutrient assimilation by the overly toxified cancer patient.

It is a time consuming process to put it together, and the organic vegetables aren't easy on the pocketbook, but Dr. Gerson felt it was imperative for proper healing. And Gail, being the almost obsessively thorough person she is, made it not every three days, but every OTHER day just for extra freshness. She often planned her social and work schedule around "soup day."

We were very fortunate that Gail already was a vegetarian, although not quite in the Gerson fashion. Because of this, she adapted readily to preparing the diet and ended up eating mostly Gerson the whole time I was on the Therapy.

With all this to do, it's no wonder the clinic emphasized that Gerson is just as difficult, if not more so, for the caregiver as the patient.

Most days, Gail was a saint. She brought me fresh flowers every week from the farmers' market downtown. They sat on the table in the upstairs kitchen brightening the room and adding a breath of new life to the air.

She made every effort not to bring her worries from work into the house, explaining I had enough to think about and that she wanted to keep a positive attitude.

Where we ran into trouble was when her practicality butted heads with my emotional neediness.

Gail comes from a tradition of completing the task at hand. There were many evenings when she got home from work and would cook for me until late at night, just barely having time to eat something herself. Then she would crash on the couch for a few hours, get up, work out, go to her job, come home and do the entire process again. And for the Gerson caregiver, days off can quickly become non-existent.

So if I approached her in the middle of all of this with a toxed-out emotional meltdown, it was a recipe for disaster.

We had one of these early on when we got home. I was arranging the upstairs kitchen "just so." I wanted an anally perfect juicing system with everything logically placed, so I wouldn't make any mistakes by missing a step in the process. My meds and the schedule for them had to be set up in a clearly understandable fashion. I naturally had a fair amount of insecurity about being away from the clinic for the first time, with no GD just down the stairs and no staff making and delivering every hourly "jugo." My fate, indeed my life, was now in my own two hands.

Plus, looking back, all this attention to setting up the kitchen was a lot about wanting some sense of control when my entire existence seemed to be one big mass of percolating chaos.

As I got things in order, Gail came up to check on me, but interpreted my intense focus as me needing "space." She withdrew emotionally, but also felt rejected and unappreciated. She wanted to help me, didn't see that she could, and felt left out in the dark. So suddenly, as I wanted to feel control over my little juice space, everything else was out of control.

Gail has never been the type of person that can just express her feelings, let it go and move on. For her, emotional disruptions have to process via several layers, protective layers perhaps, before they can siphon through her incredibly intelligent brain and generous, kind heart to be digested, mulled over and eventually resolved.

I on the other hand, usually know exactly what I think and feel and am more than willing to express it, right or wrong, timing be damned. I can be the proverbial bull in the china shop, especially when there is castor oil pumping through my liver and emotions, pulling rationality out of my consciousness along with old molecules of spilled gasoline vapor, pesticides, beer, dorm food and hundreds of mercury laden tuna fish sandwiches.

It was an unfortunate juxtaposition that would bring two well meaning people frequent and painful episodes of misunderstanding and isolation.

This particular one was not resolved until the next day after Gail got home from work. I didn't have the wherewithal that night to coax out of her what was wrong, and she coped by disappearing into cooking and bed.

A good night's sleep and simple apologies when she hit the door that evening took care of it.

But the powder keg of Gerson stress continued to roll

around the house, igniting at usually the most inopportune moments, the times when it was the last thing either of us needed.

This is not to say all days were carrot juice fueled Armageddons. Quite the contrary. Most days, Gail came home and delivered a cheerful, "How are you honey?" proceeded to ask how my day went, see if I needed anything and fill in any gaps in the conversation with jokes about enemas, the propane guy in Mexico, or speculate on what our dog, Merle or our cat, Foxy thought of the whole ordeal.

A typical thought bubble she might create for Merle would go something like this, "Well, I know Jim isn't feeling so good but I'll stay by him in case he needs me. That stuff he's doing in the bathroom is kind of weird . . . but it smells good to me, so I guess it's OK."

Or for Foxy it would go like this, "I really don't care as long as I can sleep on your face and bite your hair to wake you up."

And I think Gail really enjoyed the challenge of keeping the food interesting and tasty, day after day, week after week, month after month. I would smell something enchanting coming from the downstairs kitchen, and she would inevitably unveil a new combo of Gerson approved delicacies.

And, bless her heart, she was always tolerant when I was unable to hide any distaste for something she had slaved over.

I just tended to never see it again. Or it might be on the stove, but when I asked her about it she would tactfully say, "Oh, that's just for me."

It was truly a miracle she was able to create much variety at all. No rice, no meat of any kind, no salt, butter or cheese. No oils for cooking, no steaming allowed. No wheat, the only bread being a stoic rye, and intake of that was strictly rationed.

And yet, we were never overly hungry. I could have as much as I wanted of the approved foods and after awhile my cravings for things I had chowed down with relish only a month earlier waned. Indeed, later when I was weaning off the therapy, traditional foods tasted odd, over seasoned or way too sweet. To this day, I rarely indulge in anything most people would call a staple (staple in the traditional American diet being Doritos, French fries, chicken McNuggets, pizza, prime rib, chocolate chip cookies and Coke!).

But, there will be more on this later. The focus here is Gail. Wonderful, rapidly becoming overwhelmed, Gail.

While we plugged along fairly well the first few weeks, by week four her well meaning work ethic and amazing dedication to the task at hand, while good for me, were not letting her rest. A constant "frazzle" became her regular state of being. Even asleep, her legs would twitch, denying her a good nights respite.

And I could also tell that lurking somewhere not so deep in her subconscious was the cruel notion that if she didn't do everything just right and I died, it would be her fault. Call it Catholic guilt, call it spousal dedication, whatever, I think many family caregivers struggle silently with this, not daring to address such a concept head on because to not feel otherwise would make them a "bad person."

Of course nothing could be further from the truth.

If I croaked, I croaked. Living wasn't in the cards. My mass would not be one that magically melted into oblivion and we would have given it our best shot.

But it certainly would not be for lack of effort on her part.

For my sake, she tried to keep up a good front, not wanting me to feel responsible for her stress. But one evening she just lost it standing at the stove. It was an episode of spontaneous weeping precipitated by something minor: a spilled potato, or a burned special dish she had slaved over and thought about, unbeknownst to me, for days.

I really didn't know what to do at that point except to console her about the minor issue at hand. But I knew it was representative of other things underneath that eventually would have to be addressed.

We had almost two years ahead of us, and we would have to make them easier for both of us if we were to have any sense of normalcy, but at this point we were both far too deep into just learning how to cope on a day to day basis to think up any stress alleviating strategies.

So, after the tears, some hugs and lots of petting of ever attentive and unconditionally loving Merle, we got through that night.

And things did get better. We gradually got a handle on the routine of the Gerson therapy. It was still arduous, but at least we now knew what to expect. We got our own rhythms and rituals down, which gave us both a sense of stability in an environment that was intrinsically unpredictable.

At Easter, I was greeted with a basket of Gerson approved treats and a specially made "Oat Bunny." It had no refined sugar or wheat, but jauntily sported raisin eyes and baked oat skin. Frankly it tasted a little flat, but it brightened my life for the next several days as I savored the fun of it, nibble by nibble.

She did things like that with such wonderful consistency, I regret that I sometimes took her creativity for granted. Fortunately, she never seemed to notice and continued spoiling me rotten throughout our Gerson process.

She also, as I have mentioned, embraced the therapy to a certain extent herself. She didn't do all the juices, but found the diet quite to her liking having struggled with various food allergies for years. Wheat and dairy are particular problems for her and on Gerson food, of course, neither of those were an issue.

And, at the clinic, a bit to my surprise she mentioned that sometime she would like to try an enema. Now, I wouldn't push THAT on anyone, even though as perverse as it sounds, I had actually come to like them.

But for anyone else? Particularly someone who has no rational reason for putting their latté where the sun don't shine? I was amazed, a little shocked, but morbidly curious to see what she thought of the procedure.

The good thing was my Gerson partner would know, for better or worse, exactly what I went through during all my special "quiet time."

So, I instructed her, much as Marco had done for me at the clinic, how to specially prepare the coffee, lubricating the tip of the tube (VERY IMPORTANT), etc., and off she went to our downstairs bathroom for her first enematic adventure.

I checked in periodically, calling gently through the closed door to make sure things were flowing smoothly. Of course, had something gone awry, it's not like I would have rushed in to save the day.

Seeing one's spouse in that, uh, configuration, was not an image I wanted anywhere in my psyche, so I was grateful that it all went OK. And she actually found it relaxing, partly because she quickly realized that no one wants to bother you when you're having your coffee via reverse osmosis. "Oh, you're doing THAT!? I'll come back later . . . like . . . in a year!"

She also discovered as had I, that feeling the warm coffee fill your insides is very comforting.

She continued to do enemas periodically after that, especially after learning that Charlotte's daily regimen included, in addition to a quart of carrot juice, one coffee break. After meeting Charlotte in person and experiencing her vitality first hand, it was a good testament to continuing both protocols whether you were trying to get rid of masses or not.

And it was fun to observe Gail after a "coffee break." She was curiously very perky and energetic, which I to this day am consistently amused by, and she always says she feels better. She even braves castor oil on occasion, although for a non-cancer patient to drink it must be due to some inherent masochistic, Freudian abnormality.

But unfortunately, even her newly found affinity for coffee enemas couldn't alleviate the 24/7 stress of being a Gerson caregiver.

After a couple of months the pressure on us both was starting to occasionally boil over, precipitated by the most innocuous of events. We had one fight over who was buying water. Gail made special trips to Walmart to get distilled water because it was substantially cheaper there, and in her family finding the best deal, especially when you were going through four gallons every day, was a big deal. But as I felt stronger, I wanted to do more to lighten her load, so I picked up several gallons at Whole Foods, albeit at a higher cost, to do her a favor and feel like I was contributing more to the Gerson process. Unbeknownst to me, however, she had developed quite a sense of ownership and pride in that job, not to mention wanting to save us as much money as she could, and the turf infringement was more than she could stand.

Of course, I had almost the same reaction when, about five months out Gail came up, unsolicited, and cleaned MY kitchen. Early on, she had done it as a matter of course, but for a few months now, hard as it was to accomplish at the end of the day, I more or less got it done. It was rarely pristine, but, like her and the water, I considered it MY job.

So, when she spic & spanned it one day while I was out, rather than feeling appreciative, I felt violated, and it only exacerbated my fears of being an invalid.

We had another battle over making soup. Once again, as I began getting more energy I wanted to relieve her stress and feel like less of an invalid by taking over that omnipresent duty. But somehow she saw my request to do so as telling her she was failing, not being able to handle it all, and consequently doing a bad job of taking care of me.

Another tough one was my reaction whenever she used the word "sick" in reference to my situation. To her it was a simple description that most everyone on the planet used to describe someone with cancer. To me though, the word "sick" was the harbinger of death incarnate, with no hope of long term wellness. The "sick" people I knew were all fricking dead or soon would be, miserably, and were viewed with pity and fear and I would be damned if I would let anyone, even my spouse, unwillingly include me in that hopeless club. "Ill" was the word for me, damn it, "Ill." And as illogical as it sounds, I still to this day can't get beyond that simple, semantic differentiation.

Of course, none of these conflicts were about water, soup kitchens or "sick." They were convoluted manifestations of the pressures, fears and insecurities that I imagine all families going through cancer treatment experience.

Unfortunately, it is very difficult to jump outside the confines of the cancer box and get much needed perspective when you feel so totally surrounded by it.

But in our situation, we at least were able to recognize we

needed some help, a way to alleviate the pressure without needlessly taking it out on each other. So after brainstorming a bit, we decided to bring in some kitchen helpers; friends and family to come in and clean the kitchens once or twice a week after a long day of food prep and juicing, and to provide some in-house social interaction.

It worked wonderfully. We were able to let go of perhaps the hardest chore that faced us at the end of every day: cleaning dishes, pots and pans, the sink and even the floors, walls and ceiling if the Norwalk had gone on an explosive rampage. We got to spend fun time with people we truly liked and felt comfortable with, and they got an up close look at just what the heck we were spending all that time doing. Most of them tried a juice or two, maybe gagged a little, sampled the food and what turned out to be most important, gave us both a tremendous emotional lift.

Also, about six months into my treatment, we worked out giving Gail three days a week off. No food prep, no shopping - her own time to forget about the therapy and do or attend to whatever she wished. We continued this for the duration of my obligatory two years on Gerson. And at six months, it was a good time to give her that kind of weekly break. I was able to handle things myself for those three days, provided Gail made up at least a small cache of food I could draw upon, in addition to what I prepared myself. I am admittedly a lazy cook and food I made got the job done, but was rather Spartan in the creativity department.

This too ended up being a terrific strategy. Her chains were unshackled for almost half the week and it had a major impact on her emotional health, even though she felt a little guilty about it and found it hard to let go the first few weeks. Once I snuck in a fourth day off for her, doing what I thought was a favor, and she got mad at me for taking on too much.

Between the two of us being perhaps overly concerned for the welfare of the other, we had an inbred system of checks and balances which, most of the time, was a good thing.

And although I didn't know it at the time, the joys, the fights and the tears were deepening our bond as spouses, friends and soul mates in ways I wouldn't understand until many months later.

In September, it was time to celebrate my birthday! I was born on Labor Day, a testament to a future career as a professional jokester.

But this birthday, 48, eight months after diagnosis, was especially poignant because I was actually able to have it. At this juncture in his saga, Randy was already gone.

Thanks to Gerson, I was being reborn.

Gail of course took every effort to make it special. One of the highlights was my favorite, the baked bananas sprinkled with Mexican cane sugar, shaved from a deep brown Gerson approved cone.

But the best was coming home from a stint in Spencer Iowa (yes, I was doing shows by then, but more on that later) to find the house strung stem to stern with rolls of Charmin Ultra toilet paper, my "coffee break" staple, Sharpied in blue with "Happy Birthday!" one letter per panel.

It prompted another of my frequent "Gail is a Saint!" entries in the video diary I kept to document my Gerson journey, and emphasized just how fortunate I was to have her in my life.

One of our favorite things to do before Gerson was watching "Iron Chef," a subtitled, Japanese epicurean extravaganza. The show pits always flamboyant host, Chairman Kaga's Iron Chefs against an ever changing parade of challengers. Their amazing and sometimes bizarre dishes are judged by an eclectic rotation of grade A-C actors and actresses, current and forgotten politicians, and even a couple of very earnest fortune tellers.

It's like Martha Stewart being judged for her pound cake on American Idol.

Once on Gerson, the dishes prepared by the Iron Chefs became all the more tantalizing because they were so forbidden. The irony of having my saltless, dry baked potato, while my eyes were being fed close up images of succulent Crème Brûlée being flamed, was never lost on either of us. We would sometimes talk about creating a Gerson Iron Chef show to see who could make the most purely perfect Gerson soup, or whose oatmeal would tickle the discerning palate.

On New Year's Eve, Gail hosted festivities at our house dressed as the Chairman himself, much to the delight of all in attendance.

So even through the pressures and blow-ups, we still managed to maintain our senses of humor and have quite a bit of fun. We had to because not keeping that anchor of normalcy in our lives, regular laughter, would mean that cancer had already defeated us.

Our lives continued on much like this for the duration of the therapy, which I did in full through January of 2005 and then tapered off to half (7 juices, 3 enemas) through March of 2006. There were lots of preparations for days on the road doing shows, countless meals together watching "Iron Chef," or if we were behind that day, David Letterman. What got easier for Gail and me both was the routine, primarily because it became second nature. And I steadily, just as Dr. Gerson had promised, got more and more energy. I was able to do fewer castor oil days and by the summer of '06, it was difficult to focus totally on the Therapy every day. I felt well enough and wanted to do lots of other things besides "coffee breaks" and drinking juice.

All of this put less pressure on Gail, although she continued to be a saint. It's just her nature. In some ways, I think it was hard for her to believe she could let go a bit as I got healthier. I wonder if she didn't think that if she backed off in her diligence, even just a smidge, I might slip away like Cathy or her father.

Even in the third year when I was doing less Therapy she remained dedicated to seeing that I ate Gerson approved at home and on the road.

In July of '06 the tables got turned and it was my turn to take care of her for a while. She ripped the upper hamstring on her left leg right off the hip bone while rollerblading - tripped on a renegade horse turd of all things.

The bruise it caused looked like Stallone's decimated "in

the ring" face in all his Rocky movies combined, and the injury laid her up in a calf-to-crotch brace and crutches for six weeks, with three more months of recovery after that. Our rented wheelchair got lots of use as did a special commode she had to use because she couldn't bend low enough to use the regular toilet. And for the first few weeks, she couldn't even use that without my help.

I got a good taste of some of the same issues she had to face with me during Gerson: over protectiveness, balancing my care with her own desire for independence, and making sure all her basic needs were met.

Somehow, she even managed to squeak in some enemas with that big mass of steel and Velcro on her leg, but . . . I really don't want to even imagine how that happened.

Thankfully, as I write this, we are both healthy enough that mutual intensive care isn't necessary, so Gail turns her tireless, giving energies in other directions. When her leg healed enough, it was a triumph for her to run in our local "Race for the Cure," bitter sweetly displaying the names of an ever increasing number of friends and family on her running outfit.

As I watched her chug along that gray drizzly morning, her cheeks flushed in the chilly May air, I couldn't help but be reminded of how she ran for me, not the simple 5K she was doing today, but for two years straight with no guarantee of a happy outcome. As she finished the race and came bounding up, I had to swallow the lump in my throat welling up from thoughts of just how lucky I and the world were to have her.

I blurted out as she caught her breath, "Good job honey, you did great!". . . in more ways that you will ever let yourself admit, or I can ever tell you.

Thank you Saint Gail, thank you.

Chapter Twelve

The First Show

I had been looking forward to, and dreading, the first show. I was incredibly weak, so much so that my mother-in-law had to mow my miniscule city lawn. Most days were taken up with the monotony of juicing, coffee, read the paper then rest. As I have stated, it was all I could do to muster one extra thing each day: a run to Whole Foods, the coop, the bank.

To muster the energy for a performance quite honestly scared the hell out of me.

Fortunately, the client was truly sent from Heaven. She had booked me, contingent upon my health, for five shows over the course of the summer. It was a client I knew well, Cenex Harvest States, having done many shows for their co-op managers over the years. It was an ag crowd with families, like Yankton, which is always a good audience for me, and was taking place at one of my favorite venues, Arrowwood Resort near Alexandria, Minnesota, not far from 18 acres of recreational land I had purchased in 2000.

But what once had been an easy no brainer - a two hour drive, set up, do the gig, tear down, come back to the cities that night - now seemed almost incomprehensible because I would have to take the Gerson therapy with me.

All my food, water, produce for juices, a hot plate, coffee, coffee, and more coffee, pots, pans and complicated meds would have to be packed up along with speakers, lights, a back drop, several wooden friends and Mr. enema bucket.

As I contemplated the reality of making this happen, I kept thinking of a line from John Lennon's song, "Nobody Told Me." "Nobody told me there'd be days like these, strange days indeed, most peculiar mama."

Part of me just wanted to run like hell. I didn't need the money THAT badly. Lots of excuses and fears filled my head but I knew eventually I had to get back in the saddle, face the music and rejoin the rest of the working world.

I think what scared me most was the audience would not even have the remotest clue what I was experiencing. To them I would just look mildly frail and a bit pale, like a tree that is a wilted but will probably recover with a few glugs of water.

In reality, I felt more like a house plant that has been neglected for months, so brittle that if you brush a leaf even lightly the whole plant might collapse.

I just hoped I didn't over compensate for my condition and say or do something stupid onstage.

I was also scared of messing up the Therapy by over taxing myself. Would the exertion take me out of healing mode permanently? Would it give the mass a reprieve so it could get a foothold again?

But it wasn't like I had a bunch of shows in a row, or 54 in a month. The next show wasn't until August 24th, so I would have plenty of time to recover.

Plus, even though I could get by without it, the money would be nice and the sense of self worth created by doing a gig, making people laugh, and reawakening my sense of purpose would do my spirit wonders.

So slowly, steadily, things came together. Gail found a used hotplate called The Dainty Maid. We put together a plastic tub of road cookware: dish cloths, soup pans from Saint Vincent DePaul (or as Gail and I lovingly call it SVDP), cutting boards, everything and more than I might need went into the tub.

Meds went in one of several grocery bags that held the odds and ends of the Therapy, and three large coolers we bought held produce and cooked food.

Because of my very limited energy and logistics dictating I would have to go alone, I decided I would make the two hour drive the night before, load in, rest and then have a leisurely setup the next day between juices and coffee breaks. I didn't know it then, but I would end up using this strategy for the next year and a half.

I hadn't done a gig since Faribault and Father Flannigan, so I rehearsed, albeit at a very moderate pace, for at least two weeks before. I did one or two segments of the show at a time, rekindling the semi-dormant flame of what once had been so second nature.

I would only do the basics. Tap dancing with talking, singing, Betty Broom was out of the question. Fortunately, with years of gigs under my belt I had plenty of fun stuff without her.

I put a lot of thought into how to handle the juices. Hauling the 60 lb. Norwalk was unimaginable so, although I didn't want to spend the money, I bought a Champion Juicer and Wells Press - kind of a Norwalk in two pieces. The Champion, at 26 lbs. would grind the produce into a Norwalk style pulp and the press, operated by hand and looking much like a glorified car jack, (a 35 lb. car jack!) would squeeze the juice out. Whereas the Norwalk was a stainless steel Sherman Tank behemoth, the Champion was more like an SUV, still strong but not quite so intimidating. And quieter! That would be nice in the myriad of hotel rooms I ended up packing it into, and this system was Gerson approved to produce the quality of juice demanded by the Therapy.

As the first show date approached, I still wondered if I should even be doing this. My doctors and Charlotte said wait six months, but Rodney had gone back to work after three.

It was a huge dilemma for me. After four months of total dedication to the Gerson process, would I shut down the therapy by jumping back in the game? Would I collapse onstage?

I have to admit, part of me resented doing the show at all, but I felt pressured by my own unjustified guilt at not working for so long, and insecurity that if I stayed out another two months my agents would forget about me.

Of course, neither thought had much real validity. It's just that after working so hard for so many years, it's difficult just being a slug, in essence a semi-invalid.

But when July 22nd arrived, the day before the show, I had to put all my doubts aside. This was the choice I had made and I had to have faith in it so at 3:00 P.M., with three enemas under my belt and four juices packed in 8 oz. sealed fruit jars for the road at my side, I was off to Arrowwood.

Even though I had made this drive a million times, that day it was almost ethereal to be venturing that far from my Gerson womb. Would the umbilical reach to Alexandria? I hoped so, because as I tooled along in my Caravan, my spirit started wandering, adrift in the sea of sparkling lakes, golden grasses and miles of corn rows that define Northwest Minnesota, and I wanted to stay there as long as possible.

And while all this beauty was familiar, it was not taken for granted on this trip, as I made my way up I-94 without incident.

When I arrived it took two full luggage carts just to load in the Therapy. With my pots and pans and bags of produce, I felt like a Beverly Hillbilly invading this classy corporate golf resort. I made my way through the lobby as quickly as possible praying not to be noticed, but the bumpy tile floor jostled the cart, my cooking equipment started banging with a vengeance, and my cover was blown.

If someone had asked, "What the hell is all that crap?" I couldn't just say, "Shut the heck up, I have cancer," as much as I might have wanted to.

If I was going to be out in the world I had to play by its rules. Fortunately, no one said a thing and I rattled my way down the long halls to my room.

Getting set up to do Gerson in the hotel room was an adventure. The juicer just fit on the bathroom countertop as did the press, but it was quite an ordeal to get everything in a logical location. I set the Dainty Maid on the floor in the back of the room, put the teapot on it and promptly got shocked! Little Miss Dainty Maid apparently had issues. Too much of this and cancer wouldn't matter any more!

On the plus side, the room was beautiful with a deck looking south over the manicured grounds and expansive crystalline lake. For a Minnesotan like me it felt like home, and I was grateful for it.

Meals etc. went off without a hitch. Gail had spent hours preparing many of my favorite Gerson comfort foods and although I felt terribly self-conscious laying on the floor of a fancy resort bathroom, the enemas went fine too. Setting the bucket on the closed toilet seat gave just enough lift for good flow.

And it was actually exhilarating to be out of the house. I was doing what I love in an environment that was familiar and comforting. And even though I could absolutely not have done any of it without Gail, I had a modicum of independence. It helped diminish the "invalid" image.

It was just a drop of normality in a life full of juice and coffee chaos.

I spent the rest of the night vegging on cheesy hotel cable, and relishing the caress of the thoroughly softened sheets.

The next day they had the stage set up in the morning so

I could spread my setup out over several hours which was truly a blessing.

After my morning juices and coffee break, I loaded in the sound.

Two more juices, coffee, set up props.

Two more, sound check.

And so went the day. An hour or two before show time everything was in place and since I hadn't performed in months, double checked. One malfunctioning piece of equipment or misplaced prop could blow the rhythm of the whole program. The show would have just enough energy from me to be viable and needless distractions would be hard to overcome.

Normally when I perform, I work the room as folks come in, but I knew this night it would be all I could muster just to get through the show. To get comfy, I chatted with a couple of people and then called it quits.

This show would be James Wedgwood Lite. Good pacing, timing & skill, but running on just 40% of my usual energy like a flashlight with the battery half gone. It's a little dimmer, but you can still have fun watching the cat chase the beam.

I got the show going and basically let it work itself. What that means is the jokes, rhythms, etc. are already on the hard drive and can, if needed, be performed without much thought. Unfortunately, it might lack the impromptu embellishments and dynamic energy fluctuations that make a good show a great one. But I forgave myself that, and the audience seemed very pleased.

Gary, my agent and his wife Judy had come up to lend emotional and physical support for which I was very grateful. Their attitude during the entire episode had been one of family, which often to this day amazes me.

I have no clue if I was in Gary's shoes if I would have been as patient and understanding. On the one hand, he will be incredibly frank in his opinions, good or bad, about what you are doing and the world in general. On the other, I have seen him be incredibly compassionate. I thanked God for him and all the staff at his agency throughout this process.

They helped me pack up which I greatly appreciated because without them and adrenaline from the show, I don't think I could have done it. Then we visited my good friend comedy musician Glen, who was also there playing at the outdoor bar. It was great to see him, thank him again for his help at the gig months earlier, and to be out, almost like everything was normal without the aura of "Will he make it?" hovering over the evening like a buzzard, waiting for its shot at the remnants of a lion's kill. I did however, make an early exit, do some coffee and collapsed for the rest of the night, totally exhausted. Even the seductive lure of more mindless channel surfing on the hotel's cable couldn't keep me awake.

Load-out of Gerson took a long time, partly because I clogged the sink with carrot pulp. Too embarrassed to call the resort custodian, I ended up unclogging it by closing the main drain and blowing into the safety drain hole with enough pressure to push the obstructing orange mush through.

At least my lungs were still healthy!

In addition to loading up all the pans, juicer, produce and food, I was obsessively concerned with leaving the room hygienically pristine and spotless. Putting myself in the shoes of the next guest and housekeepers, I didn't want them to have any clue as to what I had been doing on that bathroom floor. I peroxided every surface I thought the enema bucket or tube might have touched, and tried to obliterate all evidence of my bizarre regimen. I wanted it so clean not even a CSI team with coffee-residue-detecting-lights would know I had been there.

Why did I feel so self-conscious? I'm sure worse things went on every day in hotel rooms across the country with the perpetrators not having a thought about cleaning up after themselves.

But for me, I think two things were happening. One, while I learned to joke about it with friends and family, I realized that to most people a coffee enema sounds even beneath disgusting, the stuff of late night monologue jokes, and I didn't want anyone uninitiated to be remotely involved with it. Explaining it to an uncompassionate stranger would be a degrading and useless exercise.

Second, in environments outside the house, it was wonderful to be seen as normal. Regular Jim, no problems Jim; a guy who would have a beer with you and BS about sports and cars, not a vegan-extreme-juicing-coffee-up-the-ass freak show.

So, keeping my secret mattered, especially at the start of my forays into the real world. As the months on the road went on, my comfort level gradually increased. My systems became more streamlined, and I became far less worried about being "discovered." I never got so bold as to write "Enema in Progress" on the Do Not Disturb sign, but if a maid had chanced into my room (which on multi-day stays in the same hotel, I didn't allow - no housekeeping till my expresso filled butt had checked out) and seen my bucket, it wouldn't have been the end of my emotional world. I would have made up something stupid to cover; "It's like, a silly party hat that you fill with beer, yeah, that's it! Happy birthday to me!" and then laughed about it later.

Anyway, with the sink flowing freely and the room in white glove condition, I pointed the Caravan toward St. Paul but frankly, I hated to leave. While it had technically been work, it was also a vacation psychologically from the same space day after day. And it had been successful, with a check in my pocket, the buzz of smiling, laughing faces filling my spirit, and a sense that someday I might possibly make a living at this again.

I also longed to see my land, a mere 30 minutes north of Arrowwood. Those beautiful 18 acres of grassland, oaks and aspen, nestled in between two natural, sparkling lakes filled with loons and bass and beaver, beckoned to me seductively from my pre-Gerson consciousness. But it would be a few more months before I could answer their siren's call. My healing body had to get back to the Gerson womb, and it would take all the energy I had left to make the drive.

Three uneventful hours later, I was there, being hugged by Gail, sniffed by Merle, and meowed at by Foxy. It took me three days to recover from the exertion of the outing, but I now had the outlook that yes, there probably would be life after Gerson, and that was worth the entire process.

Chapter Thirteen

9/19/03 Scan

Throughout the spring and early summer of '03 I thought a lot about when to get scanned next. I desperately wanted to know what was happening with the mass. Was the therapy working and it was happily dissolving with bits of it being escorted out four times daily on the Starbutts Express? Or was it still parked there with the meter running, just biding its time to make me feel like a chump? Or had the meter run out and the thing was now the size of a watermelon!?

Somehow my gut kept telling me, "The Miracle" was not going to be my scenario - in other words, the first and most preferable result, the mass obliterated and friends, family and doctors "ooohing" and "aaahhhing" in amazement was not going to happen.

But what would it be? If for no other reason than basic prudence and for Gail's sake, I had to find out. I couldn't ask her to give up so much of her life any longer than necessary if the Therapy wasn't doing squat.

So, how to proceed? I decided to go through Dr. Swenson and simply tell him what we were doing and why I wanted a checkup scan. At the appointment to discuss it, he was very accommodating. He strode in the door, extended one of those lanky, friendly fingered hands in greeting, sat down and basically said, "What can I do for you?"

He agreed it was prudent to see how things were, but also

wanted a followup appointment to discuss the results. That sounded fine and logical so we were all set to go. But before we closed the deal, I wanted to negotiate some terms.

I wanted to talk him into exposing me to less radiation by only shooting the images with contrast, the gunk they inject into the bloodstream to make organs show up more clearly in the CT images. It was this injection that almost caused me to faint back in Yankton.

In my earlier Abbott scan, the imaging had been done both ways, one set with injected contrast, one without, but this increased the total number of frames by nearly 100%. I had been reading about CTs and discovered one full "study" of my already compromised innards was the equivalent of 100 chest x-rays.[12] My mother would later send me an article about a study describing the radiation from one full CT study as the equivalent of being a Hiroshima survivor. Yikes![13]

Concerned about this, I had also spoken with Thomas Payne, Ph.D., Director of Medical Physics at Abbott Northwestern Hospital, the guy that makes sure all the radiological machines are in working order. He said, "You need to look at the exposure allowed for radiological workers. They are allowed the equivalent of exposure to two full 'studies' a year." I'd already had two "studies," so I was understandably concerned about having more.

He continued, "Of course, you have to weigh the diagnosis benefit against the risk. But if you get up in the 5-10 (studies) per year range, the CTs can definitely be an issue."

To this day, no doctor has ever asked my total CT exposure or even seemed concerned with it. I think this gap in medical diagnosis management is one of several issues Western medicine needs to take a close look at as it continues to evolve its long term procedures. I think there should be a central patient data clearing house where all the info from every appointment is filed and categorized. That way no matter where the patient roams in their lifetime, their history is easily accessible to whomever is trying to help them, rather than being squirreled away in who knows how many separate, disconnected medical offices.

Until that happens, I was sure keeping track of how many CTs I had endured. Neither Dr. Swenson nor Dr. Hampton had seemed to reference those first non-contrast frames in the studies anyway, so to me it didn't seem like a big deal.

When I broached Dr. Swenson about it, he said he would make the request, sort of, but I'm not sure I convinced him and somehow wasn't positive it would go exactly the way I wanted.

Regardless, he was cordial and to his credit I think he was balking a bit only because he wanted to be thorough.

We set it up for September 19. As the day approached, of course I became more and more anxious. Would I be the chump? Or God forbid, would the darn thing actually have gone postal on me? The waiting just sucked.

I was deliberately vague with friends and family about the exact date because I knew they would be chomping at the bit to know if my treatment was succeeding. For many of them it was as much about their comfort and peace of mind as mine. But my thought was, "I'm going through this and they will know when and only when I have had the time to process the information the new scans might yield." I would not let the house be flooded with calls when my guard was down, especially if the news was bad.

I couldn't stand the "Oh no's" and the awkward pauses in conversation until I had "Oh no'ed" myself for a couple of days. I wanted to have a plan and feel in control before anyone else chipped in their two cents.

Finally 9/19 arrived, almost six months to the day from my arrival at the clinic in Mexico. Our appointment for the scan was set for mid-morning and Gail had made arrangements with work so she could accompany me to the medical center, where Dr. Swenson's patients get their radiology done.

Unlike Abbott, the medical center had me drink clear contrast, not milky white, and only after I got to the hospital, not at home beforehand. Theirs even tasted better. So far so good.

But then they made me get into that damn gown that immediately dehumanizes you. I hate those gowns. Why? They take away your individuality and some of your dignity and change you in the eyes of the staff from a human on equal footing to a slightly damaged piece of goods that now will be managed in their system. Directed, sterilized, poked and prodded.

I know not everyone sees it this way, but my own fierce sense of independence and general mild paranoia denies me any other perspective.

Some of it also stems from watching this system chop up and radiate Randy and give Cathy pain meds that would pilfer her lucidity in the waning days of her life.

Or hearing my father referred to by a male nurse as "one of these older models," not Mr. Wedgwood.

Anyway, I put the butt ugly thing on and dutifully polished off the remaining contrast. I also ordered an extra set of the CTs for myself. I was very anxious to do my own compare and contrast with previous scans, especially if it might be awhile before I could follow up with Dr. Swenson.

Full of fruity fluid and with a chill down the open gap of the gown on my back, we sat down and waited. And waited. Our scheduled time came and went. We soon found out the difficulty: There was a backup at the main CT because it was being used to aid in a biopsy procedure.

When they do this the CT creates a live image while they insert a needle into the desired tissue. Sometimes it's the only way to accurately sample a mass. Dr. Swenson had suggested this for me and immediately my brain screamed, "Uh, no, THAT ain't gonna frickin' happen!" Zap me with possibly even more radiation than a regular CT for results that, by the good doctor's own admission, might still be inconclusive?

Would someone rein these people in PLEASE? I had to wonder, was all this really for my benefit or was it so the doctors can say, "Well, we did everything we could," to cover their ass in case of a lawsuit.

Anyway, because of the delay they decided to send us

down to a second CT scanner in their ER.

As we waited in our new location, orderlies wheeled in an emergency patient, a young woman in her early 20's, unconscious from a blow to her head. We were seated in the hall, but immediately next to the booth where the images being recorded by the CT showed up on monitors. As they scanned her cranium, I asked the tech about her through the open door of the booth. He said she was homeless and had been found unconscious by the police. The scans showed fluid between her brain and her skull, caused most likely by a beating.

"What will happen to her?" I wondered.

My problems suddenly seemed miniscule by comparison. Even if I did die, I had lived a full and very fun life. This young woman had God only knows what existence in front of her. I had support and resources. She had poverty, fear, and apparently no one, assuming she even recovered.

My wife sat lovingly by my side. The person who beat this girl was still out there, possibly just waiting to get his hands on her again.

I was truly lucky, even spoiled by comparison. I thought, "If I make it through all this, I have to give back somehow, I can't just go back to my former existence and that's that. Going through this has to mean SOMETHING, it has to make a difference."

There was another woman in front of me getting a follow up CT after a round of surgery and chemo to treat her cancer. We chatted with her nervous husband who had brought her in from Iowa. She was doing OK, but you could hear the weariness and a touch of fear in his voice. This disease had touched so many people in so many ways. Each one I just wished I could make better. The whole thing seemed so brutally cruel, senseless and unforgiving.

Her scan went quickly. There wasn't much to say afterward. We all knew what was at stake for her and me without speaking a word, so we just wished them well and then it was my turn.

I had chatted with the tech in the booth quite a bit by this point, and talked him into letting me peek at the images on screen after they came in from the scanner to his computer.

I also tried to emphasize that I only wanted images with contrast, per my discussion with Dr. Swenson, but for that he referred me to staff in the imaging room and they were a bit ambivalent about it. Had my request not been passed on? Could they not think outside their usual protocols? I didn't know, and that day, with everything backed up it wasn't the time to make a stink. Maybe I would end up with 25 extra images worth of radiation, but hopefully it wouldn't be the end of the entire world . . . or at least my part of it.

A fun thing though, was that because I had done so much research about scans, and my proficient use of CT jargon, the staff thought I was some sort of health professional, not just a grown man that plays with dolls for a living. I chuckled at that concept. "Ventriloquist Doctor, the man with the healing dummies, next on Oprah," but I was also gratified with the sense of self-empowerment it afforded me.

The scan went smoothly, again with much whirring and

the disembodied, robotic voice droning, "Please hold your breath."

Gail was in the booth with the imaging tech, and I was a bit jealous she might get to see the truth before I would, but if she did, she didn't let on. She understood my need for ownership of the results. It was my mass, damn it, I should know what's up first, good or bad.

I teetered back to the booth once I was freed from the overgrown doughnut, and still in my chilly gown anxiously watched as the tech scrolled through the images.

There were slices of my stomach, liver, miscellaneous parts that do God knows what, and then the tops of my kidneys came into view. Grayish white on the scans, each orb got bigger as we scrolled down and then, when we got about half way through the left one . . . there it was, still happily hangin' in there, my little buddy the "indeterminate mass," the cause of juicing, coffee up my butt and an entire shift in focus for my life and Gail's.

The good news - it really didn't look any different than before! The bad news - it really didn't look any different than before!

Now what? A little 1.8 cm wad of gunk was dominating my life and grinning maniacally at me from that glowing computer screen, like a sick, 1970's smiley face caught in a 1950's black & white horror movie.

"Yeah, see . . .whatcha gonna do now puppet boy? Hmmmmm? I dare you to cut me out . . . I double dare ya! How you gonna face your friends and family now, huh, chump?" I could almost hear it chanting in an Edward G. Robinson tone of voice.

On the other hand, though not dramatic, the mass still being there was completely consistent with Gerson success. I thought of the fellow in Charlotte's kidney cancer booklet with at least five masses in one kidney and three in the other who was doing well several years later and thought, "Well . . . OK . . . OK."[14]

I had told myself if it was the same or smaller I would continue. Gail was willing. I asked her as we walked away, "Well, do you want to keep on?" She, God bless her, was more than game despite the stress and the meltdowns. She was in it to the finish, which to this day totally amazes me.

I remember walking down the hall thinking, "Hmmmm, hmmmm. No drama, no failure, just . . . ambivalence."

We went home, I did my 13 juices, multiple coffee breaks and went to bed with a head full of confusion, joy, disappointment, hope and a little bit of anger at the inconclusiveness of it all.

What the hell would I do next?

When we went to see Dr. Swenson and follow up, he didn't know I had already seen the images. I brought in my Abbott scans for comparison.

Again, he greeted us with his wonderful graciousness, but when we got to the scans, he seemed all too anxious to dismiss what I was doing with the Gerson therapy. He said, "Well we've got basically what we had six months ago with no changes." He still thought we should schedule a biopsy and urged surgical removal of the mass.

Since our last visit I had seen a fascinating program on NOVA, produced by PBS (Cancer Warrior, Feb. 27, 2001).[15] In it they addressed the disconcerting topic of why, once a tumor is removed, frequently the cancer spreads with vicious abandon. This was certainly true in Randy's case. Three months after surgery it was in his lungs, liver and brain. Six months later he was dead.

Cathy's, although stopped for a while with surgery and chemo, came back with a vengeance in her colon, liver and lungs.

This fact had weighed heavily in my therapy decision. VERY heavily. And yet when I mentioned this "Cut and Spread" scenario to Dr. Swenson in reference to my mass, he seemed unconcerned, as though my case existed in some other reality, where cancer wasn't cancer and surgery always handled everything.

I then described the NOVA program. In it they said the primary tumor site emitted a chemical signal called an angiostatin that went throughout the body and when it found potential metastases, it prevented them from stimulating blood vessel growth, thus depriving them of nourishment and keeping them in a nonexpanding quasi-dormant state. Simply put, it kept the potential mets from growing.

They did experiments on two groups of mice. In one group, the primary tumor site was removed and angiostatin was administered. The second group received no angiostatin. When the mice were examined, the angiostatin group had no growth of metastases, while the second group was riddled with them throughout their vital organs.

Not being a scientist and being a bit nervous, I bobbled some of the chemical names and mass types as I described the program to the good Doctor, but nonetheless got the concept across.

Dr. Swenson's response to what I deemed critical cutting edge medical revelations? He dismissed it out of hand as "Cartoon Science."

Cartoon Science?! CARTOON SCIENCE?!! That comment told me then and there he would not be removing MY kidney anytime soon. By calling this enlightening NOVA program "Cartoon Science," he communicated such disrespect for my intelligence, such callousness for my position.

I have done shows for CEOs, brain surgeons and national celebs. I am not intimidated by anyone and wanted to challenge his statement and all its implications right then and there.

I wanted to question his thought process, push him to think outside the box that was his office, his education, his golf club.

His choice of words, "Cartoon Science" represented to me all that was wrong with traditional medicine. Stick with the program, right or wrong, put down anything that threatens the status quo.

Probably for the better, Gail was there. My lovely wife

abhors conflict, especially with a perceived authority figure. She takes the tension on herself like a human sponge, trying to wash it away and make everything happy again.

And I knew from past experience that the residual effects of a "Confront the Doctor" scenario would linger in the house for days, especially since we had come to Dr. Swenson through her beloved brother. She would feel embarrassed at best, and furious at worst.

Alone, I have no compunction about being perceived as a jerk. But with her potentially absorbing intense feelings of shame and humiliation because of me, it just wasn't worth it.

So I let it ride but knew, if surgery came, it wouldn't be here.

After Dr. Swenson left his nurse sidled in and asked for a urine sample. She had a look on her face that said, "You are frickin' insane juice boy."

I was confused because I thought I was just there to discuss CTs, not to get any sort of check-up.

Obviously, they thought I was committing the suicide of ignorance and wanted to look for blood in my urine. But she never really said why they wanted it and seemed kind of sneaky about it, as though they had to save me in spite of myself.

But I complied, all the while trying not to chuckle to myself about this cloak and dagger act lest I jiggle and miss the all too tiny collection cup.

As we left, I tried to sort out the muddle of emotions in my head and realized I felt violated again by traditional Western medicine, and became even more convinced to persevere on Gerson. Although I didn't convey my frustration with what had transpired in the office to Gail, we did discuss continuing with the therapy.

She, of course, just like at the CT in the ER, was game, not an ounce of hesitation. What an amazing woman. Hell, lots of days *I* didn't think I was worth it, and yet she was still on board. All for a mere puppet boy.

I guess there was a miracle happening after all.

Looking back, I realize Dr. Swenson was just being prudent within the parameters of his background. Indeed, he wanted to get another opinion from a colleague and then follow up. But at the time, I didn't want to see that. I was under stress and working my tail off to make the Gerson Therapy work. I had circled the wagons and anyone who was not inside with me was suspect, regardless of their obvious credentials.

So how did I channel the anger I was still feeling over Dr. Swenson's "Cartoon Science" comment? As we drove off, I felt more determined than ever. I would call my friends in Mexico and get support. I would call Charlotte for the same reason. And even if I died, I would have done it my way, not full of radiation, surgical scars and hallucinatory pain meds.

I tried to fax a jpeg of the scans to my Gerson Doctor at the clinic, but technical problems prevented a clear image from coming through. Nonetheless, she was encouraged, emphasizing "It's not any bigger and you're feeling better." Yes, I was damn it! Plus I had several shows under my belt and though still arduous, the therapy was manageable.

And my blood tests were in essence always perfect. My HDL's were a bit low, but that was due to not being able to exercise as much as I would like.

I also resolved to do five enemas every day. Until now, four was all I could bear, but now I would make the extra coffee break happen. My GD had always recommended five, but even at the clinic doing that many seemed so incredibly overwhelming.

But now, damn it, I had to load both barrels and let that mass have it!

I called Charlotte and she was equally encouraging. I had sent her the scans and to her there was a definite recession of the mass. Where Dr. Swenson had only done a cursory visual comparison, Charlotte took the time to fine tooth them.

She also emphasized the absence of metastasis (a word that still terrifies me) and cited the case study previously mentioned of the man whose masses remained but had not spread, and whose growth had been arrested. Her tone and support went a long way to boost my shaky morale. She also made a point, just as she had at the clinic, to ask about Gail, realizing more than anyone how vital spousal/partner support is to the success of the therapy. What a wonderful and amazing soul Charlotte Gerson is.

I also Photo-Shopped side by side comparisons of the

previous and current scan and e-mailed them to all my friends and family so they could see the results for themselves, rather than me having to describe them over and over. Most were very encouraging, a couple were diplomatically skeptical, but all were gracious. Almost everyone said they thought the mass looked smaller too, and whether they said it truthfully or hid their real thoughts to make me feel better, I didn't care. Real or illusionary, I was taking all the truth I could get.

The hardest person to convince that actual empirical progress was being made was Gail.

She looked at the comparisons of the two scans. I explained the image process and what all the grey blobs and shadows meant, but she remained reserved about the whole thing, which drove me nuts. Her support was so important in placating my insecurities that I pushed the issue. It wasn't really fair, but I had to know why she was hesitant in seeing what I thought was infinitely clear, THE DAMN THING WAS A LITTLE SMALLER!

She, understandably upset, said, "I just lost a sister after four years of this and a father the same way. I can't let myself get hopeful because if it doesn't work it will hurt too much. I have to keep my guard up."

I couldn't argue with that and was glad to know why she remained reserved. Even though it was excruciatingly difficult for me, it made perfect sense.

With images of Cathy and Randy dying still simmering just behind my eyeballs, how could I not understand completely?

For the rest of the therapy I would try never to push her again.

Life went on, although for a few weeks I continued to obsess over the scans. Eventually, I realized I had to move on and forget about it. What would be would be.

And I had to remember, only 2700 enemas to go and it would all be over!

---

12. D.J. Brenner and C.D. Elliston, *"Estimated Radiation Risks Potentially Associated with Full-Body CT,"* Radiology, 232, no.3 (2004): 735-738, www.ncbi.nlm.nih.gov/pubmed/15273333.

13. Mark Kantrowitz, Radiation Exposure from Diagnostic Tests, accessed June 19, 2010Tests,"www.kantrowitz.com/cancerpoints/radiationexposure.html.

14. Charlotte Gerson, *Healing Brain and Kidney Cancer The Gerson Way*, (Bonita: Gerson Institute, 2002 paperback), 17-18.

15. *Cancer Warrior: Will Endostatin Revolutionize Cancer Treatment?,* directed by Nancy Linde (2001; Boston: WGBH Educational Foundation), DVD.

Chapter Fourteen

Going Ballistic

During the first months of the therapy, I had several incidences where I went irrationally ballistic.

I would completely overreact to relatively innocuous situations. It took me about three of these to identify the pattern and then figure out it was meds related.

The most typical of these was once when I took Merle, my ever faithful canine companion, for a walk in a park by the Mississippi River. The park is called Harriet Island and has been beautifully redeveloped in recent years with a new band shell, creative riverboat inspired playgrounds, comfortable walking paths bordered by native prairie grasses, and towering ancient cottonwoods. However, it is so under used that Gail and I joke about it being "our personal" park. Invariably, when we take jaunts there we have the park virtually to ourselves, which always amazes us since it is located just across the river from downtown St. Paul.

The absence of people at Harriet Island made walking there during the therapy a real treat for me. I could get some much needed relief from being homebound and not have to worry about interacting with strangers. I would prepare one or two juices for the car, load Merle up and escape my Gerson cocoon for an hour.

But early on in the Therapy with my body in healing overdrive, I felt so vulnerable I still took great pains to keep a safe zone around me, even at desolate Harriet Island. My state of being was like a wounded animal with mental defenses splintered at best, and any unthinking word or action, however inadvertent, could put me in an emotional tailspin. I didn't want to interact with anyone, just walk and go home. Today was no different.

It was an exquisite spring day and when we pulled into the parking lot Merle was anxious to go, his nose filling up with all the new life making its first appearance after the long Minnesota winter.

As we got out of the car, I did a 360° check for any situations we should avoid. The coast looked clear except for three kids playing with a 4-5 week old puppy. It was on a very long leash, and they were having trouble controlling the little bugger.

Even though it looked innocuous enough, we would give them a wide berth.

Merle and I took our usual route, a leisurely circumnavigation of the park with him gleefully sniffing and marking to say to other dogs, "Hey, I was here, Merle was here, yes I was, whoo hoo!" It was so relaxing and beautiful. My nose enjoyed different but no less intoxicating smells than Merle's did. Freshly mowed grass, budding wildflowers, and the water of the Mississippi merged into an aromatic cocktail more uplifting than any martini imaginable.

Riding that buzz and hoping it would buoy my spirits through the rest of my evening Gerson rituals, we approached the parking lot again and the kids and their puppy were still there. From a distance, I carefully sized up the length of the puppy's leash to make sure we would be out of range, knowing that a dog that age would be itchy to interact with any new "buddy" it could find, and Merle was the only candidate in sight. Even though our jaunt had been relatively short, and as uplifting as it had been, I became fatigued and was looking forward to getting in the van.

But then, suddenly, without warning, the young dog was somehow loose and running straight toward us. It had slipped out of its collar and when it reached us began running taunting circles around Merle and me, nipping at Merle's legs and flaunting its own youthful exuberance.

I realize most people would have brushed it off. With dogs these things certainly happen. Merle was keeping his cool, realizing that this was simply a kid sowing his oats. But unlike my level headed canine companion, I was unable to find any sort of rational perspective.

Immediately, adrenaline flooded my veins. I started screaming at the hapless kid, "Your dog is attacking my dog! He's supposed to be on a leash. Get your dog! If you don't get him I will kick him!"

The dog was young and fast and the boy had quite a time corralling him, but I didn't let up. "He should be on a leash; he's trying to bite us!"

Of course the difference between biting and being playful is difficult to assess, especially with puppies, but looking back I don't think Merle or I were really threatened.

The boy however didn't help matters. Rather than offering any apology, which would have placated my over-reaction somewhat, all he could muster was, "You don't have to yell!"

And then, with the puppy still nipping at Merle and this child now nipping at my pride, things got worse.

A big burley guy, with his bleached blonde girlfriend and a white Huskie in tow, had decided to flex his testosterone by verbally jumping into the fray.

"Hey, he just slipped his leash man," Bubba chimed in from about 25 yards away.

"Oh, oh great," I screamed back, "I'm getting attacked by a dog and now you're yelling at me. I've got cancer, I get out for the first time in weeks and I get attacked by a dog and you're yelling at me. This isn't even your issue," I emphasized, surmising he was just trying to be the big man in front of his woman.

About this time the kid finally caught his damn dog, and I walked toward my car with the Huskie wielding goon and now his girlfriend and I exchanging insults, each trying to get the last word in (which by the way were, "For a little guy you've got a big mouth!" to which I replied, "Yes and at least I've got a BRAIN to go with it!"). I said this as he feigned running what was now about the 100 yards between us to pulverize my ass.

I got into the car feeling very sorry for myself. The thing I had tried so explicitly to avoid, couldn't have turned out worse. A lovely relaxing spring walk had left me quaking in mixed emotions.

I was mad, resentful and trying to figure out what the hell

was going on. I had tried to protect myself by doing something good for my psyche and gotten screwed anyway. Does God really enjoy hitting people when they're down? It sure seemed so that day.

I had three more incidents like that over the next couple of months. They were under different circumstance but the same pattern; big emotional reactions to things that most people could cope with in a rational, calm and reasonable manner. When I realized these blowups weren't isolated, I began to seriously question how much of this was just me. Was it possible something in or about the therapy was triggering these potentially dangerous episodes?

Unfortunately, it wouldn't be easy to sort out. I had always been a bit of a hothead, the classic diminutive man with a big chip on his shoulder. But in recent years, as a matter of growth and trying to be a better spouse to Gail, I had eliminated much of this self destructive behavior. When I was younger, I was much more of a sponge, letting every perceived slight soak into my core. But before my diagnosis, I had become much more like the proverbial duck, letting negativity slide off and drain away without impact.

But when I melted down on Gerson it was different. I could barely control it, if at all. I could see what was happening rationally from the outside, the adult watching the child doing something stupid, but I couldn't always override the behavior. The child had way too much control, like a spoiled-single-parent-rich-kid whose busy mom feels so guilty she lets him get away with anything.

It had to stop. Poisons being pulled out of my tissues could account for some of it, and early on it was obvious castor oil was a major contributor. As I have mentioned, Gail and I had a tacit understanding on those days. I cloistered myself away like a smoker withdrawing from nicotine, and she would busy herself in the kitchen making soup, potatoes, whatever and cautiously test the water with a tentative, "How ya doin' COD (Castor Oil Day) boy?" before coming upstairs to my juicing lair. I made a point to be honest about my condition, lest she inadvertently push my freak out button, prompting a day of emotional alienation for both of us, victims of the now all too familiar "Male PMS."

But "Male PMS" was not anything like the vitriolic, bile-laden response I had to the bounding puppy. COD day tended to evoke tears and mild paranoia. Not fun stuff, but certainly not the hair trigger emotional implosion of the dog/child testosterone-laden-Bubba incident.

I thought part of it might be my generally elevated state of metabolism. I was on thyroid and niacin, the latter according to my Gerson Doc, opening up my blood vessels, and the former working like premium gas to rev up my systems a bit.

I tucked that possibility in my "hyper response" file, but continued to look for something more specific.

I systematically went through the supplements I was on. I went back to *A Cancer Therapy* to analyze dosage and type. After a lot of thought, I realized that the episodes tended to happen when I took a natural Pancreatin I got at Whole Foods, instead of the Pancreatin the clinic provided.

We tried throughout the Therapy to find local sources for

some of the meds to make access to them easier and to have a backup if our primary supplies from Mexico ran out. I did not use the new Pancreatin exclusively, but had taken it intermittently on a trial basis.

The tablet size on the new stuff was larger and the consistency was different, so I cut them to what I thought would be a comparable dosage to the clinic's Pancreatin.[16]

But perhaps there was a real difference between the two. I decided to test my theory and took the locally obtained Pancreatin exclusively for several days to see what would happen. Sure enough, edginess and irritability reared their ugly heads, like the husband on that old TV ad that drinks too much coffee and screams at his family.

Whether it was the Pancreatin itself, an extra ingredient in the Whole Foods version or my own unbeknownst mis-dosage, I never took the new ones again.

Just to be sure, I went a few steps further. I asked my GD during a phone consult what the Pancreatin was for anyway. She said it helped digest all the juices.

OK, but my digestion worked fine. That prompted me to go back to the source, Dr. Gerson, and read all I could about Pancreatin in his thick blue book that had now become my medical Bible.

Like my GD, Dr. Gerson said Pancreatin was to help make digestion more comfortable and efficient. Interestingly though, he also mentioned that some patients could not tolerate Pancreatin, and it had to be discontinued.[17] It did not, however, seem that this eventuality - not taking

Pancreatin at all - was in any way damaging to the overall effectiveness of the therapy.

I said "screw it" and cut Pancreatin out altogether. I still had my mass damn it, albeit a wee bit smaller, and I was tired of taking so many pills anyway.

The juices continued to go down just fine and I didn't worry about going ballistic on anyone anymore.

I not only questioned the heavy use of Pancreatin, but when the results of the six month scan were so maddeningly ambivalent, I decided to give some of my other meds a bit of analysis as well. Why? Rodney's masses were gone in three months, and he was back at work.

At six months, mine was still hanging around and I was tired as hell. I didn't get it. I was doing every darn thing every day. I called Rodney to ask him what he took and did or did not do that might be different from my process.

He religiously did the juices and enemas. He took thyroid and niacin. He was ecstatic about COQ10. He took Pancreatin.

The one thing he did not take was Inflazyme. Inflazyme - at $94 a bottle - is a supplement containing a broad mix of "do good" things including a fair amount of Pancreatin. I asked my Gerson Doctor about it, and she said it was to help dissolve the tumor tissue.

As I mentioned, I speculated it was to help replace the raw liver juice which was no longer administered at the clinic. Liver juice was discontinued in 1989 because of a history of being associated with Campylobacter fetus bacterial infections.[18] This was a very unfortunate development for the therapy, because raw liver is full of all kinds of live, powerful enzymes and nutrients.[19]

Jaquie Davison had taken it as part of her regimen and while just reading about it made me gag, her melanoma, one of the absolute deadliest cancers, had miraculously disappeared. At times on the Therapy, I wished I could have taken it too. Since Doctor Gerson had prescribed it, that meant it was a seminal part of the treatment, the best way to a full cure.

But, for the reasons described earlier, that just wasn't possible. So, in place of liver, we took dessicated liver tablets several times a day. Rodney had taken these too. We also got liver in the form of daily injections of liver extract along with the B-12, that wonderful daily shot in the Gluteus Maximus. Rodney? Yep, he got the shots too.

But that Inflazyme stuff? It was nowhere to be found in Rodney's regimen. It was the one thing he did not take that I got lots of - to the tune of 9 tablets per day.

And yet, I sat here with my mass gleefully intact. I decided to see what specifically was in Inflazyme. The label said Papain, Trypsin, Chymotrypsin, Rutin, Lipase, Zinc, Superoxide Dismutase, Catalase, L-cysteine.[20] OK, I had no clue what any of this white-bread-dough-ingredient-sounding stuff was for, but if the clinic thought this was good, who am I to argue?

But then, under "Other Ingredients" I noticed the first one listed was CALCIUM PHOSPHATE. Being first, it means it is one of the larger components if not the largest component of the medication.

I remembered from *A Cancer Therapy* something about Calcium Phosphate, and so I checked the index. The impression I had was vaguely negative, so I turned to that page with some trepidation.

Dr. Gerson told the story of trying Calcium Phosphate supplements on several of his patients with advanced decalcification. When the Calcium Phosphate got in their systems, their tumors grew "immensely." Several of these patients died.[21]

I was impressed by his honesty, describing these terminal failures in a presentation to the US Senate. Losing cases must have been emotionally devastating for him. Somehow he carried on and continued to tweak the therapy.

I was grateful he did.

But would he have approved of the Calcium Phosphate in Inflazyme? Was it beneficial in this application, combined with all those other ingredients, or could it be preventing the dissolution of my mass?

I had to know. I called Charlotte immediately. She said the Calcium Phosphate in Inflazyme was a trace amount that held it together and was not enough to cause trouble.

My GD? Same thing.

But being mildly paranoid me, I wasn't convinced, even after hearing from Charlotte, the reigning Godhead of the

Therapy. I was taking boatloads of this stuff every day. What if they were wrong? Had any clinical trials been done? And who had made the call to administer Inflazyme?

I called the manufacturer to find out exactly how much Calcium Phosphate was in each tablet. The woman I spoke with gave me the same "trace amount" statement I heard from Charlotte and my GD, but when I persisted in trying to get an exact amount she had to say she didn't know. Didn't know?! Crap! My life is riding on this, and no one knows exactly how much of a potentially therapy halting ingredient is in it?!?

I never took it again. Rodney got well without it and so, by God, would I.

Anyway, I thought this was all about LIVE enzymes, not some powdered gunk crammed into a tablet.

I looked at other parts of the Therapy and questioned everything - for about a week. And then I had to focus on what I thought was right and move on.

Was I jeopardizing the Therapy with all my second-guessing and the elimination of Pancreatin and Inflazyme?

Medical treatments of all types improve BECAUSE they are questioned, BECAUSE they are forced to evolve with trial and error. Dr. Gerson developed the Therapy with pain-staking analysis of each success and failure.

Me being me, I just couldn't accept anything carte blanche. And hopefully, despite my questioning of some of the meds, the mass would be gone in six months and I would then be unequivocally singing the Therapy's praises.

But now I would have to leave it in the frustratingly slow moving hands of Time and Perseverance.

I was consoled by one thing that was definitely good. I WAS still alive and ever so slowly feeling better.

Six months after his diagnosis, my best friend Randy was dead.

---

16. "Vitamin B3 (Niacin)," accessed June 18, 2010, www.herbs2000.com/vitamins/v_b3.htm.

17. Max Gerson M.D., *A Cancer Therapy: Results of Fifty Cases and the Cure of Advanced Cancer by Diet Therapy*, 6th ed. (San Diego: Gerson Institute, 2002), 211-212, 236.

18. Helen Cooke and Helen Seers, "Gerson Therapy," accessed June 18, 2010, www.cam-cancer.org/CAM-Summaries/Biologically-Based-Practices/Gerson-Therapy/Is-it-safe.

19. Max Gerson M.D., *A Cancer Therapy: Results of Fifty Cases and the Cure of Advanced Cancer by Diet Therapy*, 6th ed. (San Diego: Gerson Institute, 2002), 196.

20. Accessed June 18, 2010, https://www.momentum98.com/inflazyme.html,

21. Max Gerson M.D., *A Cancer Therapy: Results of Fifty Cases and the Cure of Advanced Cancer* by Diet Therapy, 6th ed. (San Diego: Gerson Institute, 2002), 220.

Chapter Fifteen

Teeth: Is it all in my Head?

Before Gail and I went to Mexico the institute sent us *The Gerson Handbook*, their straightforward guide to all things Gerson. This book put in lay terms the diet, the coffee breaks, shopping, what help the patient will need, etc.

As I perused the handbook, I came across what seemed at the time an odd statement. They strongly suggested having all root canals removed before starting the Therapy.[22] And by that they meant having any root canalled tooth extracted, yanked out, hasta la vista baby . . . ow! Why on earth were they suggesting what seemed to me like a very painful, potentially disfiguring and unnecessary procedure? They said the therapy had not been as successful for folks with root canals.

Huh? What the heck was THIS about? I had one root canal in the tooth behind my upper right canine (my dentist told me it was #5). That darn tooth had been a source of chaos in my mouth for years, first with decay then an infection that left me sick as a rabid dog, followed by an abscess that was misdiagnosed by an oral surgeon as a "bone anomaly" on my upper jaw!

After much internal debate and on the advice of my NEW dentist (I dumped my former dentist after her referral to the aforementioned wacko oral surgeon), I decided to get the root canal to hopefully take care of the problem tooth once and for all. But there was something about the thought of killing the tooth I didn't like.

In a root canal, they ream out the nerves, blood vessels and infection from the canals of the tooth and then fill them with a material called Gutta-percha, a rubbery substance derived from Sumatran tree sap. The procedure usually cures the infection, but leaves the tooth without the benefit of blood and nerves that carry energy and nutrients to its structure.

Given my options though (pain and a continuing abscess, versus at least keeping the tooth and eliminating the problem), and with the assurances of my dentist, I had it done and unlike the urban myth of being horrendously painful, the whole procedure was very straightforward and actually a great relief. The swelling above the tooth on my jaw immediately went down and I had no more trouble whatsoever. They were even able to drill through the old porcelain crown I had on the tooth and fill the hole saving me a bundle because I wouldn't need a new crown. I thought, "Well great, that's over and done with."

Or was it? When the Gerson Handbook said root canal teeth should be removed, I called the clinic to ask why. They referred me to a book, *Root Canal Cover-Up,*[23] which I ordered immediately. I wondered, "How could this thing be so dangerous as to warrant removal of the whole tooth?" I had no pain, nothing.

When the book arrived, Gail and I were in the thick of preparing to go to the clinic in Mexico. I was selling a car, arranging transport, canceling show dates and doing a myriad of other things, so the root canal book did not get my full attention. I did ascertain from a quick perusal the gist of it though.

The dead, root canalled tooth was not as solid as it might seem. It actually was very porous and without blood and nerves, so small microbes and other nasties could take up residence there. They would, in the safety of their little enamel caverns, party, reproduce, and then take field trips to the rest of the body via first the surrounding gum and bone tissue, and then the bloodstream.

The book claimed these were the eventual cause of a myriad of physical problems as the vicious little guys found new places to live. Arthritis, cardiac difficulties and a host of other health issues and yes, cancer, were attributed in the book to these terribly toxic teeth.

All this was based on research done by Dr. Weston Price in the 1920's. It started when he removed a root canalled tooth that had no apparent issues from a patient suffering from severe arthritis. He placed the tooth under the skin of a live rabbit as an experiment, and lo and behold, the rabbit developed the same arthritis as the human patient. What's more, the human patient recovered almost completely from her illness!

Fascinated, Dr. Price began repeating the experiment, not just on a couple of patients but hundreds, and almost each time the rabbit contracted the same disease as the human. Over the years, he refined his research and published two extensive books on the subject containing countless case studies.

Compelling - yes. Did I buy it? Heck, I didn't know what to think. For God's sake, I was about to go and put coffee up my ass for two weeks in Mexico!

On the other hand, it had a lot of logic to it. But yanking a darn tooth? There was no going back after that. I hated the thought. I would become one of the "Dentally Challenged" folks I occasionally, well more than occasionally, made fun of in my shows. I had a nice smile with attractive, straight teeth, and I had no idea how, or even if, you could replace it once it was gone.

I heard vague references to expensive implants and cumbersome bridges, but it was all more than I could fathom in the short time we had before departure, even though my dentist was willing to extract the tooth.

I decided to take a wait and see approach. Rodney's mass had vanished in three months. If mine did the same, no problem. I could have my tooth and eat with it too. If it didn't, then we'd go back to square one. I just wasn't ready in my mind to be disfigured. Vain? Absolutely. But damn it, with CT radiation and contrast infiltrating my cells, urologists chomping at the bit to slice and dice me, and Randy's ghostly visage looming ever in front of my eyes, enough was e-fricking-nuff! One little tooth that was not causing me any trouble could wait!

So we went, mouth intact. I felt very OK with that. Maybe I was ill, but at least I was whole.

But the issue wouldn't go away. In fact once we were at the clinic it got more complex. As I mentioned earlier, during my initial physical my Gerson Doctor said something that surprised me. When I opened my mouth for a check of my tongue, throat, etc., she said "Ah, metal," the undertone being that all the gold in my mouth was not a good thing. She didn't say anything else about it during our stay, offered no specificity, but that comment remained with me.

The root canal? Well, I at least understand the concept of a possible hazard. But gold? I had always been told by my dentist that this was the best dental restoration you could have. Strong, long lasting, very biocompatible. Plus, I kind of thought it looked cool. Like jewelry in my mouth in a tacky, trailer park kind of way. And as classless as it sounds, those gold crowns sort of made me feel wealthy too.

I had six teeth with gold in my mouth - five crowns and one onlay. The only trouble I had ever had was chronic soreness in back of my left molar, and I really didn't know why. Whether it was the crown or my gums, I didn't know. It was not a big deal though, I thought.

Still, when we got back to St. Paul, I was curious about my Gerson Doctor's comment. I kept remembering a vague reference to metal fillings somewhere else. Then I remembered an odd book my mother-in-law had given me, apropos of nothing, a few months earlier, *The Cure for All Diseases* by Dr. Hulda Clark (not a medical doctor, a Dr. of Physiology).

I remember when she handed it to me I was polite saying "Oh, thank you," as I did with all the myriad of unsolicited health advice I got throughout this process. But inside I scoffed. "Cure for all diseases? Riiiight! Get a frickin' clue Dr. Clark."

Nothing could be that simplistic. But, as I'm sure it was designed to, the title had piqued my curiosity and I flopped on the couch to peruse it.

Dr. Clark addressed root canals and the benefits of non-metallic dentistry at length. Her position was that all metal was bad.[24]

A few years before I had gotten all the amalgam (mercury/silver) fillings taken out of my mouth because even though most dentists told me they were perfectly safe, I didn't want anything containing mercury permanently mounted in my head.

But Dr. Clark said even gold was a "no no" because it set up bad electrical fields in the body and many gold alloys weren't nearly as pure as they were made out to be. According to her, gold fillings were hardened with nickel, an element which could potentially cause numerous health issues.[25]

Worse yet, some dentists put gold crowns over old mercury fillings, encasing them in the tooth forever!

Crap! Really? To me, that could be the whole thing. Three of my gold crowns had been put in at a dental school in the 80's, long before I had even the slightest notion of researching dental materials and techniques. Could mercury from my teenage years still be under there leaching away? Could it have accumulated in my kidney causing my mass? Was I totally off base and overacting? All these scenarios were possible.

I checked the ADA's (American Dental Association) website, and many dentists say amalgam mercury fillings are perfectly safe because the mercury stays stable and within the filling matrix.[26]

But mercury, based upon frequency of occurrence and exposure, is the third most toxic material on the planet, behind only such lovely charmers as arsenic and lead.[27] They no longer recommend using it in children. Duh! I speculate they only still put it in adults because it has been around since the 1800's, and it's familiar and easy to work with. Plus, if it ever was clinically shown to be toxic can you imagine the lawsuits? It would be right up there with the tobacco and asbestos settlements, because it is in millions of people's mouths all over the world.

There are countless online articles about mercury, blaming it for everything from autism as part of childhood vaccinations to breast cancer, leaching straight down out of fillings into breast tissue.[28] And I might still have some in my head!

I had to know. I wasn't going to go through two years of gluteal expresso if the process was already sabotaged by God knows what toxic metals molded into my dentition.

I called my dentist and asked if he would be willing to check it out. In other words, lift a crown or two and check what was underneath. If there was mercury, we would get it out immediately. He told me we risked damaging the crown so much it couldn't be put back in place, but I didn't care.

If this was the cause of my mass, I had to deal with it. It was life or death to me.

I went in, we checked underneath those shiny gold globs in my mouth and there was . . . no mercury, none - whew! And better yet, my dentist was able to reseat the crowns without damage. Well, at least that was OK.

At the same time it crossed my mind to ask about the cement used to glue the crowns on. I don't know why, but I figured that was almost as important as what the crown itself was made of. After all, this is what actually came in contact with the tooth. Did it have any nasty stuff in it?

I asked my dentist. He said the cement he used, a Fuji Glass Ionomer cement, was very safe. He said some cements contain fluoride. I asked him if the Fuji contained fluoride and he said no. I was greatly relieved by this, because on Gerson fluoride is a big no no. I was keenly aware of not consuming it in any form, not in toothpaste, water, anywhere. This was a big reason for drinking only distilled water.

At the clinic, Charlotte Gerson told us fluoride displaces iodine in the body because it is higher on the periodic table of elements. So why is that important? Well, it is the iodine in our systems, in our glands, in the Lugol's solution added to the juices that the body uses to kill nasty things. Without it, the immune system is compromised.

I also asked my dentist not to use any fluoride products on me for any other dental purposes and he assured me he wouldn't.

Still, cynic that I am, I decided to double check the cement he used, just in case he had overlooked anything. As I was quickly learning, medical professionals are human and are perfectly capable of screwing up too. If it had been in the cement, it could have meant that the last several months of arduous work on the therapy could have been for nothing, done in by my teeth!

OK, great, no mercury and hopefully, according to my dentist, no fluoride. But I still continued looking into gold.

Little did I know that checking this out, along with my curiosity about my GD's metal comment and Gerson's stance on root canals, would begin a process that wouldn't end until ALL my gold fillings had been removed, the cement researched and changed to an ancient recipe, and my root canal yanked out of my head.

It all began online. I started with the cement - glass ionomer. I had been thinking about it quite a bit because, as I mentioned, this was the material that actually came in contact with the surface of my tooth. Not the gold, but this glass ionomer, whatever that was. There were lots of listings when I Googled it, referencing brands, clinical studies and crown retention. As I scanned through though, one thing alarmed me. Many brands had "fluoride release." What did this mean? In addition to containing their own fluoride, (see endnote for Fujicem, page 18) the cements also had ". . . a capacity to absorb fluoride from the fluoride in toothpaste and then release it."[29] Holy crap! And this might be in my mouth? Are you kidding? That would mean I would have to have six crowns removed ASAP! And at around $750 a pop, this was no small undertaking not to mention hours of grinding and prepping to get this fluoride laden adhesive out of my head. Yikes!

I prayed that the glass ionomer my dentist used had no fluoride. Why was it there in the first place? To strengthen enamel. It is also added to many municipal water supplies for the same reason, whether we want it or not.

Is it good? Is it bad? That has been debated for decades. I recall a girl giving a speech in 7th grade (1967) on the evils of fluoride. But lots of folks obviously thought the effects on teeth were worth it.

But for me there was no choice. It was expressly forbidden for the reasons mentioned earlier, and after doing other research, it just seemed too controversial to risk it. An interesting website on the negatives of fluoridation is www.nofluoride.com/.

Anyway, I was seeing my dentist in a few days and I made a point to ask him again about it. He said the glass ionomer he used, Fujicem, had no fluoride. I again was relieved. At least, in addition to everything else, I had dodged one bullet. Or so I thought.

Next, I started researching gold. Online there is a wealth of information that basically only dental professionals would be interested in. But I was fascinated.

My dentist had told me he used a very high quality gold - "Bio Gold"- a mixture with the highest gold content available. Typically it is 86.5% gold, 10.5% platinum and a small amount of other elements.[30]

But as I researched more and asked my dentist questions, I found out there is an immense variety in the make up of "gold" tooth restoration products. Some have much lower proportions of gold, the balance being made up of cheaper materials such as silver and copper. In Europe, a material called Palladium had been used extensively.

My dentist told me that during the early eighties, when

gold went up to $800+ per ounce, there was even less gold, and even some tin in what were called "gold" crowns.

Hmmmm. I had two crowns in my mouth from that very period on my back left bottom molars. Could they be harboring toxic metals that leached down into my kidney? And, what was that palladium all about?

I dug in some more.

Apparently palladium is some pretty nasty stuff. It has been used in crowns in varying percentages, some as high as 78.5%.[31] It has been identified as the cause of a myriad of health problems, including dying teeth, depression, insomnia and bronchitis just to name a few.[32]

It is so nasty that is has been banned for use in dental applications in Switzerland.[33]

Could I have any of that crap in my mouth?

As to the crowns put in at the dental school, I checked historic gold prices. Sure enough, they were put in at the exact time the price of gold was skyrocketing. I called the school to ask them about the composition of the crowns, but at that time they could not locate my records. As I mentioned, I'd had chronic mild pain in back of the lower left molar for years, regardless of how much I flossed, and at this time a constant mild discharge of fluid from the left corner of my mouth and from the left corner of my left eye. I never associated these with my teeth, thinking instead I just had some type of chronic sinus infection. But, as I'll explain later, they may have been related.

Not being able to get information on these oldest metal crowns in my head, I decided I couldn't afford to keep them in and made the decision to have them removed. If they were toxic, they would be gone and I had the money for two new ones. We could put a temporary on while I decided what to replace them with (which became in itself a huge issue).

My dentist thought this was prudent anyway, given the age of the crowns and their degree of deterioration. And so, within a couple of weeks and with a few tugs and pries they were out, and that part of my dental saga was complete.

The third gold crown on that side, just in front of the two from the dental school, had been put in by my previous dentist. It had never given me a lick of trouble and looked just fine. It had been put in the late eighties and I really didn't want to mess with it. But when I called that dentist's office to ask about its composition, she said it had palladium in it! Not a lot, but here in my already compromised body, in my very mouth was a deadly substance banned by Switzerland! Why in the hell had this ever been put in my head in the first place? Did any dental professional even give a rats fricking ass about what they were installing, permanently, in their patient's mouths?

I was truly amazed, shocked and angered by this revelation.

Within two weeks, that crown was out of my head too.

The fascinating thing was that with each hunk of gold removed from my overwhelmed head I felt lighter, better, cleaner. Was that feeling real or just psychological mind games? I don't know and frankly I don't care. For me it was VERY real and even though it was tedious, time consuming, confusing, painful and expensive, I was damn glad to be getting it done.

I was also glad to be on Gerson during this process, because I strongly believe whatever junk this old metal had put into my body, Gerson was the best possible way to clean it out.

But now, what the heck to replace it with?

This issue was definitely not cut and dry. I could go porcelain, high quality "Bio Gold," or use composite, a white, strong plastic material used in fillings, but generally not strong enough long term for crowns.

My dentist greatly preferred gold for its strength and its ability to fit well on the tooth it was topping. But I was not convinced.

In my continuing research, I discovered there were some dental practitioners who believed in no metal whatsoever. The reasons ranged from toxicity to adverse electrical fields.

I needed more information so I found two holistic, non-metal dentists in the Twin Cities. Each had seminars on non-metallic dentistry which I attended. Many of the people in attendance were like me, ill with serious diseases and trying to totally clean out their bodies.

Most were very concerned about mercury, but others had also read about non-pure gold crowns and the effects of heavy metals leaching into their bodies. Gail always complained about the "zing" she would get when metal silverware touched her gold crowns.

And, although I didn't know it then, when my mouth was eventually metal free, an odd sensation in my eardrum, whenever I used my cell phone, disappeared. It had been so strong that I was only comfortable using it with a hands free earpiece.

Another reason I was leaning toward non-metal crowns was the reaction I had to rings and watches. Whenever I wear them too long, they begin to ache and feel uncomfortable. Especially, even though this may not go over too well with Gail, my wedding band. It is beautiful Black Hills gold and has, of course, tremendous emotional significance. But I can only wear it two days and then it has to come off, because my finger and the surrounding joints just start hurting too much.

Why should my mouth be any different? But what to use instead?

Hulda Clark recommended composite as the most innocuous crown. She called them "plastic." The problem was, they don't last as long as other options, about 10 years.[34]

Porcelain? Both my dentist and Hulda Clark said beware, because they are made of alumina silicate, and of course I didn't want aluminum in my mouth. Like most people, I had heard all sorts of things about the hazards of using aluminum cookware.

While I was mulling all this over, I also took a Clifford

Materials Reactivity Test.[35] It had been mentioned by both of the holistic dentists as a good indicator of one's biocompatibility with a variety of dental products. You send in a blood sample to a lab and they send you back an extensive list of dental products, by brand name, that your body likes and doesn't like.

I was specifically interested in gold reactivity, but curious about anything else too.

This was all now becoming an obsession, as you can tell. But damn it, whatever went back in my mouth would be there a very long time. And I wasn't so sure that dental products hadn't caused my trouble in the first place. Plus, I had no confidence that the dental profession, for the most part, had any clue about what their products might be doing to the rest of a person's body. For the most part I felt, accurately or not, that the attitude was, "Well, it's always worked before, so how can it be bad?"

They said that about asbestos and early high x-ray radiation too. Asbestos is virtually gone now and each medical x-ray taken now uses far less radiation than in the pioneering days of radiology. And who can forget the numerous drugs that were approved by the FDA only to be pulled later for causing serious health risks? Vioxx, anyone?[36]

I had to be sure, darn sure, that whatever went back in my head was as innocuous as possible.

I must admit I had my doubts about the Clifford test because I had no idea how one test could yield all that information, but what the heck. And it was very interesting to read about the vast array of products it tested for.

After lots of contemplation I decided to revisit porcelain. I figured what's best to have in my mouth: metal, a hunk of plastic, or a piece of a nice coffee mug? I had to simplify it down to that just for my own sanity, because the complexity of all the different materials was becoming overwhelming.

With my favorite mug in mind, I began researching options. I called the head of Clifford testing, Walter J. Clifford, to see what he thought about putting alumina silicate in my mouth. He said it was fine and that alumina silicate was a bad misnomer.

Alumina silicate is, in essence, sand. That's right, plain old sand. It was no more like an aluminum pot than a tree would be. Well thank you Mr. Clifford! I guess he and his test did know what they were talking about. This was reconfirmed as I called and e-mailed various porcelain crown manufacturers. No aluminum in them.

Was this another case of very smart people, my dentist and Dr. Clark not doing their homework? Apparently.

Yep, no aluminum. Well, I guess it truly was "mug like." Great. And even better, new technology in recent years allowed the manufacture of totally ceramic crowns. In the past, to fit well, porcelain crowns had to be mounted on gold or other metal to mate to the tooth which would defeat the purpose of going non-metallic. But now that little nugget of alumina silicate could be glued right to the tooth. Well, hooray at least for that advance in dental technology.

There was a wide variety of all ceramic crowns to choose

from, and after a lot of research I decided on Procera, because they do a computer scan of your tooth for a good fit. Also, the ceramic they used was designed to not be as tough on opposing natural teeth. And when I called the company, they had been very forthcoming with specifics about the exact makeup of their products.

But there was a hitch. Not all dental labs use every available dental product. They use what they think is best, are familiar with or have the most comfortable business relationship with. I called my dentist's lab to see if he used Procera and he said no, he wasn't set up for it. I called other labs in town. Some used Procera copings, the base computer designed part of the crown, but not Procera ceramic on top. Why? I have no clue. It seems to make sense to me to stay with one company for the whole thing, a system designed to work together. But lots of things I encountered on my cancer journey defied logic, so I didn't give it too much thought.

Finally I found a lab that used both the Procera coping and ceramic together, as they were designed to be used, and loved the product. The owner of the lab, Dennis Lemke, took a lot of time with me, explaining pros & cons, design and installation processes, etc. He was very gracious and I was quickly sold. Even though they wouldn't be as strong as gold, I didn't care. And they would look perfectly natural, just like real teeth, a look my mouth hadn't enjoyed for several decades.

When I told my dentist he wasn't very happy about working with another lab - vendor relationships and all that, but you know what? Tough. Ten years from now these little mugs would still be in my head but mean nothing to him, mere footnotes in hundreds of gaping mouths.

By the time I finally got all this figured out though, months had passed. The temporaries on my three back teeth where my gold crowns had been had long since come off, but I really didn't care. I had been in the dentist's chair so much it wasn't worth it to me to replace them so I just chewed on the other side.

Now, with my product selected and my dentist more or less on board, came the fun part: Prepping my teeth for my new Procera crowns. Years ago a dental student had nailed me in a nerve while administering anesthetic. I couldn't open my mouth for three days and it hurt like hell. Even full-fledged docs had missed a bit from time to time so for years, except in extreme instances, I went without anesthetic for all dental procedures.

Did it hurt? Sure, but I had learned to go to kind of a 'Happy Place" in my head, and apart from my toes curling anxiously, always came through just fine.

So, three crown preps in one sitting. Did that warrant anesthetic? Naaah. Screw it. I recovered more quickly without it and wouldn't have to walk around drooling and slurring my speech for the rest of the day. It actually made my dentist more nervous than me, which I rather enjoyed. Let him be anxious during a procedure for a change.

I mean really, if only other pains in life could be like that: Intense, uncomfortable for an hour at most and then everything is OK.

At the appointment, he dug in and we got 'er done,

including installing a new temporary. It would be three weeks for the new crowns to come in.

During that time I explored what cement to use. Amazingly, I couldn't find a single glass ionomer cement that didn't have fluoride. This included, much to my dismay, the FujiCem that my dentist had so assuredly told me was fluoride free! My trust in him took another hit, and glass ionomers, despite their excellent retention abilities, were out of the question.[37]

After more discussion with my dentist, (I delicately relayed my findings about the FujiCem, but didn't rub it in) we ended up using Mizzy's Zinc Phosphate cement to mount the crowns. While not as strong and more tedious to use and mix, it has no fluoride. Indeed, according to my dentist, it has been around since ancient Egyptian times, having been found in several mummies. I just hoped it wasn't what killed them!

And when I called the rep from Mizzy's to double check what was in it, he was more that happy to discuss his product and its makeup with me.

My own version of vendor relations with dental suppliers was taking shape quite nicely.

And even though my dentist said he had some Zinc Phosphate in house, I went out and bought my own to have on hand, should I change dentists, or should they stop making it, etc.

Mind you, only dental professionals are supposed to be able to get it, but I just walked into the dental supply place, acted like I knew what I was doing, and they sold it to me.

Which was good, because when we mounted the crowns, my dentist was unable to find his own stash of Zinc Phosphate, and was apologetically relieved when I pulled mine out of my pocket. I speculated he was actually a bit peeved at my wanting to use fluoride free ancient technology and was secretly trying to get out of it.

Regardless, it worked great, the crowns looked and felt terrific and needed no adjustment; a nice testament to Dennis Lemke's lab and my dentists technical skills.

It was almost shocking to see real looking teeth in my mouth after so many years. They hadn't been this natural looking since Junior High and it would take a bit of getting used to. I must admit, my vanity was appeased! Most importantly though, they felt like they should be there; safe, non-toxic, electrically inert little mugs that hopefully would last a lifetime.

The other major oral issue I had to deal with was my one and only root canal on infamous tooth #5, the one I couldn't bring myself to yank before we went to the clinic. After my scan in September, with the mass still staring starkly back at me from the murky grayness of the CT, I made the decision to yank it.

I had to cover all my bets. It would suck to die not having tried everything. "Well, he should have pulled the root canal," they would say staring at my prone coffin enclosed body. "I'm sure that was the reason it didn't work. All that effort, and he let one stupid tooth mess it up!"

But the stigma of missing a tooth was still very hard for me, as petty as that sounds. The image of a backwoods hick cleaning his shotgun in his freshly-possum-blood-stained overhauls loomed before my eyes every time I thought of a gap in my pearly whites. But still, I had to do it. The books *Root Canal Cover-Up* and Hulda Clark's dental insights were compelling and "coulda, woulda, shoulda" was now more important than Bubba and his possum.

We set up the appointment and off I went. But extracting the tooth was a bit more complex than just pulling it out. According to one of the non-metal dentists I visited, Dr. King, for complete healing of the bone socket you must also snip and or grind out the periodontal ligament, something most dentists don't normally do.[38]

I ran this by my guy beforehand and he assured me he would take care of it, although I made a mental note to remind him that day, recalling the "Oops, I can't find my Zinc Phosphate" and "Fujicem has no fluoride" incidents all too clearly.

By the time extraction Tuesday arrived, I had already decided to let him numb me up. Digging around on a tooth is one thing, digging it out of solid bone and grinding out a ligament is quite another. I kept hearing my Marine Corp father's words echoing in my ear, "Don't try to be a hero Jim, don't try to be a hero." As I said earlier, I can take more pain than most people, but this would border on sado-masochism and probably have crunchy sound effects thrown in just for effect!

After what seemed like 47 doses of anesthetic injected in my jaw, my dentist started working ol' #5, rotating the tooth slowly with some Spanish Inquisition looking device to loosen it up. "How you doin' Jim?" he would periodically say. "Well how the hell do you think I'm doin' pardner!!" I thought. "You're crankin' a chunk of my mouth out of my frickin' head!"

But all I could muster through the numbness and the gurgle of the omnipresent suction tube was a grunting "Ugghhh!" He could interpret that as "Wonderful!" or "Screw you!" whichever he wanted.

Could I feel it even through the anesthetic? Oh yes, not much . . . but just enough to make me very, very afraid of it wearing off!

But I could at least partially go to my Happy Place as he continued to yank, rotate, and grind. It was kind of like a kid trying to play his favorite game upstairs, while his parents argue in the living room. Your Happy Place can't quite tune it all out, and eventually you know you'll have to face the ugly, painful reality lurking just beyond your bedroom door.

And that reality was getting to the crunchy stage, like chewing Shredded Wheat without enough milk. I made a note to myself; next time bring an iPod with industrial-strength earplugs.

And then suddenly, without fanfare, it was done. Ol' #5 almost kind of oozed out after all that grinding, like a reluctant piece of escargot being sucked from its shell. When he held it up I was amazed at its length, like it belonged to Merle, not me, or something harvested from a new species on a National Geographic TV special. "Ah, the canine from one of the last living ventriloquists! There were thousands during Vaudeville, but now only 50-60 remain. Your contribution will help us build habitat where they can play with their dummies in complete safety, far from lumberjacks and hecklers."

I asked once more about the periodontal ligament, and he again assured me it had been ground out. Indeed, he said if he dug any further, he risked puncturing the maxillary sinus!

At the same time he installed a wing bridge, a temporary arrangement where a composite tooth is attached to the teeth in front of and in back of the hole. It would be a little cumbersome, but cosmetically looked fine.

They sent me home with some serious pain meds, and I made a point to ask for my now disembodied tooth. Why? One, it was the only record of what my original tooth had looked like and two, I had saved every tooth I ever lost; baby, wisdom and now ol' #5, and this massive gem would be the biggest in my collection. As odd as it sounds, the bottom line was I just couldn't quite part with something that had been an integral part of my being for 47 years.

And a few weeks later, a close examination of the darn thing would yield chilling information. It was a crown where the porcelain part of the crown was attached to a metal base, which then fit over what was left of the original tooth. The base was a silvery metal that according to my previous dentist could easily contain palladium. Yikes! Another validation of my decision to have it removed!

During recovery from the extraction I experienced by far the worst pain of the entire Gerson process. I took Vicodin or the first couple of days and the Gerson pain triad for several thereafter. The Triad consists of one niacin tablet, 500 mg of vitamin C and one aspirin. It is very effective against most types of pain, and both Gail and I have used it almost exclusively since Gerson came into our lives.

My entire right jaw, the entire right side of my face ached incredibly. But my temptation to indulge in too much self pity was tempered by the constant TV coverage of our new war in Iraq. It reminded me of brave wounded soldiers with far more serious injuries than my little tooth, and how they must feel, God bless them. My discomfort would be gone in a week or so - for many of them who had lost limbs, fingers and faces, their lifetime of pain was just beginning.

I could easily deal with this.

Apart from the pain and a couple of sleepless nights, the other difficult, but interesting thing was the God awful, revolting beyond belief, gut wrenching smell of the matter oozing out of the hole where the tooth had been. I described the odor to Gail as horse manure spread on top of a rotting corpse. Not even Listerine or hydrogen peroxide could cut it completely.

The thing that intrigued me about the smell was, if it was that bad, had all that toxic junk been bound up in my jaw all this time? As we say in Minnesota, "ish!"

And if any of that was leaching into my body, I was surprised I was even still alive.

If a root canal caused all of that goopy, pussy, putrified nastiness, I was GLAD to get the damn thing out of my head and good frickin' riddance. Where else could it come from? The tooth was, after all, a piece of dead tissue locked in my upper jaw bone. Ewe!

But the good part? At the very least I had covered all the bases. #5 was gone, finito. It had been eliminated as one more source of toxicity. And with the prosthetic wing bridge in, no one was the wiser cosmetically. Was it bulky? Yep. Did I like it? Not really. And now that the tooth was out, did I feel like a Gomer? No. I felt a bit less complete; it was the first one of my original parts I could never really get back. But compared to losing a kidney and the total physical trauma of that surgery? This was nothing.

I did have another minor issue though.

While the Gerson folks had been great in guiding me to resources about the hazards of root canals, no one told me that all that juice you drink can wreak havoc on your teeth.

Despite brushing, mouthwash and my semiannual flossing, I developed cavities in spots I hadn't had trouble with for years, specifically my front teeth. By the time I put two and two together I had to have one filling done twice! I asked my new dentist (Dr. "No fluoride in Fujii" had since moved on to another dental opportunity) if using a straw would help and he said definitely.

I didn't think that even though they were organic and pure, the juices were still loaded with sugar and acid.

The straws have since helped immeasurably, and I use them to this day.

Over the course of 2003 and 2004, I continued my dental cleanup as finances allowed. Each crown was now $850, so spreading this cost out made it easier until eventually I was, for the first time since age 14, metal free.

As I felt lighter with each gold removal, I also felt, especially after the last one came out, less hyper, less prone to snap or overreact. Less prone to go "Ballistic!"

I had not expected this at all. Life just didn't seem to bother me as much. Although there is no empirical way to judge this, to me it was palpable.

Had the metals interfered with my systems to that great an extent as to affect my very personality? From age 14 on?

Currently the controversy rages over the relationship between childhood vaccinations and autism. My autistic nephew reminds me a bit of myself at his age. Could tooth metal have caused a milder form of this in me? Indeed, because of a recently settled lawsuit with consumer advocacy groups such as Moms Against Mercury, none other than the FDA has put the following statement on their website, "Dental amalgams contain mercury which may have neurotoxic effects on the nervous systems of developing children and fetuses."[39]

And yet, the American Dental Association still stands behind the use of this mercury infused filler. Their site states, "Dental amalgam is considered a safe, affordable and durable material that has been used to restore the teeth of more than 100 million Americans."[40]

Of course if it is so darn safe, why do they have a 7 page

PDF on their website describing in detail how to safely dispose of it?

But at least now, that wasn't one of MY worries. I was relatively orally pure, as if every time I smiled Shirley Temple shone from my teeth singing, "On the Good Ship Lollipop."

I wore my wing bridge for longer than I was supposed to and it caused some decay, exacerbated by the juices, in the tooth behind it. I was delaying making what would be an expensive and difficult decision as to what to replace it with, and had kind of hoped the wing bridge could be a long term solution. I'd just get a new one every few years - but it was obvious now that couldn't happen. It just wasn't designed to be a permanent installation.

But this was a much bigger deal than just a crown. It would mean either grinding down the teeth on either side of the gap and fitting a bridge over the stubs with the fake tooth in the middle or, getting a dental implant. The implant is a titanium post, implanted surgically in your jawbone. Once the bone has healed around the post, an extension is added to which the porcelain tooth is attached. They have been a very successful solution but are very expensive (my cost for one implant, post, crown and labor as of 6/15/05 would be about $4000). Plus it would mean more metal in my head and I had just gotten all of that out!

But the thought of grinding the two relatively healthy teeth adjacent to the gap didn't excite me either. I needed more time to think. I called Dennis Lemke again to see if there were any other alternatives. He recommended a Biostar, a plastic thing that fits inside your teeth along the front of the upper palate, and has the fake tooth hanging off it.

I went for that. It bought me time. It worked fine, although my articulation suffered a bit. But it wasn't metal and only cost $345. And by that point, I had been through enough damn dental trauma for a while. Of course I could have just left the hole in my face, but #5's gap was prominent enough that I would have been very self-conscious doing shows.

Like the wing bridge, I hung onto the BioStar longer than I should. I was working up the courage to pull the lever on an implant. While expensive, it was the best alternative for my situation. My mouth and its shape were critical to my success long term as a ventriloquist, and in that regard the implant would be the closest thing to the original in tooth function, root structure and hygiene care I could get. Plus, I hated the thought of sacrificing two more teeth with a bridge and not having an actual gap between the teeth.

When the BioStar finally bit the dust hours before a show, and I had to do it gap and all, that was the final push I needed to getting the implant process started.

And quite a process it was. First my oral surgeon (As with labs, I had to shop around for one that used the implant product I wanted - Nobel Bio Care, the same folks that make Procera) drilled a hole into the bone where #5 had been and installed the bottom of the post my porcelain crown would eventually attach to. After that healed for six weeks, my dentist completed the process by casting a crown and fitting it to the top part of the post and installing it. The first crown we got from the lab unfortunately wasn't designed well and didn't look right, so I had it sent back and they happily made another one that cosmetically was much better.

Since then the Titanium implant/Procera crown combo has worked well, looks great and it will never rot or decay. Apart from having to adjust the inside of the crown a few times to get it just right for articulation and comfort, I have had no trouble with it whatsoever, and it actually feels stronger than my natural teeth.

And with that, I was done, until I needed other cavities filled or whatever.

Did all these dental issues have anything to do with my kidney mass? Who knows. But for certain it made life a bit easier for my whole body, and my teeth have been eliminated as future sources of toxicity. Plus my mouth looks and feels great, and metal utensils touching my teeth no longer zing them. I also don't feel any "current" when I use my cell phone.

As to long term success, only time will tell. But at least concerning dental issues, I knew I had covered all my bases as best I possibly could.

---

22. Max Gerson M.D., *Gerson Therapy Handbook: A Companion to A Cancer Therapy,* rev. 5th ed. (San Diego: Totality Books, 2007), 24-25.

23. George E. Meing D.D.S, F.A.C.D., *Root Canal Cover-Up,* (Ojai, CA: Bion Publishing, 1998) 1-6.

24. Hulda Regehr Clark, *The Cure for All Diseases* (Chula Vista CA: New Century Press, 1995), 409-420.

25. *Ibid.,* 124-126.

26. American Dental Association, "Oral Health Topics: Dental Filling Options," www.ada.org/6605.aspx?currentTab=1.

27. Agency for Toxic Substances & Disease Registry, "Priority List of Hazardous Substances," www.arsdr.cdc.gov/SPL/index.html

28. Search "Mercury Fillings Toxicity" or "Mercury Autism" in Google.

29. S. Hatibović-Kofman and G. Koch, "Fluoride Release from Glass Ionomer Cement in vivo and in vitro," *Swedish Dental Journal* 15, no.6 (1991): 253-258, accessed June 21, 2010, www.ncbi.nih.gov/pubmed/1817351.

30. "BioGold Plus from Elephant Dental B.V.," accessed June 21, 2010, www.dentalcompare.com/details/8931/BioGold-Plush.html.

31. Corinne Vizcarra D.D.S., "Palladium - Dental Danger Alloy," accessed June 21, 2010, www.naturalhealinghouse.com/hm_palladium.htm.

32. "Adverse Health Effects of Palladium," www.holisticmed.com/dental/palladium 1.html.

33. *Ibid.*

34. Gordon J. Christensen, "Longevity of Posterior Tooth Dental Restorations," *Journal of the American Dental Association* 136, no.2 (2005): 201-203, accessed June 21, 2010, http://jada.ada.org/cgi/content/full/136/2/201.

35. "Clifford Materials Reactivity Test," accessed June 21, 2010, www.ccrlab.com.

36. Rita Rubin, "How Did Vioxx Debacle Happen?" *USA TODAY,* October 12, 2004, accessed June 21, 2010, www.usatoday.com/news/health/2004-10-12-vioxx-cover_x.htm.

37. "GC FujiCEM™ Automix: Glass Ionomer Luting Cement," accessed June 21, 2010, www.gcamerica.com/products/operatory/GC_FujiCEM_Automix/features.php.

38. Michael Rehme, D.D.S., C.C.N., "Unexplained Dental Pain Explained: Tooth Extractions, Cavitations and the Periodontal Ligament," October 13, 2011, accessed June 14, 2012, http://thehealthyplanet.com/2011/10/unexplained-dental-pain-explained-tooth-extractions-cavitations-and-the-periodontal-ligament/.

39. David Gutierrez, "FDA Reluctantly Admits Mercury Fillings Have Neurotoxic Effects on Children," accessed June 17, 2012, www.naturalnews.com/024993.html.

40. ADA Council on Scientific Affairs, "Statement on Dental Amalgam," accessed June 21, 2010, www.ADA.org/1741.aspx.

Chapter Sixteen

Coffee and Cruisin'

When I was on the therapy, several people asked me how I passed the time during all those "coffee breaks." After all, it was at a minimum two hours a day of lying on my side, alone, waiting for my liver, pancreas and colon to do their own lower GI version of binge and purge.

It was the ideal time to read. And read I did. Books, magazines, newsletters, and countless catalogues full of things I couldn't afford and didn't need, but of course thought I desperately had to have.

One of my favorites in the first weeks was Miata magazine. I had two old British sports cars crammed into our miniscule one car garage that were a lot of fun, as long as you really didn't want to drive them. The Spitfire and TR3B sat forlornly on their slowly sagging tires, pining for my ever codependent attention. I say codependent because Triumph cars are truly a labor of love . . . or serious masochism. For every one hour of driving pleasure, there are at least four under the hood. And when the car is actually moving, one hand is on the steering wheel with your fingers crossed, and the other is clutching your cell phone and AAA card.

So, as much as I was inextricably bonded with my Britmobiles, I yearned for something easy. Especially after going through Gerson, I didn't want to waste what life I had left on my back on a cold garage floor with road-grit-encrusted grease and the occasional drop of transmission fluid plopping down in my face.

A Miata seemed like a good call. Reliable Japanese engineering, easy parts availability and actual dealerships still in existence (Triumph closed its doors in the early '80's), and it would probably, actually work most of the time. Amazing!

I fantasized frequently about lazy, top down cruises to nowhere in particular, the wind, sunshine and delicious fragrances of spring engulfing my senses - and not a thought of cancer in my head.

My body in this imaginary scenario was whole and energized and my spirit full of optimism. Age and time and pain were nonexistent, banished to a special Alcatraz where they would slowly rot into oblivion.

Looking back, it was a vision that I needed more than I would ever admit. While I continued to slowly feel better, I was still inextricably chained to the Therapy. The umbilical connecting me to my Gerson cocoon could not be severed for long time, and would only stretch beyond the confines of our upstairs kitchen for a day or two.

But what I was imagining reinforced my will to survive, to see this thing through, so I could take that Miata drive in the real world, indulging in one of the simple pleasures that make life worth living.

So I devoured each issue of Miata magazine (yes, I subscribed) with relish. I figured out which model I would buy, contemplated adding a supercharger so I could compete with the Beemers and Boxters, and never made myself figure out how to pay for it all. Somehow, if it was meant to be, it would happen.

All that really mattered was that the thought of countless carefree cruises could give me a regular mental and spiritual vacation during the long tedious months to come.

Chapter Seventeen

"Ewe, Ewe, EWE!!!"

In the late spring of '03, as Gail and I were just getting our Gerson regimen dialed in, my agent Tim called about a nice gig for the fall. I would be part of an arts series in western Nebraska. If it all worked out there would be two family style shows and they would pay a nice chunk of change, but there would be a lot of driving and Gerson logistical issues, so Tim wanted my input before we sealed the deal.

I knew I couldn't make it happen alone, so it would all depend on Gail. The very thought of a road trip of that magnitude on the Therapy was incredibly overwhelming - just thinking about it made me feel exhausted.

But it was a few months out and God willing, I would be feeling better by then, the money was great and heck, I had never been part of an "Arts Series." So, even though it made me nervous, I said, "Let me check into the practicalities and call you tomorrow."

I had thought a lot about how I would handle gigs like this in my considerable "prone" time, that is when I wasn't thinking about Miatas. I couldn't avoid them for two years, so I had preemptively developed some Gerson travel strategies.

After lots of contemplation, I realized the only way to continue the therapy and stay mobile was to rent a motor home. A stove, fridge, and the ever important toilet would all be there, and I could if necessary, juice in transit. It would hopefully work for Nebraska, and if I did any county fairs that summer, a mobile Gerson womb would be a must.

I started making some phone calls to see if it would even be worth it though. Once I had motor home rental prices and estimated gas costs, I figured I could net $1500 for the two days, so that was plenty of profit to justify it.

But could Gail go? Would she be game? Would I indeed have the strength by then or was I deluding myself?

Or, would I take a turn for the worse and have to cancel the whole tour a week before?

Would I even be alive?

As with any major decision, I had to take it one step at a time. To focus on unknowns was fruitless, so first I asked Gail. Without a thought of unwillingness or doubt she said, "Let me check my schedule." She was such a trooper. It was obvious, if she could work things out at the library, her part of the formula would fall into place.

Indeed, by the next day she had it cleared with work and was amazingly up for the challenge of a multi-day sojourn across the plains of South Dakota and Nebraska, in a rented motor home, with an organic-juicing-anally-coffee-infused ventriloquist and Merle, our ever faithful canine companion.

With Gail on board I almost impulsively decided to go for it. Worst case? I totally jeopardize the therapy by overdoing it. Best case? I feel great, we have some fun and make some money. Reality? Who the heck knew?

I called Tim and asked if the clients could work with the

caveat of my health. I did not want to mislead them and have to cancel unexpectedly if my body went in the crapper along with all that coffee.

I also explained to Tim the magnitude of putting this journey together so that we didn't end up booking things like this every month. One or two in the next year would be about all my kidney-mass-stressed-psyche could handle.

Tim was great as always, and amazingly the clients were OK with my conditional acceptance of the shows. And so, that was that. In the fall Gail, Merle, the Therapy and I would be tooling out West.

It certainly gave me something to look forward to, but not necessarily in a good way. The instant I hung up the phone with Tim after the date was confirmed, I had an anxiety attack.

What was I doing? I was sure my Gerson Doctor would not approve. Was I sacrificing the rest of my existence for a nearsighted gain? Was I doing this only because I felt like a schmuck for not working much - for receiving so much from so many without having a chance to give back?

I had to respect the Therapy, but languishing at home was beginning to take its toll too. Gigging gave me purpose, self respect and . . . revenue. It was a cure for the insecurity that was constantly trying to seep in through the cracks of my self worth brought on by being involuntarily sidelined, just when the game was getting good.

And with a little luck we might just pull it off.

As October approached, I began dusting off bits I hadn't done in months because the shows would each be 75-90 minutes. I practiced "Betty the Dancing, Talking Broom" with whom I tap dance to Louis Prima's "Sing, Sing, Sing." I brought out my Danny slide show, a "Behind the Music" style story of my first dummy and our breakup. It would be fun to do all these creative pieces, ones that take me out of the traditional realms of "Guy with Dummy." Typically I only perform for 45 minutes or so, and in a corporate or county fair environment there isn't time to explore the non-traditional applications of ventriloquism, but for an "arts" show, I could wander outside the lines a bit.

And of course just as important as the act was taking the therapy on the road. I reserved a medium sized motor home a few months out, so I knew exactly what our ride would be like.

There would be nowhere to restock our organic food supplies (I checked online for stores or co-ops), so we would have to take several coolers on the five day junket. The fridge in the RV would help, but not be nearly enough for all the carrots, apples, soup, lettuce, etc.

Plus, we had to leave room for our trusty, devoted, if not somewhat confused by the whole prospect furry friend, Merle.

As departure day neared I got both anxious and excited, but Gail's presence helped keep both emotions in healthy check. And with her along, we were sure to have some of those serendipitous road adventures that you talk about the rest of your lives.

Plus we were staying one night at a place we had joked about for years on our way to the Black Hills: Yogi Bear's RV Park just outside Sioux Falls, South Dakota. Golly gee, it had hookups, showers and everything! Forget that no one born after 1970 knows who or what the heck Yogi Bear is, much less what his name is a parody of (baseball legend Yogi Berra). We were going to fulfill childhood "Pikinik Basket Boo Boo" fantasies neither of us had been able to indulge in as kids.

My family are hotel folks, not RV'ers, and Gail never went to South Dakota as a child. So to the part of our souls that remembered and embraced being 10 years old, this was big stuff.

I would also get to see the fascinating sand hills of western Nebraska, whose endless waves of sand and grass had engaged my imagination as a boy. Were they really a petrified ocean? How were they formed? And most importantly were there dinosaur skeletons under them?!

These things would be fun. But my anxieties kept both feet firmly in reality. This was no vacation. I had pressure and a schedule and even though I felt better, I was still worried about my energy.

On the other hand, I realized long ago that if I don't have something to be anxious about, I'm not really happy anyway.

Our departure day loading took forever because of all the details that had to be considered. As I mentioned, there would be nowhere to reload our coffers once we got out of the Twin Cities, so we had to be thorough. But after several hours, too much lifting and countless double checks, we were off: Me, Gail, Merle, a ventriloquist show, juicer, press, veggies, meds, five days of food and of course, Mr. Enema Bucket. Everything you need for a swingin' time in the Corn Husker State!

The RV lumbered like a Thai elephant with too many logs on

its tusks. We waddled down I-35E out of St. Paul about 2:00 P.M., and took the big turn west toward South Dakota on I-90 an hour and a half later. In past years that turn had symbolized adventure, fun, escape, and usually the start of a trip to the Black Hills. But by this time in the day, after so much effort getting everything together it was more like, "Let's just get there."

As we tooled toward Sioux Falls we had a stiff wind from the south making steering a bit trying, but all in all things were going fairly smoothly. At Blue Earth, we got a fleeting glimpse of the 55-foot Jolly Green Giant statue that towers over the local Walmart. At Jackson, I recounted to Gail tales of hosting the Jackson County fair talent contest, and as we neared the South Dakota border we reminisced about dining with my Dad at a supper club in Luverne, with its giant chicken out front and miniature chapel for penitent travelers next door. He had been in the area for his 50th high school reunion. I was just hoping to see my 31st.

On this leg of the trip the dog was still trying to settle in and find his place. Between us? Not quite enough room. Back by the coolers? Too far away. He looked a bit lost in this hulking turtlesque mass of vehicle, glad to be with us but obviously hoping this outing wouldn't last too long.

Finally after five hours of driving there it was - Yogi Bear Campground - not teaming with laughing kids and mellowing adults soaking up summer sun, but cold and desolate with a dispassionate self-sign-in box.

It was almost eerie to be there at this time of year, like pulling up to a ghost town waiting to happen. But we got settled in quite nicely, and within the metallic cocoon of the RV were reasonably comfortable. I had finished juicing before we left home, so I just had dinner and one coffee break to do. Even with Gail, who by now was infinitely comfortable with all things Gerson, I was self conscious about doing a "coffee break" in such close quarters. She grabbed a book and pulled the curtain around the bed in the back of what was now our mobile clinic, which left the rest of the RV to me and the task at hand. It was the most privacy available, and I would just have to cope.

Somehow, I wedged myself in the narrow isle of the RV, putting my bucket on top of a cooler and towels underneath. My legs were contorted in at least three directions and despite my best efforts, I did feel idiotic. I imagined myself stepping out of my body, looking at myself sprawled there like a ski jumper who's missed the end of the ramp and thinking, "Yep, this IS weird!"

On the other hand, I needed the "break." It had been six hours since my last one, two hours past my normal time and I was feeling it. I was a bit lightheaded and my ability to focus was waning. I was also getting a bit anxious about not being able to detoxify, so even in the confines of Yogi Bear RV Park it was comforting to finally indulge in a nice warm bucket of organic Mexican brew.

As I got the process started, I began to realize this whole crazy journey just might work. Apart from the plumbing being a bit finicky in the RV, this was a functional, if somewhat cramped, setup.

I felt much better after my little "quiet time." When I was done, Gail and I stored extraneous items and went to bed, exhausted. Next day it took us an hour more than I thought to get underway, but we had time and after 24 hours on the road, we were getting our space organized and systems in place.

Gail was constantly cleaning dishes, pots, juice glasses etc., and I was running my road juicer and press. We would make up four carrot/carrot apple juices in advance, drive for a few hours and then stop to make more, eat, and then I would do "coffee" while Gail walked Merle.

A truck stop in lovely Murdo, South Dakota was a place where we made one of these extended stops. The wind had picked up considerably. As I walked back from the truck stop after picking up a few items and saw the RV sitting there with the dust swirling around it in that isolated parking lot, it brought home just how much making this work was totally up to us.

We were an island oasis, not just in the RV, but the whole process. No Gerson doctor around the corner, no meds from Walgreen's, nothing for insurance to cover - just our faith in the Gerson Therapy and ourselves. That thought invigorated me and my sense of fierce independence, but at the same time it engendered a bit of anger at the traditional American health care system. I had to be independent because my chosen treatment is not supported by the government here, for reasons I still can't get my head around. [41]

But I never liked to dwell on that too long. Anger got me nowhere and perhaps eventually I could help make Gerson more mainstream, and hopefully save a few lives.

But first I had to lie on the floor of a rented RV in the middle of a desolate, dusty South Dakota truck stop parking lot and do an enema.

We sojourned on after our Murdo break. The wind picked up and blew us like a land born tsunami. We had to turn the steering wheel into it 75° just to go straight.

The RV started lurching more and more intensely with each successive gust. As we jostled along, anything not tied down clanged with increasing intensity.

It was about this time Merle began to realize this wasn't a one day junket and started sighing frequently. It was that kind of fed up Charlie Brown sigh that dogs who know they're resigned to a fate not of their choosing frequently indulge in. "No walk this afternoon?" - sigh- "No Frisbee?" -sigh- "A thousand more miles in this rattle trap behemoth?" -sigh-.

Dog and decibels notwithstanding, we pressed on passing towns with signs that said "The railroad's gone, but we're staying," shortly after which the remaining tracks in town ended abruptly.

We went by remote wells stuck in pastures pumped by incessantly turning windmills. We encountered numerous ranchers in old pickups and new cowboy hats, who would raise one gnarled finger in greeting as they passed by in the opposite lane.

Mile after mile we continued, drinking a juice each hour, taking my meds and munching on rosemary potatoes and Gerson soup.

We got into Alliance, Nebraska late in the evening a day before the show the following night. It was another desolate campground, but associated with a hotel so we actually saw a human being. It had gotten colder, so we had to drain all the water tanks in the "rig," including the infamous "black water" tank. What is "black water?" The holding tank for the toilet refuse.

To drain it, you put on your Playtex elbow length rubber gloves, cram a big hose down a hole in the ground, open a valve and let 'er fly. Ewe . . . ewe, ewe, ewe. Especially on enema intensive Gerson. Ewe!

I made Gail come out to see, just to hear her say "EWE!" Merle came out and even for a creature that identifies friends by the smell of their poop, this was too much. I swear, he barked out an "ewe" too.

I think our cache of peroxide for hand washing went down by half each time we dumped that tank. And God forbid you got any of that disgusting slurry on your shoes! Ewe! And where did it go once it had been in that hole for awhile? I didn't even want to know or imagine.

Next morning I took a frigid walk with Merle, but there wasn't anything very interesting to sniff and the wind bit mercilessly in our faces. We had tried to liven up the trip for him by making a big deal of crossing the Missouri River, but by that time he had adopted faking being asleep as a coping mechanism. He conveniently forgot all words except "walk" and "dinner," and with each of his ever increasing sighs he seemed to be saying, "You know, you COULD have boarded me at the kennel!"

More juices, more meds, more coffee breaks and a trip to Shopko for supplies and distraction, and then it was time to jockey the big rig to the American Legion to set up for the show.

The client and two volunteers cheerfully greeted me, even though I had lost track of time and arrived a bit late.

The odd thing was, this process of meeting the client, set-up, etc. was usually SO routine for me. But with the undercurrent of Gerson and my mortality in the lurch, it was anything but. I felt odd not telling the client all about it, but instead put on the facade of normality to reinforce their confidence in having a great event. These things take lots of planning, organization, press, etc. and the last thing the client wants is to have the act show up and be needy.

They worked their butts off to make this happen and damn it, you'd better work yours off for them! Even if it is highly caffeinated!

Forget that I still felt a little shaky. Forget that 45 minutes before the show I would be power loading oatmeal, plain fat free organic yogurt (which I could now eat in limited amounts) and apple sauce, since I had no fat reserves to draw from. The show must go on, and I was committed to being a hit.

And I was.

The audience was a perfect demographic for me; all ages, small town, wanting a clean fun show reminiscent of Ed Sullivan.

Patrick my leprechaun joked, Betty Broom and I tap danced without missing a beat, and my wit sparkled during the audience participation.

And afterward I was totally fried.

But it felt so damn good to be doing what I was born to do: Making people laugh, forget their worries, escape from their everyday cares, annoyances and yes, illnesses. For that hour and fifteen minutes we all journeyed to an endorphin filled, wonderful reality where cares cannot enter and pain is nonexistent.

I needed it as much as they did. And the check didn't hurt either.

The whole experience of getting here, surviving the journey and then killing at the gig went far in dissolving any image I had of myself as an invalid. My self esteem and self worth got a big boost, and it made all the juice, coffee and struggles seem worth it. I could be a vehicle of great joy for people of all walks of life, a return blessing to a world that was blessing me with a wonderful therapy, an even more wonderful spouse to help me with it and the funds to carry it out. That night I counted myself very fortunate indeed.

The next night we were in Valentine and what I was afraid might happen did. I didn't have enough umph left to make that performance sparkle as much as the one the night before.

That's not to say it wasn't entertaining. It was and people were appreciative, but I knew in my heart two in a row with the travel and Gerson complexities was a little much for my healing body, and the performance suffered accordingly.

Fortunately having done thousands of shows, you know not every night is brilliant, and sometimes just "good" is good enough.

Of course the real reason I was not 100% was probably that

I was distracted by the amazing monument we had visited earlier in the day just outside Alliance. The Ranchers Hall of Fame? The Sand Hills Interpretive Center?

No, it was bigger than any of those could be, if they even exist.

This was an American-Druidic monument of immense historic proportion, none other than emotion stirring, awe inspiring, internationally renowned Carhenge!

Yes, that's right, Carhenge. Old autos, slathered in battleship grey paint and meticulously mounted in the exact configuration of their sarsen stone counterparts across the Atlantic.

Stoic relics of Detroit's finest marked the solstice and equinox and presumably were a valuable tool in Nebraska agriculture. "Well by golly, the sun's peekin' over the Caddy Mother, time to plant the corn."

Gail and I had thought it would be hokey, but we ended up being duly impressed and enjoyed it immensely.

It was the one actual bit of vacation kitsch we had on the trip.

It would become the major thing we would share with friends about our sojourn, that along with the dog's homeward yearnings. Juice and coffee and thoughts of cancer gratefully almost paled by comparison.

On the way home we saw the sand hills, just as fascinating as I remembered them as a boy, and of course we had our regular extended Gerson rest stops. Endless grassland and empty roads slowly yielded to cultivated fields and more traffic. I attempted a couple of times to juice in motion but that was not a happy event. The juicer kept trying to wander off the counter and filling the 8 oz. jars would have been tough even for one of my circus trained juggler friends.

But all in all, the journey back to St. Paul was uneventful, until we had to return the RV.

The rental place understandably asked that all the tanks, including the black water tank, be empty and the rig thoroughly cleaned.

We had dumped all the tanks at a rest stop just outside the Twin Cities, but the RV was on a bit of a slant when I did it. It made me nervous that the gauge for the black water tank still showed a bit of enematic sludge remaining, but surely it was in error, or hopefully just a few drips were left . . . surely.

Once we pulled up to our welcoming Edwardian on Superior Street, in a medium drizzle we unloaded the juicer, press, coolers, pans, the show, the much glad to be home dog, sound, lights and several ventriloquist dummies.

We scrubbed the inside of the RV from stem to stern and headed for the car wash to clean off what seemed to be a couple of acres of Nebraska and South Dakota dust.

Because the RV was too big to fit in the stall, we had to park it just outside in the drizzle, wash one side, turn the thing around and then repeat the process. In rereading the RV rental contract it mentioned they wanted the thing returned with the tank valves open, black water included, to guarantee they were empty.

What better place than here at the car wash to double check the emptiness of the tanks before we returned our mobile Gerson cocoon? They had drains and it was already drizzling. I could hose the valves openings off and bring the thing in sparkling.

Armed again in my yellow Playtex living gloves, I gingerly opened the gray water valve (gray water comes from the sinks) . . . two little drips trickled out onto the asphalt of the carwash lot. I hosed it and closed it.

Feeling confident now, I moved on to the imposing black water valve. Not foreseeing a problem because of my gray water success, I opened the valve quickly with a cocky twist . . . and out spewed at least 5 gallons of murky, chunky fluid best described as well used Gerson coffee. "Ewe! Ewe!" I screamed louder than necessary just for dramatic effect. When Gail saw it, she joined in to make a horrified, reverberant chorus of "Ewes!"

They resonated through the carwash stalls in a swelling mantra of disgust. It was so intense a situation that as the slimy effluent spread across the stall floor and parking lot we just broke into uproarious "ewey" laughter.

What else could we do? We began doing a car wash *River Dance* to keep our shoes out of the creeping sludge. We were so giddy after six days of road warrior escapades, we just kept squealing "Ewe! Ewe! Ewe!" interlaced with healthy amounts of raucous giggling. We needed a giant vehicular Depends, a Super Squeegee, or a Godzillian Sponge Bob Square Pants and quickly.

Thank God there was no one else in the car wash. Like Vesuvian lava, the ooze, smelling faintly reminiscent of Hazelnut expresso, continued slithering across the floor of the car wash stall and parking lot. The stall had a drain that we could rinse with the sprayer, but the parking lot flowed to grass and shrubs.

I rationalized, "Well, the plants will actually appreciate the extra nitrates! Yeah, that's it!"

Ewe!

Fortunately, our guardian angels were "Ewe!"ing with us. The drizzle was changing to heavy cleansing rain so after monitoring the situation for about half an hour with EPA diligence, we were able to depart without leaving so much as a coffee stain.

The entire time though we prayed that no one in the restaurant next door had witnessed our Exxon Valdezesque loss of containment. If we had been caught, what would our punishment be? "Yes, yes your honor, I'm guilty. No, cleaning Portolets at the State Fair for the next 10 years is more than appropriate. Thank you!"

It was a fitting end to a truly amazing adventure and God willing, I would live to have many more of them.

---

41. "The Gerson Therapy," http://livingfood.hubpages.com/hub/The-Gerson-Therapy.

Chapter Eighteen

May '04 Scan

In the spring of '04, after a solid year on the therapy, Gail and I both thought it would be a good idea for me to get scanned again. Plus, my family, friends, and even family and friends once removed, had been asking Gail and me about it.

It was obvious why most people close to me wanted me to undergo what would be my fourth scan in two years. They loved me and were genuinely concerned for my welfare. It wouldn't have mattered what course of treatment I had pursued, they just hoped for my sake I would survive.

But it took me awhile to figure out that other folks in my inner circle, and more than a few on the periphery, weren't so magnanimous about seeing what was going on inside my little kidney.

It was never really articulated, but from subtexts of conversations and implications unspoken, it was clear some thought, "OK, he'll do this thing, the mass will continue to grow, he'll come to his senses and hopefully get surgery just in the nick of time . . . and finally WE can relax a bit."

Of course enabling their relaxation meant drinking contrast and getting even more radiation zapped into the very tissue I was trying so arduously to heal (not to mention the disturbing sensation of having one's privates glow like a black light at a Janis Joplin post-concert party).

This subset of friends, family and acquaintances were concerned about their own peace of mind first, and my welfare second. For them, Gerson was way too ambivalent. Far from seeming like concrete action, to them it was more like warm Jello, amorphous, vague and insecure. It left them wondering if they should intervene on my and Gail's behalf and dramatically save us from ourselves. I'm sure some of them were more concerned about her, thinking what I was doing was cruel and unusual spousal abuse and that she would end up a widow if no one slapped me into reality . . . their reality of course, not mine.

It made me all the more appreciative of those who were able to let go and let God, trust in my choice of what path was best for me and be willing to live with that choice . . . or let me die if need be.

Because of the varied motivations of people wanting to know the results I decided I would get a scan, but I would do it on my own time and not tell a soul the results until I had digested it well myself and felt secure enough to answer every question from a position of confidence, ownership, and with a good post-scan plan of action already in place.

And what would that plan be? The same as in September. If it was bigger, surgery would seem very likely. If it was smaller or the same size, I would consider that consistent with success on the therapy according to the case studies that I had read and have described earlier.

But now, how to do it? I had no desire to go through Dr. Swenson again. I would fear another round of needless grilling and second-guessing.

Dr. Hampton was out for the same reason. I mentioned this dilemma to Gail and in talking with her brother Paul about it he mentioned that some imaging facilities did scans on an outpatient basis. I wouldn't need to go through a hospital at all, and hopefully avoid a lot of hassle.

It sounded great so I looked - where else? - in the Yellow Pages. I found several radiology clinics that indeed would do an abdominal CT for me and they were FAR cheaper than going through the medical center or Abbott Northwestern. My initial scans, which I paid for through my insurance, were each about $2000. Going to St. Paul Radiology, less than two miles from my house, would be $750 with contrast, $550 without. Why so much less? I speculate it was a couple of things. There were fewer layers of institutions to pay. No hospital check-in or hospital fees and no urologist's group involved made for lower overhead. All I needed was a prescription from my doctor.

Hmmmm. My doctor. I had all but burned the bridges with Dr. Swenson and Dr. Hampton. I doubted the imaging clinic would take a prescription from a physician in another country so unfortunately my GD was out too.

But what about Dr. Taylor, my wonderful, smiling, open minded GP, who had been so gracious and helpful at the start of this whole ordeal? Perhaps she would agree? I would deck myself out in my most innocuous, yet charming, persona and try to schmooze her into it. Without telling anyone, I scheduled an appointment.

When I arrived, she listened graciously, and I told her about my journey on Gerson to this point. While she didn't necessarily endorse it, she didn't blow me out of the water either. She understood the prudence of having the imaging done and even took a look at my CTs from the medical center and Abbott.

Before I met with her, I thought a lot about the contrast issue too. It was cheaper to do the scan if I didn't use any, and I knew from examining my previous scans, you could see quite a bit without it. In Yankton, they had done a pass sans contrast before starting the injection and while the internal make up of the mass did not stand out nearly as well, the size was easily distinguishable, especially since my mass protruded beyond the edge of the kidney wall.

And for me at this juncture, size was ALL that mattered.

Plus if they did it without contrast there would be fewer passes and consequently less radiation. As I mentioned above, they typically do a pass without and then one with contrast, and any radiation I could avoid would be less I would carry around with me for the next, God willing, 40+ years.

God bless her, Dr. Taylor magnanimously agreed to write the prescription but said I would have to take up the contrast issue with the radiologist whose interpretation of the images was included in the price.

Wonderful. Somebody on my side! And it looked like this would be easy, which I really needed because just doing the therapy was such a chore in itself, and the whole CT issue made me incredibly anxious.

I set up a date for my "shoot." I asked, however, to meet with the radiologist beforehand to negotiate on the contrast.

His name was Dr. Mark Bowen, and he was remarkably open minded. When I told him about my desire to avoid more radiation by foregoing the contrast, he said something no one else had even broached with me. He said, "I would be more worried about the total amount of contrast you have had than the quantity of radiation. The contrast destroys some of the cells in your kidneys that manufacture urine. Sometimes we don't give that enough consideration and hand out contrast like candy."

What? Why the hell hadn't any other medical professional bothered to tell me that I was damaging the very organ I was so desperately trying to save? Uh, oops! Guess that wasn't important to my former urologists, radiologists, ER staff or CT technicians.

Once again it was hammered home how important it is to ask questions and be your own best advocate.

I was VERY grateful for his candidness. We discussed it for a good 10 minutes and though it wasn't his first choice, he reluctantly agreed to no contrast with the caveat that if he saw anything else in there we would run it again, but this time with my tank full of leaded and my great balls afire.

Ok. I liked this guy. Honest and flexible. Cool.

I also had decided to simplify things by paying cash for the whole deal. On the surface that may seem odd, but by this point I was so sick of seeing what seemed like 300 pieces of paperwork each time I sent anything through Blue Cross. For instance, when I saw Dr. Hampton there was a notification from his office of what was being submitted to my insurance then later a bill, the same for Abbott

Northwestern and also from the radiologist and then three notifications from Blue Cross, first about what would be paid to each entity and what I would cover, then the actual bill from Blue Cross for each one.

I was sick of it. Enough. It gave me a headache and the interminity (Yes, I made up that word!) of it was maddening. You would think you were finally done with it all, only to have another bill show up six months after the procedure.

Screw it. I'll write a check. It's done. Paying the $550 was worth the peace of mind.

And so, by simplifying the payment with cash this scan continued to be easy. Since it would be my fourth one the whirring donut was not at all intimidating and with no contrast, it was simply a walk in, "hold your breath" a few times, and walk out. Nothing to drink, no IV's and gratefully, room temperature testes.

I was unable to see into the booth afterward as I had at the med center, but they did give me films of the shoot on the spot and later sent me the images on a CD and unlike the med center, there was no extra charge. While I had an appointment with Dr. Bowen to discuss the results in a couple of days, of course I checked out the films in the parking lot, anxiously sliding them out of the envelope and squinting to find my left kidney among the amorphous blobs of white and gray.

Would it be there? Would it be gone? Bigger? Or maddeningly the same!?

OK, there's my liver, my empty and now somewhat

growling stomach, the top of the kidney, lower, lower . . . and there it was, happily residing where I had first seen it after my racquetball fiasco a year, two months and 5600 juices ago.

And it looked exactly the same frickin' size.

I didn't know what to think. Part of me was pissed, but part of me was very grateful. And, as I had done in September, I remembered it WAS consistent with the successful testimonials I had read about in the Gerson kidney cancer booklet.

Now what to do, who to tell. I decided not to jump the gun and instead sit on it until I had seen the radiologist so I would have all the information from this set of images I could get. And when we met, he gave me the most encouraging news any traditional health professional had offered.

First, he had just been at a symposium on small renal masses, where a collection of doctors, radiologists and specialists who deal with these on a daily basis concluded they didn't know exactly what the best way was to treat them.

Leave them in or take them out? There was apparently a quandary about the whole thing.

According to what Dr. Bowen had heard, they were often rather innocuous, a tolerated nuisance to be monitored for sure, but major surgery right off the bat was not necessarily the best course of action.

And they were fairly common. Not that everyone on the planet had one bouncing around inside them, but they also weren't some rare and mystifying occurrence.

The next words he said were the best of all. He thought that because the mass was still its happy 1.8 centimeter self after 14 months, there was a far less likelihood that is was malignant.

Really! Was I actually hearing this? Whoa! This is cool. "What percentage?" I of course asked next.

"Oh I'd say 50-60% chance it's malignant."

All right! Now we were jammin'!. Good damn news! Whoo Hoo! All right!

I wanted to scream it to the world! I was glowing from stem to stern. 50-60%? What a world of difference from the 95% my two urologists had given me.

So, was it due to Gerson that the mass was apparently "arrested?" Or was it benign and going nowhere anyway? Or, or . . . I didn't care. It was the first really encouraging information I had gotten from any traditional medical professional. And the guy was nice to boot. He also gave me the name of a urologist he had been with at the conference who concurred with the, "We don't know really what to do with them" realization. I loved the honesty. No one protecting their turf or egos or insurance rates at my expense.

How refreshing!

I didn't tell anyone for several days. I wanted to ride this joyous buzz as long as I could and all too often, even with family, they aren't sensitive to that and say something negative or discouraging.

I don't know why so often people feel some bizarre obligation to buzz kill your most uplifting moments.

But with this, I wasn't about to let that happen.

When I finally came down from Cloud 9, no, make that at least Cloud 19, and told folks, reactions were mixed. Some, especially Gerson people, were ecstatic like me. Other folks saw it as a failure. Nothing but the complete dissolution of the thing would constitute a "cure." One person said, "So now you're going to get it cut out, right?"

But what they didn't understand was that the body does what it thinks is best, and if leaving it in there but shutting it down or encapsulating it is the right course of action, then who am I to second guess that? Our bodies, with the proper boost from gallons of juice and colonated coffee, CAN get it done . . . or at least that's what I thought.

My favorite uncle, Frank, served as a Lieutenant Colonel in Patton's army during WWII and his tank suffered a direct hit, leaving him with shrapnel in his body until he passed at the ripe old age of 91. He joined my father and me on a backpack trip at 65, was an avid golfer, gardener and all around active, great guy. Somehow HIS body dealt with unwelcome toxic visitors for almost two thirds of a century and if his body could do it, by God so could mine.

That scan and the radiologist's comments changed a lot of

things for me. My outlook improved, my fears began dissolving and I started worrying much less about leaving the planet and planning what I could do for it - once Gerson was done.

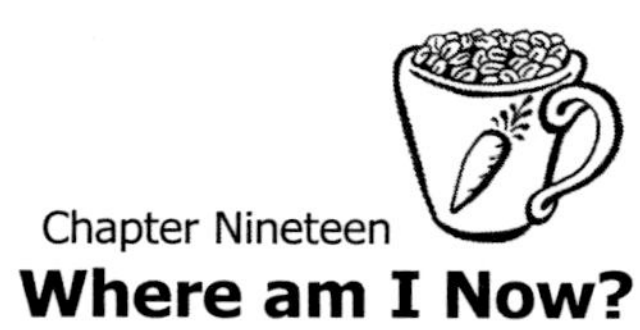

Chapter Nineteen

Where am I Now?

It is August, 2008, five and a half years after my diagnosis in Yankton on that fateful Valentine's Day. I am sitting in my van between shows at the Eastern Idaho State Fair. To keep the heat out I have stuck newspapers up against the windows to block out the sun creating a sort of Want Ads, Presidential campaign news, Dear Abby chrysalis.

And I feel great. While I am no longer doing 54 shows in a month in boiling summer heat, it is a choice predicated on mental rather than physical health. The past few months have taken me to Louisiana for their Rural Water Association Convention, Miles City, Montana for a fair and several times to Indianapolis to help care for my father during his recovery from a grand mal seizure.

Gail and I have finally taken up painting the trim of our Edwardian on Superior Street, one of several projects interrupted by months of enemas and juice. I purchased the home next to my land North of Alexandria and have been rehabbing it over the past two years, with that process serving as a nice retreat from hours of road time, gigging demands, and the intensity of city life.

My good friend Ralph had a reoccurrence of cancer two years ago, but after extensive surgery and followup chemo he, gratefully, is doing fine. We compared notes during his recovery and had a bet as to who got the skinniest during their extra cellular debacles. And damn it, he beat me by two pounds, sinking to a gaunt 127 on his 5'8" frame.

And yes, I did ask him if he wanted to pursue Gerson as his treatment of choice. He, as much as anyone, knew what I went through. I didn't have to explain about toxicity elimination, live enzymes or even castor oil. I simply stated if he wanted to look into it, I would be there to provide whatever help he needed. But he politely declined with a gracious and oh so true to his nature, "It's not my path."

I knew by that point that those are very key words. Everyone does have their own path, and there is no right or wrong in treating one's own illness. With Ralph I had to trust, hope and then . . . let go.

I had to take the same approach with my 6'+ strapping brother-in-law who, after being diagnosed with breast cancer, didn't even let me offer Gerson assistance. His preemptive statement, after he and my sister had informed us of his diagnosis was, "And I'm not putting any coffee up my ass!" which served to give us all a chuckle in what was otherwise another one of those, "Crap, here we go again" moments.

He too is doing very well, although camouflaged behind his friendly eyes you can see the toll the rigors of chemo and repeated surgeries have taken.

And to top it all off, my mother was diagnosed with cancer in the lining of her . . . yep, kidney. Golly Mr. Wizard, that's three out of four in my nuclear family. They removed the entire kidney endoscopically and while she has had a few complications, is also doing well. The worst part of her recovery was the development of Sundowners syndrome, a fairly common problem in seniors placed on opiate based pain protocols.

After surgery she was on a morphine drip and because of intense pain, was also given an opiate based suppository. Her pain subsided and we left her in the afternoon resting comfortably. Later that night, I decided to swing by the hospital just to tuck her in. I was shocked when I came into her room to find two beefy security guards standing next to her bed. They had been called because my tiny 80 year old mother had ripped out her IV's, lashed out at any staff within punching or kicking distance, and was screaming that they were all out to get her in some massive retirement-nest-egg-grabbing conspiracy.

And then my heart was crushed when I approached her bed and the first words out of her mouth were, "Oh God Jim, you're in on it too."

Nothing I could say would convince her that she was experiencing a horrible, aberrant, illusionary reality. She was seeing things that weren't there and for her, everything her morphine infused brain was telling her was absolutely true.

They brought in a syringe of Haldoll to settle her down and as they injected it into her thigh she blurted out wryly, "OK, here I go, just like Soxy" (our dog in the sixties who was put to sleep by injection). She truly believed we all were killing her for her money.

I couldn't help but think about Cathy and how we lost her forever when her pain meds got out of whack. Was Mom about to go the same way? Surely I wouldn't have to endure that torture again! I was furious, confused and scared as hell.

Thank God Gail eventually talked her down (apparently Mom saw her as Switzerland, totally neutral) and after three intense days and a total change in pain management, she was reasonably back to her old self. The whole episode just reinforced my skepticism about the western medical system although to be fair, as I mentioned earlier, Mom too is doing quite well.

But could she have stayed in our reality and been cured with Dr. Max? As with Ralph and my brother-in-law, Gerson was not her path.

I have not really been surprised that no one in my immediate circle or even peripheral circle of family, friends and acquaintances has opted to try Gerson.

This is not because I know it is intense and somewhat intimidating, but because I have just gotten used to it. I think most people just see it as too far out of the parameters that define their daily existence. When I bring it up and am usually summarily rejected, however politely, I can almost hear, "Leave doctorin' to doctors. I will do what they say and use the down time to watch hours of Matlock reruns."

So be it.

In the mean time, I will continue to be a living example of the Therapy's possibilities, and hopefully my experience can help someone, somewhere who resonates with it as much as I did.

And speaking of my own health, here's the synopsis: 5 ½ years down the line from my fall in Yankton I have far more stamina, my hearing is greatly improved, I am much slower to anger in general and my tolerance of others has increased dramatically. I mention these non-medical specifics because they are what stand out for me the most in the aftermath of my treatment.

Am I calmer because of some vegetarian chemical change in my general makeup, or is it because I looked death in the eye and that makes day-to-day perturbations seem insignificant?

I don't know. But I am grateful for the changes. It is only now looking back at how I used to react to difficult situations, that I realize just how edgy I had been in my pre-Gerson existence. It's almost scary and embarrassing when I see other people making the choices I used to; anger and impatience, judgment and hostility, when in the long haul those emotions usually mean nothing.

For that change alone I do feel grateful indeed.

As to other post-Gerson aspects of my life, my weight is up a bit, to 145 from a low of 129 in the middle of the Therapy (again, Ralph beat me by TWO frickin' pounds), but my blood pressure is consistently around 110/64 and my heartrate a steady 62 bpm. My overall cholesterol is always under 200, but I have to watch my genetically high LDL's.

And, after reading this entire book, I imagine more than a few readers are wondering, "Do you still juice and enema?"

Since adhering to Gerson strictly from 2003 to 2005 and doing it about half (7 juices and 2 or three enemas) through 2006 I backed off quite a bit. I felt I was out of the woods if

I had lasted that long without incident and frankly . . . I got sick of it. I wanted a break.

Oh, I didn't go on banana split binges, or start ordering Dominos double cheese and pepperoni every night. I, to this day, remain mostly vegetarian except for wild caught salmon, and can't even stomach the thought of nachos with melted Velveeta.

But I will now let myself have a night out at an Indian restaurant or have vegetable sushi and vegan scones from our local food coop. And when I am on the road, I no longer pack and cook all my food. I bring enough reasonably healthy stuff to get by and try to include enough organic produce for the entire run. Occasionally I will bring an Omega centrifugal juicer to keep that enzyme rich carrot juice flowing through my veins.

And I have to admit, I have also been corrupted by coffee, not through a plastic tube but from a cup like most of the planet puts it in their bodies. Of course it's shade grown, organic, and made with distilled water when I'm at home, but I indulge in it far too much.

Call it a desire for "Comfort Jitters," a subliminal desire to be a Bad Boy, or wanting a ritual most folks on the planet indulge in, I just dig the hell out of it.

I wish I could be more faithful to the therapy at this point, but I have had to make a choice: Do more things - shows, house renovation and tending to my elderly parents, or spend more time with the Norwalk and my bucket and food preparation. At this point in my life, I have to defer to other callings besides spending hours on my upstairs bathroom floor next to the purple claw foot tub.

In particular, my parents' needs at this juncture outweigh my own, so I hope my indulgence in a more traditional lifestyle will work for the next few years - like building up Gerson Credits that will carry me through a bit of retoxification until time allows me to get back to a more consumptively pure existence.

The one thing I still am very sensitive to and find hard to avoid in the non-Gerson universe is salt. It is packed into everything most Americans eat and when I encounter it in excess or even at "normal" levels, food can become unpalatable.

And I finally understand Gail's comment that something is "too sweet." Pre-Gerson you couldn't give me enough sugar. In college I was a serious Coke-a-Cola junkie and frequently OD'd on chocolate chip cookies whenever they were offered.

But now, those former delicasies have no appeal. Give me a Fuji apple any day over a Ding Dong, a mint tea instead of root beer.

And of course there is the big question: Am I Cured???

Well, if "Cured" means the mass is gone, then absolutely not. It is still there, its happy little 1.8 cm self doing whatever a little indeterminate mass does all day, probably watching "Dancing with the Stars" and "Deal or No Deal."

But if "Cured" is to be defined in Gerson terms, then I will be fine. As with other Gerson kidney mass cases I read about, mine seems to be arrested and God willing, will placidly remain where it is, unobtrusive and harmless, for the rest of my hopefully long life, especially if I can continue to keep my body reasonably detoxified.

And that is all based on the supposition that it was not benign in the first place! It is infinitely possible that the thing was harmless all along, just hanging out, a simple genetic anomaly or an aberration caused by a damaged rib rubbing against my kidney as I drove mile after mile after mile jostling up and down on the way to shows.

Maybe I didn't even have to worry about it at all!

If that is the case, would I regret having done Gerson? Would I regret the hours and hours laying on my right side, purging myself of everything nasty inhabiting my being? Would I regret sucking down gallons and gallons of carrot, carrot apple and dirt tasting green juice, giving myself B-12 shots in the ass and suffering through countless days of castor oil induced male PMS?!!

Not for a minute.

I have been blessed with the opportunity to confront my own mortality and survive, whether it was ever really in jeopardy or not. That alone has taught me invaluable lessons in humility and as pathetically cliché as it sounds, to seriously examine what matters in life in general and mine in particular. My personal purpose changed from achievement motivated by an intense need for external approval, to manifesting my gifts for the betterment and enjoyment of others.

Why? Because external approval, when faced with the possibility of non-existence, suddenly didn't matter. Making people feel good for their sake instead of mine seemed far more important.

And an odd thing happened when I embraced that philosophy. The shows got better. Because I was there for the audience and was not so worried about me, I relaxed.

I took the act places I was too nervous to explore when I was so worried about what others might think. I now trust the flow, God, the Universe, (fill in your own term for omniscient consciousness here), to keep me in sync with the folks just beyond the spotlights, and it's better for them and more enjoyable for me.

And that translates to the rest of my life too. Things just don't upset me like they used too. The little man chip I had going into Gerson has mellowed into mostly comedic self-deprecation. My judgment of other people has morphed into an appreciation of their process, an acknowledgement that a first impression can be totally opposite of what the whole person is about.

And I've learned that life is too short to hate or hold grudges about anything. It just isn't worth it. To die with a gut full of vendettas would mean I really hadn't lived at all.

And so I move on in my life. Hopefully my experience will help someone else in their cancer process, whether they choose Gerson or not. It certainly helped me, not just in getting physically healthy again, but in healing my spirit as well.

Would you like **James Wedgwood** to speak about his journey on the **Gerson Therapy**, or perform his hilarious ventriloquist show at your event? Or do you need to order more copies of **3000 Coffee Breaks**? For information contact:

James Wedgwood
info@jameswedgwood.com

For more information on the **Gerson Therapy** contact:

The Gerson Institute
P.O. Box 161358
San Diego, CA 92176

858-694-0707
www.gerson.org
info@gerson.org

Bibliography

Books

Clark, Hulda Regehr. *The Cure for All Diseases*. Chula Vista, CA: New Century Press, 1995.

Davison, Jaquie. *Cancer Winner: How I Purged Myself of Melanoma.* Pierce City, MO: Pacific Press, 1977.

Gerson, Charlotte. *Healing Brain and Kidney Cancer the Gerson Way*. Bonita, CA: Gerson Institute, 2002.

Gerson, Max, M.D. *A Cancer Therapy: Results of Fifty Cases and the Cure of Advanced Cancer by Diet Therapy.* 6th ed. San Diego: Gerson Institute, 2002.

Meing, George E., D.D.S., F.A.C.D. *Root Canal Cover-Up*. Ojai, CA: Bion Publishing, 1998.

Platt, Richard. *Stephen Biesty's Incredible Body.* New York: DK Publishing, 1998.

Articles and Reports

"Appendix I: Summary of Changes to the Classification of Dental Amalgam and Mercury." *U.S. Food and Drug Administration*. July 28, 2009. Accessed June 17, 2012. www.fda.gov/MedicalDevices/ProductsandMedical Procedures/DentalProducts/DentalAmalgam/ ucm171120.htm.

Brenner, D.J., and C.D. Elliston. *"Estimated Radiation Risks Potentially Associated with Full-Body CT." Radiology* 232, no.3 (2004): 735-738. www.ncbi.nlm.nih.gov/ pubmed/15273333.

Christensen, Gordon J. "Longevity of Posterior Tooth Dental Restorations." *Journal of the American Dental Association* 136, no.2 (2005): 201-203. Accessed June 21, 2010. http://jada.ada.org/cgi/content/full/136/2/201.

"Colorectal Cancer Facts & Figures Special Edition 2005." *American Cancer Society*. http://www.cancer.org/Research/CancerFactsFigures/ColorectalCancerFactsFigures/colorectal-cancer-facts-figures-special-edition-2005.

Hatibović-Kofman, Š. and G. Koch. "Fluoride Release from Glass Ionomer Cement *in vivo* and *in vitro*." *Swedish Dental Journal* 15, no.6 (1991): 253-258. Accessed June 21, 2010. www.ncbi.nih.gov/pubmed/1817351.

DVD Video

Cancer Warrior: Will Endostatin Revolutionize Cancer Treatment? Directed by Nancy Linde. 2001. Boston: WGBH Educational Foundation. DVD.

Websites

ADA Council on Scientific Affairs. "Statement on Dental Amalgam." *American Dental Association*. Revised August 2009. Accessed June 21, 2010. www.ada.org/1741.aspx.

"Adverse Health Effects of Palladium." *Holistic Healing*. http://www.holisticmed.com/dental/palladium1.html.

"BioGold Plus from Elephant Dental B.V." *Dentalcompare*. Accessed June 21, 2010. www.dentalcompare.com/details/8931/BioGold-Plush.html.

"Clifford Materials Reactivity Test." *Clifford Consulting & Research Inc.* Accessed June 21, 2010. www.ccrlab.com.

"Colon Cancer." *Yahoo!® Health*. http://health.yahoo.com/coloncancer-treatment/colorectal-cancer-metastatic-or-recurrent-treatment-overview/healthwise--tv7575.html.

Cooke, Helen, and Helen Seers. "Gerson Therapy." *CAM-Cancer*. Accessed June 18, 2010. www.cam-cancer.org/CAM-Summaries/Biologically-Based-Practices/Gerson-Therapy/Is-it-safe.

"GC FujiCEM™ Automix: Glass Ionomer Luting Cement." *GC America*. Accessed June 21, 2010. www.gcamerica.com/products/operatory/GC_FujiCEM_Automix/features.php.

Gerson, Charlotte. "The Evolution of the Gerson Therapy: Changes and Updates to the Therapy." *Resource Library*. 2008. http://findarticles.com/p/articles/mi_6818/is_6_23/ai_n31160785/.

"The Gerson Therapy." *HubPages*. http://livingfood.hubpages.com/hub/The-Gerson-Therapy.

Gutierrez, David. "FDA Reluctantly Admits Mercury Fillings Have Neurotoxic Effects on Children." *Natural News*. December 2, 2008. Accessed June 17, 2012. www.naturalnews.com/024993.html.

"Hemodyialysis." *American Kidney Fund*. Accessed June 18, 2010. www.kidneyfund.org/kidney-health/treatment/hemodialysis.html.

Kantrowitz, Mark. "Radiation Exposure from Diagnostic Tests." *Cancer Points*. Accessed June 19, 2010. www.kantrowitz.com/cancerpoints/radiationexposure.html.

Mercola, Joseph M., D.O. "FDA's Mercury Ruling Defies ALL Scientific Reasoning." *Mercola.com*. August 22, 2009. Accessed June 17, 2012. http://articles.mercola.com/sites/articles/archive/2009/08/22/fda-has-the-audacity-to-claim-mercury-is-completely-harmless.aspx.

Momentum98. Accessed June 18, 2010. https://www.momentum98.com/inflazyme.html.

"Oral Health Topics: Dental Filling Options." *American Dental Association*. www.ada.org/6605.aspx?currentTab=1.

"Priority List of Hazardous Substances." *Agency for Toxic Substances & Disease Registry*. www.atsdr.cdc.gov/SPL/index.html.

Rehme, Michael, D.D.S., C.C.N. "Unexplained Dental Pain Explained: Tooth Extractions, Cavitations and the Periodontal Ligament." *The Healthy Planet*. October 13, 2011. Accessed June 14, 2012. http://thehealthyplanet.com/2011/10/unexplained-dental-pain-explained-tooth-extractions-cavitations-and-the-periodontal-ligament/.

"A Timeline of the Trip." *PBS: Public Broadcasting Service*. Accessed June 18, 2010. www.pbs.org/lewisandclark/archive/idx_time.html.

"Vitamin B3 (Niacin)." *herbs2000*. Accessed June 18, 2010. www.herbs2000.com/vitamins/v_b3.htm.

Vizcarra, Corinne, D.D.S. "Palladium: Dental Danger Alloy." *Natural Healing House*. Accessed June 21, 2010. www.naturalhealinghouse.com/hm_palladium.htm.

"What You Need To Know About™ Kidney Cancer." *National Cancer Institute*. Accessed June 18, 2010. www.cancer.gov/cancertopics/wyntk/kidney/page4.